Eastern Europe
phrasebook

Daniel Condratov
Krzysztof Dydyński
Koronczi Katalin
Richard Nebeský
Dr Angel Pachev
Katarina Steiner

Eastern Europe phrasebook
2nd edition

Published by
Lonely Planet Publications
Head Office: PO Box 617, Hawthorn, Vic, 3122, Australia
Branches: 155 Filbert Street, Suite 251, Oakland, CA 94607, USA
                10 Barley Mow Passage, Chiswick, London W4 4PH, UK
                71 bis rue du Cardinal Lemoine, 75005 Paris, France

Printed by
Colorcraft Ltd, Hong Kong

Published
December 1994

Cover Photo
Facade on Radnične Square, Bardejov, Slovakia (Richard Nebeský)

National Library of Australia Cataloguing in Publication Data
Eastern Europe phrasebook
   2nd ed.
   ISBN 0 86442 260 1.

   1. Slavic languages - Conversation and phrase books - English.
   2. Europe, Eastern - Languages - Conversation and phrase books - English.
   I. Dydyński, Krzysztof. (Series: Lonely Planet language survival kit).

491.8

text © Lonely Planet Publications Pty Ltd 1994
cover photo © photographer as indicated 1994

Contents

Acknowledgements

Bulgarian was written by Dr Angel Pachev. Richard Nebeský wrote the Czech section, with assistance from his parents. The Hungarian section was written by Koronczi Katalin, with assistance from James Stewart. Polish was written by Krzysztof Dydyński. Romanian was written by Daniel Condratov, with proofreading by Dana Lovinescu. Katarina Steiner wrote the Slovak section.

The book was edited by Sally Steward and James Jenkin. Valerie Tellini was responsible for design and cover design. Rachel Black designed the title pages.

From the Publisher

In this book Lonely Planet uses a simplified phonetic transcription, based on the International Phonetic Alphabet. While this can only approximate the exact sounds of each language, it serves as the most useful guide for readers attempting to say the various words and phrases. As you spend time in a country, listening to native speakers and following the rules offered here in the pronunciation sections, you should be able to read directly from the language itself.

Five of the six languages in this book have masculine and feminine, and sometimes neuter, forms of words. The different forms are separated in the text by slashes and/or the bracketed abbreviations (m), (f) and (neut), when appropriate. Many words share the same form, in which case no indication of gender is required. You will find a handful of words which exist in one gender form only and have not yet developed a corresponding word in the other gender. For instance, 'business person' exists in Romanian only as *om de afaceri*, 'businessman'.

Each of the languages in this book has both formal and informal ways of speech, which means that for one word in English (especially 'you') you may find two in another language, one being the polite, formal word, and the other being more casual and informal. For the purposes of this book the formal way of speech has been adopted throughout, as this will ensure that at least you will not offend anyone by using a more intimate style. In instances where the informal is more appropriate, we have included it, indicated by the letters (inf).

Bulgarian

Bulgarian

Introduction

Modern Bulgarian belongs to the group of South Slavonic languages. It is the descendant of the oldest Slavonic literary language, Old Bulgarian (Old Slavic or Old Church Slavonic). Originally formulated in connection with the missionary work of the Salonica brothers, Cyril and Methodius, during the 9th century AD, Old Bulgarian flourished in the Bulgarian lands for several centuries, thus giving rise to an original literary and cultural tradition which continues to thrive.

Today Bulgarian is the native language of more than eight million speakers who make up the Slavonic ethnic majority of the Republic of Bulgaria. It is the second language of several linguistic minorities in the country, including Turkish, Romany, Armenian, Greek and Romanian. While Contemporary Standard Bulgarian is the official literary language of the Republic of Bulgaria, historical and social factors have brought about the emergence of regional varieties in neighbouring areas. Bulgarian is also spoken by some fairly sizable groups in the former USSR, Canada, Argentina and in some other countries. In Bulgaria itself a number of regional dialects (most of them highly urbanised) appear in common speech.

Bulgarian has affinities with all the other Slavonic languages. Closely akin to Russian, it shares the Cyrillic alphabet (with a few minor differences). But unlike Russian, Polish, Czech, and other Slavonic languages, Modern Bulgarian features a general loss of grammatical case endings. A number of shared linguistic similarities with other Balkan languages (Greek,

Albanian and Romanian) also adds up to the unique place of Bulgarian among the Slavonic languages.

Some features of Contemporary Standard Bulgarian are:

1. All the attributes, pronouns and ordinal numerals agree in number and gender with the noun they qualify or specify: този хубав град, 'this nice city' (masculine, singular); тази хубава жена, 'this pretty woman' (feminine, singular); това хубаво дете, 'this beautiful child' (neuter, singular); тези хубави къщи, 'these nice houses' (plural).

2. Almost every verb is used with an ending denoting grammatical person, number and tense: говоря, 'I speak/am speaking' (1st person, singular, present tense); говорихте, 'you spoke/were speaking' (2nd person, plural, past tense), etc.

3. Bulgarian has no equivalent to the English indefinite article 'a'. However, you can add a particle to the end of a noun equivalent to the English definite article 'the'. This particle has special forms for the three genders and the plural: градът 'the city' (masculine, singular, definite), жената 'the woman' (feminine, singular, definite), детето 'the child' (neuter, singular, definite), къщите 'the houses' (plural, definite), etc.

4. Use of special noun forms for addressing a person, such as господине 'Mr!', госпожо 'Mrs!', etc.

Throughout the chapter the polite verbal forms, and the polite forms of the pronoun 'you' (Вие, Ви) are used.

You may at first feel a little uneasy when trying to match the above shortlisted grammatical peculiarities as you speak. But you should always be at ease with the Bulgarians for they are generally friendly people who like to speak and be spoken to. And if you don't have the time to learn their speech etiquette and body language involved in communicating, rest assured that the use of the polite forms, accompanied by a friendly smile, will take you a long way in Bulgaria. There are few, if any, aspects of body language that are likely to cause confusion, with one important exception: Bulgarians shake their head from side to side to signify 'yes', and nod their head up and down to indicate 'no'. Have a great time in Bulgaria!

Pronunciation

To a great extent, the Bulgarians write as they speak, so Bulgarian spelling (unlike English) generally provides almost one-to-one representation of letter-sound correspondences. The application of this principle and the exceptions to it are well represented throughout this Bulgarian chapter by using the simplified phonetic translation.

Most Bulgarian sounds occur in the English language as well, with some slight differences in the way sounds are produced. With a little practice you will have no problem making yourself understood.

Vowels

In Contemporary Standard Bulgarian there are six vowels which differ from the English vowels both in quality (the Bulgarian vowels are tenser and more rounded in articulation) and in quantity (all Bulgarian vowels are of medium length whereas in English there are two distinct classes of short and long vowels).

а	ah	is pronounced approximately as 'a' in 'father', 'rather' (but shorter)
е	eh	is pronounced as 'e' in 'bet', 'egg'
о	o	is pronounced as 'o' in 'pot', 'sorry'
и	i	is pronounced as 'i' in 'it', 'shilling'
ъ	a	is a characteristic Bulgarian vowel sound which roughly resembles 'a' in 'soda' or 'address'
у	u	is pronounced as 'u' in 'pull', 'put'

All these vowels occur in stressed and in non-stressed syllables. The non-stressed vowels are shorter, laxer and weaker, and they approach one another in a pairwise fashion: а – ъ, о – у (educated speech) and е – и (Bulgarian dialect). This process of vowel reduction is not shown in the present phonetic translation of the Bulgarian vowel sounds.

Consonants

Bulgarian consonants are pronounced much less energetically than English ones, and most of them should be easily produced by English-speaking learners:

б	b	as in 'boy', 'husband'
в	v	as 'v' in 'vice', 'never'
г	gh	as 'g' in 'get', 'girl'
д	d	as 'd' in 'door', 'kind'
ж	zh	as 's' in 'treasure', 'evasion'
з	z	as 'z' in 'zoo', 'zero'
й	y	as 'y' in 'yes', 'yellow'
к	k	as 'k' in 'king', 'kill'
л	l	as 'l' in 'last', 'greatly'

М	m	as 'm' in 'mind', 'swim'
Н	n	as 'n' in 'name', 'then'
П	p	as 'p' in 'pen', 'help'
р	r	as the rolled Scottish 'r' in 'bring'
С	s	as 's' in 'say', 'thinks'
Т	t	as 't' in 'tip', 'pot'
Ф	f	as 'f' in 'foot', 'safe'
Х	kh	as the Scottish 'ch' in 'loch'
Ц	ts	as 'ts' in 'tsetse'
Ч	ch	as 'ch' in 'Charles', 'much'
Ш	sh	as 'sh' in 'ship', 'English'
Щ	sht	as the two consonant sounds of 'shed' in 'pushed', 'rushed'
Ю	yu	as 'yu' in 'youth' (but shorter)
Я	ya	as 'ya' in 'yard' (but shorter)

In order to produce standard Bulgarian speech, you need to follow a number of rules which often differ from those in English. When at the end of a word or before a voiceless consonant, the voiced consonants б, в, г, ж, з, д become voiceless: 'fraction', дроб sounds like дроп; the preposition 'in', ВЪВ – ВЪф; 'snow', СНЯГ – СНЯК; 'knife', НОЖ – НОШ; 'subway', подлез – подлес; 'lunch', обед – обет; 'to sign', подпиша – потпиша, etc.

Voicing or devoicing affects the final consonant of a preceding word under the influence of the initial consonant of a following word: 'I am', аз съм – ас съм; 'with a bath', с баня – з баня, etc.

In word-final position the consonant 't' is dropped out: 'six', ШЕСТ – шес; 'the back', гърбът – гърбъ; 'night', НОЩ – НОШ, etc.

Greetings & Civilities
Top 10 Useful Phrases

Hello.
*zdrah-**vehy**-teh*　　　　　Здравейте.

Goodbye.
*do-**vizh**-dah-neh*　　　　Довиждане.

Yes./No.
dah/neh　　　　　　　　Да./Не.

Excuse me.
*iz-vi-**neh**-teh*　　　　　Извинете.

May I? Do you mind?
*mo-ghah li. **i**-mah-teh*　　Мога ли. Имате
*li **neh**-shto pro-**tif***　　ли нещо против?

Sorry. (excuse me, forgive me)
*sa-zhah-**lya**-vahm*　　　Съжалявам
*pro-**shtah**-vahy-teh*　　　(прощавайте).

Please.
***mo**-lya*　　　　　　　Моля.

Thank you.
*blah-gho-dah-**rya***　　　Благодаря.
*mehr-**si***　　　　　　　мерси.

Many thanks.
*mno-**gho** vi*　　　　　　Много (Ви)
*blah-gho-dah-**rya***　　　благодаря.

That's fine. You're welcome.
*mo-lya, **nya**-mah zah-**shto*** Моля, няма защо.

Greetings

Good morning.
*do-**bro** u-tro*　　　　　Добро утро.

Good afternoon.
do-bar dehn   Добър ден.
Good evening/night.
do-bar veh-chehr   Добър вечер
leh-kah nosh   лека нощ.
How are you?
kahk steh?   Как сте?
Well, thanks.
blah-gho-dah-rya,
do-breh sam   Багодаря, добре съм.

Forms of Address

These are used only as special forms of address:

Madam/Mrs	*ghos-po-zho*	госпожо
Sir/Mr	*ghos-po-di-neh*	господине
Miss	*ghos-po-zhi-tseh*	госпожице
friend	*pri-ya-tel-yu*	приятелю

Small Talk
Meeting People

What is your name?
kahk seh kahz-vah-teh?   Как се казвате?
My name is ...
kahz-vahm seh ...   Казвам се ...
I'd like to introduce
you to ...
poz-vo-leh-teh dah vi   Позволете да Ви
preht-stah-vya nah ...   представя на ...

I'm pleased to meet you.
*pri-**ya**-tno mi eh dah seh*
*zah-poz-**nah**-ya z vahs*

Приятно ми е да се
запозная с Вас.

I like ... /I don't like ...
*khah-**rehs**-vahm ...*
*neh khah-**rehs**-vahm ...*

Харесвам ...
Не харесвам ...

How old are you?
*nah **kol**-ko ste gho-**di**-ni?*

На колко сте години?

I am ... years old.
*nah ... (gho-**di**-ni sam)*

На ... (години съм).

Nationalities

Where are you from?
*ot-ka-**deh** steh?*

Откъде сте?

I am from ...
ahs sam ot ...

Аз съм от...

Australia	*ahf-**strah**-li-ya*	Австралия
Canada	*kah-**nah**-dah*	Канада
England	*ahn-ghli-ya*	Англия
Ireland	*ir-**lahn**-di-ya*	Ирландия
New Zealand	*no-vah zeh-**lahn**-di-ya*	Нова Зеландия
Scotland	*sho-**tlahn**-di-ya*	Шотландия
the USA	*sa-eh-di-**neh**-ni-teh*	Съединените
	shtah-ti	Щати
Wales	*u-**ehls***	Уелс

Occupations

What is your profession?
*kah-**kaf** steh po*
*pro-**feh**-si-ya?*

Какъв сте по
професия?

I am a/an ...
ahs sam ...   Аз съм ...

artist	*khu-dozhnk* (m)	художник
	khu-do-zhnich-kah (f)	художничка
business person	*bi-zneh-smehn*	бизнесмен
doctor	*leh-kahr* (m)	лекар
	leh-kahr-kah (f)	лекарка
engineer	*in-zheh-nehr*	инженер
farmer	*sehl-ski sto-pah-nin,*	селски сто-
	fehr-mehr	панин, фермер
journalist	*zhur-nah-lis* (m)	журналист
	zhur-nah-lis-kah (f)	журналистка
lawyer	*ahd-vo-kaht*	адвокат
manual worker	*fi-zi-cheh-ski*	физически
	rah-bo-tnik	работник
mechanic	*meh-khah-nik*	механик
	teh-khnik	техник
nurse	*meh-di-tsin-skah*	медицинска
	sehs-trah	сестра
office worker	*chi-no-vnik* (m)	чиновник
	chi-no-vnich-kah (f)	чиновничка
scientist	*u-chehn*	учен
student	*stu-dehnt* (m)	студент
	stu-dehnt-kah (f)	студентка
teacher	*u-chi-tehl* (m)	учител
	u-chi-tel-kah (f)	учителка
waiter	*kehl-nehr* (m)	келнер
	kehl-nehr-kah (f)	келнерка
writer	*pi-sah-tehl* (m)	писател
	pi-sah-telkah (f)	писателка

Religion

What is your religion?
kahk-vah re-li-ghi-ya
is-po-vya-dah-teh?
Каква религия
изповядате?

I am not religious.
neh sam vyar-vahsh (m) Не съм вярваш.
neh sam vyar-vah-shtah (f) Не съм вярваща.

I am ...
ahs sam ...
Аз съм ...

Buddhist	*bu-dis* (m)	будист
	bu-dis-kah (f)	будистка
Christian	*khris-ti-ya-nin* (m)	християнин
	khris-ti-yan-kah (f)	християнка
Hindu	*in-dus* (m)	индус
	in-dus-kah (f)	индуска
Jewish	*eh-vreh-in* (m)	евреин
	eh-vrehy-kah (f)	еврейка
Muslim	*myu-syul-mah-nin* (m)	мюсюлманин
	myu-syul-mahn-kah (f)	мюсюлманка

Family

Are you married?
zheh-nehn li steh? (m) Женен ли сте?
o-ma-zheh-nah li ste? (f) Омъжена ли сте?

I am single.
neh sam zheh-nehn (m) Не съм женен.
neh sam o-ma-zheh-nah (f) Не съм омъжена.

I am married.
zheh-nehn sam (m) Женен съм.
o-ma-zheh-nah sam (f) Омъжена съм.

How many children do you have?
kol-ko deh-**tsah** i-**mah**-teh?

Колко деца имате?

I don't have any children.
nya-mahm de-**tsah**

Нямам деца.

I have a daughter/a son.
i-**mahm** da-shteh-**rya**/sin

Имам дъщеря/син.

Is your husband/wife here?
sa-**pru**-ghat/sa-**pru**-ghah-tah vi tuk li eh?

Съпругът/съпругата Ви тук ли е?

Do you have a boyfriend/girlfriend?
i-**mah**-teh li pri-**ya**-tehl/pri-**ya**-tehl-kah?

Имате ли приятел/приятелка?

brother	*braht*	брат
children	*deh-**tsah***	деца
daughter	*da-shteh-**rya***	дъщеря
family	*seh-**mehy**-stvo*	семейство
father	*bah-**shtah***	баща
grandfather	*dya-do*	дядо
grandmother	*bah-bah*	баба
husband	*sa-**pruk***	съпруг
mother	*mahy-kah*	майка
sister	*seh-**strah***	сестра
son	*sin*	син
wife	*sa-**pru**-ghah*	съпруга

Feelings

I am angry.
- *ya*-do-sahn sam (m) — Ядосан съм.
- *ya*-do-sah-nah sam (f) — Ядосана съм.

I am cold/hot.
- stu-**deh**-no mi eh — Студено ми е.
- gho-**reh**-shto mi eh — горещо ми е.

I am grateful.
- blah-gho-dah-rehn sam ... (m) — Благодарен съм.
- blah-gho-dahr-nah sam ... (f) — благодарна съм.

I am happy/sad.
- **rah**-do-stehn/**rah**-do-snah sam **ta**-zhno mi eh — Радостен/радостна съм тъжно ми е.

I am hungry.
- **ghlah**-dehn sam (m) — Гладен съм.
- **ghlah**-dnah sam (f) — Гладна съм.

I am right.
- prahf sam (m) — Прав съм.
- **prah**-vah sam (f) — Права съм.

I am sleepy.
- spi mi seh — Спи ми се.

I am sorry. (condolence)
- sa-zhah-**lya**-vahm — Съжалявам.

I am thirsty.
- **zhah**-dehn sam (m) — Жаден съм.
- **zhah**-dnah sam (f) — Жадна съм.

I am tired.
- iz-mo-**rehn** sam (m) — Изморен съм.
- iz-mo-**reh**-nah sam (f) — Изморена съм.

I am well.
   do-breh sam   Добре съм.

Language Problems

Do you speak English?
   *gho-**vo**-ri-teh li*   Говорите ли
   *ahn-**ghliy**-ski?*   английски?

Does anyone speak English?
   ***nya**-koy gho-**vo**-ri li*   Някой говори ли
   *ahn-**ghliy**-ski?*   английски?

I speak a little ...
   *gho-**vo**-rya **mahl**-ko ...* Говоря малко ...

I don't speak ...
   *neh gho-**vo**-rya ...*   Не говоря ...

I (don't) understand.
   *rahz-**bi**-rahm*   Разбирам
   *(neh rahz-**bi**-rahm)*   (не разбирам).

Could you speak more
slowly please?
   ***bikh**-teh li mo-**ghli** dah* Бихте ли могли да
   *gho-**vo**-ri-teh **po** bah-vno* говорите по-бавно,
   ***mo**-lya?*   моля?

Could you repeat that?
   ***bikh**-teh li mo-**ghli** dah* Бихте ли могли да
   ***pof**-to-ri-teh to-**vah**?*   повторите това?

How do you say ...?
   *kahk **kahz**-vah-teh?*   Как казвате ...?

What does ... mean?
   ***kahk**-vo o-znah-**chah**-* Какво означава ...?
   vah ...?

Some Useful Phrases

Sure.
*dah, rahz-**bi**-rah seh*

Да, разбира се.

Just a minute.
sah**-mo zah mo-**mehnt

Само за момент.

It's (not) important.
***vah**-zhno eh*
*(neh **eh** vah-zhno)*

Важно е.
(Не е важно.)

It's (not) possible.
*va-**zmo**-zhno eh*
*(neh **eh** v a-**zmo**-zhno)*

Възможно е.
(Не е възможно.)

Wait!
*po-**chah**-kahy-teh!*

Почакайте!

Good luck!
*us-**pehkh**!*

Успех!

Signs

BAGGAGE COUNTER	БАГАЖ
CHECK-IN COUNTER	КОНТРОЛА
CLOSED	ЗАТВОРЕНО
CUSTOMS	МИТНИЦА
EMERGENCY EXIT	АВАРИЕН ИЗХОД
ENTRANCE	ВХОД
EXIT	ИЗХОД
FREE ADMISSION	ВХОД СВОБОДЕН
HOT/COLD	ГОРЕЩО/СТУДЕНО
INFORMATION	ИНФОРМАЦИЯ
NO ENTRY	ВХОД ЗАБРАНЕН

NO SMOKING	ПУШЕНЕТО ЗАБРА-
	НЕНО
OPEN	ОТВОРЕНО
PROHIBITED	ЗАБРАНЕНО
RESERVED	ЗАПАЗЕНА

Emergencies

POLICE	ПОЛИЦИЯ
POLICE STATION	ПОЛИЦЕЙСКО
	УПРАВЛЕНИЕ

Help!
po-mosh!   Помощ!

It's an emergency!
i-mah speh-shehn   Има спешен случай!
slu-chahy!

There's been an accident!
stah-nah-lah eh   Станала е
kah-tah-stro-fah!   катастрофа!

Call a doctor!
po-vi-kahy-teh leh-kahr!   Повикайте лекар!

Call an ambulance!
po-vi-kahy-teh bar-zah   Повикайте бърза
po-mosh!   помош!

I've been raped.
iz-nah-si-li-khah meh!   Изнасилиха ме!

I've been robbed!
  *o-**ghrah**-bi-khah meh!*   Ограбиха ме!
Call the police!
  *po-**vi**-kahy-teh*   Повикайте полиция!
  *po-**li**-tsi-ya!*
Where is the police station?
  *ka-**deh** seh nah-**mi**-rah*   Къде се намира
  *po-li-**tsehy**-sko-to*   полицейското
  *u-prah-**vleh**-ni-eh?*   управление?

Go away!
  ***mah**-khahy-teh seh!*   Махайте се!
I'll call the police!
  *shteh iz-**vi**-kahm*   Ще извикам полиция!
  *po-**li**-tsi-ya!*
Thief!
  *krah-**dehts**!*   Крадец!

I am ill.
  zleh sam/neh seh   Зле съм/Не се
  chuf**-stvahm do-**breh   чувствувам добре.
I am lost.
  *zah-**ghu**-bikh seh*   Загубих се.
Where are the toilets?
  *ka-**deh** i-mah*   Къде има тоалетни?
  *to-ah-**leh**-tni?*
Could you help me please?
  ***bikh**-teh li mi*   Бихте ли ми
  *po-**mo**-ghnah li?*   помогнали?

Could I please use the
telephone?
*iz-vi-**neh**-teh mo-ghah li
dah **pol**-zvahm
teh-leh-**fo**-nah?*
    Извинете, мога ли
    да ползувам
    телефона?

I'm sorry. (I apologise)
*pro-**shtah**-vahy-teh*
    Прощавайте.

I didn't realise I was doing
anything wrong.
*neh **znah**-ehkh cheh
var-shah neh-shto
neh-**reh**-dno*
    Не знаех, че
    върша нещо
    нередно.

I didn't do it.
*neh **gho** nah-**prah**-vikh
ahs*
    Не го направих аз.

I wish to contact my
embassy/consulate.
*zheh-**lah**-ya dah seh
svar-zhah s **nahsh**-to
po-**sol**-stvo/**kon**-sul-stvo*
    Желая да се свържа
    с нашето посолство/
    консулство.

I speak English.
*gho-**vo**-rya ahn-**ghliy**-ski*
    Говоря английски.

I have medical insurance.
*i-**mahm zdrah**-vnah
zah-strah-**khof**-kah*
    Имам здравна
    застраховка.

My possessions are
insured.
***veh**-shti-teh mi sah
zah-strah-**kho**-vah-ni*
    Вещите ми са
    застраховани.

My ... was stolen.
    *ot-**krah**-dnah-khah mi* ...   Откраднаха ми ...
I've lost my ...
    *iz-**ghu**-bikh si* ...   Изгубих си ...

bags	***chahn**-ti-teh*	чантите
handbag	***rach**-nah-tah*	ръчната
	***chahn**-tah*	чанта
money	*pah-**ri**-teh*	парите
travellers'	***pat**-ni-chehs-ki-teh*	пътническите
cheques	***cheh**-ko-veh*	чекове
passport	*pahs-**por**-tah*	паспорта

Forms

name	***i**-meh*	име
address	*ahd-**rehs***	адрес
date of birth	***dah**-tah nah*	дата на
	***rahzh**-dah-neh*	раждане
place of birth	*meh-sto-rozh-**deh**-ni-eh*	месторожде-ние
age	*va-zrahs*	възраст
sex	*pol*	пол
nationality	*nah-**ro**-dnos*	народност
next of kin	***nahy bli**-zak*	най-близък
	*ro-**dni**-nah*	роднина
religion	*veh-ro-is-po-veh-**dah**-ni-eh*	вероизповеда-ние
reason for travel	*tsehl na*	цел на
	*pa-**tu**-vah-neh-to*	пътуването
profession	*pro-**feh**-si-ya*	професия

marital status	seh-**mehy**-no po-lo-zheh-ni-eh	семейно положение
passport	pahs-**port**	паспорт
passport number	**no**-mehr nah pahs-**por**-tah	номер на паспорта
visa	**vi**-zah	виза
identification	do-ku-**mehnt** zah sah-mo-li-chnos	документ за самоличност
birth certificate	svi-**deh**-tehl-stvo zah **rah**-zhdah-neh	свидетелство за раждане
driver's licence	svi-**deh**-tehl-stvo zah prah-vo-u-prah-**vleh**-ni-e	свидетелство за правоупра-вление
car owner's title	i-meh-**nah** nah **sop**-tveh-ni-kah nah ko-**lah**-tah	имена на собственика на колата
car registration	**no**-mehr nah ko-**lah**-tah	номер на колата
customs	**mi**-tni-tsah	митница
immigration	i-mi-**grah**-tsi-ya	имиграция
border	**ghrah**-ni-tsah	граница

Getting Around

ARRIVALS	ПРИСТИГАЩИ
BUS STOP	АВТОБУСНА СПИРКА
DEPARTURES	ЗАМИНАВАЩИ
STATION	СПИРКА (СТАНЦИЯ)

SUBWAY	ПОДЛЕЗ
TICKET OFFICE	БИЛЕТНО ГИШЕ
TIMETABLE	РАЗПИСАНИЕ
TRAIN STATION	ЖП ГАРА

What time does (the) ...
leave/arrive?

	f kol-ko chah-sa	В колко часа
	zah-mi-nah-vah	заминава
	pri-sti-ghah ...?	пристига ...?

(aero)plane	*sah-mo-leh -tah*	самолетът
bus (city)	*ghraht-ski-ya*	градският
	ah-fto-bus	автобус
bus (intercity)	*mehzh-du-ghraht-*	междуград-
	ski-ya ah-fto-bus	ският автобус
the train	*vlah-kah*	влакът
the tram	*trahm-vah-ya*	трамваят

Directions

Where is ...?
   ka-deh seh nah-mi-rah ...? Къде се намира ...?
How do I get to ...?
   kahk dah sti-ghnah do ...? Как да стигна до ...?
Is it far from/near here?
   dah-leh-cheh/bli-zo Далече/близо
   li eh ot tuk? ли е от тук?

Can I walk there?
*mo-ghah li dah **sti**-ghnah
peh-**shah** do tahm?*

Мога ли да стигна
пеша до там?

Can you show me (on the map)?
*mo-zheh-teh li dah mi
po-**kah**-zheh-teh na
kahr-tah-tah?*

Можете ли да ми
покажете на
картата?

Are there other means of getting there?
*kahk **mo**-zheh dah seh
sti-ghneh tahm po
druk **nah**-chin?*

Как може да се
стигне там по
друг начин?

I want to go to ...
*is-kahm dah o-**ti**-dah
do ...*

Искам да отида до ...

Go straight ahead.
*var-**veh**-teh nah-**prah**-vo*

Вървете направо.

It's farther down.
*po-nah-**do**-lu eh*

По-надолу е.

Turn left ...
*zah-**viy**-teh nah-**lya**-vo ...*

Завийте наляво ...

Turn right ...
*zah-**viy**-teh nah-**dya**-sno ...*

Завийте надясно ...

 at the next corner
*nah **slehd**-vah-shti-ya
a-ghal*

на следващия
ъгъл

at the traffic lights
*pri sfeh-to-**fah**-rah*

при светофара

behind	*zaht*	зад
in front of	*preht*	пред
far	*dah-**leh**-cheh*	далече
near	***bli**-zo*	близо
opposite	***sreh**-shtu*	срещу

Booking Tickets

Excuse me, where is the
ticket office?

> *iz-vi-**neh**-teh ka-**deh** eh
> bi-**leh**-tno-to ghi-**sheh**?*

Извинете, къде е
билетното гише?

Where can I buy a ticket?

> *ka-**deh** mo-ghah dah si
> **ku**-pya bi-**leht**?*

Къде мога да си
купя билет?

I want to go to ...

> *is-kahm dah
> pa-**tu**-vahm do ...*

Искам да
пътувам до ...

Do I need to book?

> *tryab-vah li dah si **ku**-pya
> prehd-vah-**ri**-tehl-no
> bi-**leht**?*

Трябва ли да си купя
предварително
билет?

You need to book.

> *tryab-vah dah si
> **ku**-pi-teh bi-**leht**
> prehd-vah-**ri**-tehl-no*

Трябва да си
купите билет
предварително.

I would like to book a seat
to ...

> *bikh **is**-kahl bi-**leht** saz
> zah-**pah**-zeh-no **myas**-to
> do ...*

Бих искал билет със
запазено място
до ...

I would like ...
mo-lya dahy-teh-mi ...   Моля, дайте ми ...
a one-way ticket
bi-leht f eh-dnah   билет в една
po-so-kah   посока
a return ticket
bi-leht zah o-ti-vah-neh   билет за отиване
i vra-shtah-neh   и връщане
two tickets
dvah bi-leh-tah   два билета
tickets for all of us
bi-leh-ti zah fsich-ki   билети за всички
nahs   нас
a student's fare
u-cheh-ni-cheh-ski   ученически
(stu-dehn-ski) bi-leht   (студентски) билет
a child's/pensioner's fare
deht-ski/pehn-si-o-   детски/пенсионерски
nehr-ski bi-leht   билет

1st class
par-vah klah-sah   първа класа
2nd class
fto-rah klah-sah   втора класа

It is full.
nya-mah meh-stah   Няма места.
Is it completely full?
ni-kahk-vi meh-stah li   Никакви места ли
nya-mah?   няма?

Can I get a stand-by ticket?
*mo-zheh li eh-din bi-leht
zah prah-vo-sto-ya-shti?*

Може ли един билет
за правостоящи?

Air

CHECKING IN	КОНТРОЛА
LUGGAGE PICKUP	БАГАЖ
REGISTRATION	РЕГИСТРАЦИЯ

Is there a flight to ...?
i-mah li po-leht do ...?

Има ли полет до ...?

When is the next flight to ...?
*ko-ghah eh slehd-vah-
shti-ya po-leht do ...?*

Кога е следващият
полет до ...?

How long is the flight?
*kol-ko vreh-meh pro-dal-
zhah-vah po-leh-tah?*

Колко време продъл-
жава полетът?

What is the flight number?
*koy no-mehr eh
po-leh-ta?*

Кой номер е полетът?

You must check in at ...
*tryab-vah dah
preh-mi-neh-teh pres
kon-tro-lah-tah v ...*

Трябва да
преминете през
контролата в ...

airport tax	*sah-mo-leh-tnah tahk-sah*	самолетна такса
boarding pass	*bor-dnah kahr-tah*	бордна карта
customs	*mi-tni-tsah*	митница

Bus

BUS STOP	АВТОБУСНА СПИРКА
TRAMSTOP	ТРАМВАЙНА СПИРКА

Where is the bus stop?
ka-deh eh *ahf-to-bu-*
snah-tah **spir**-*kah?*

Къде е автобусната
спирка?

Which bus goes to ...?
koy ahf-to-bus o-ti-vah
do ...?

Кой автобус отива
до ...?

Does this bus go to ...?
to-zi ahf-to-bus
o-ti-vah li do ...?

този автобус
отива ли до ...?

How often do buses
pass by?
nah kol-ko vreh-meh
mi-nah-vaht ahf-to-bu-si?

На колко време
минават автобуси?

Could you let me know
when we get to ...?
bikh-teh li mi kah-zah-li,
ko-ghah-to sti-ghnehm
do ...?

Бихте ли ми казали,
когато стигнем до ...?

I want to get off!
is-kahm dah slya-zah!

Искам да сляза!

What time is the ... bus?
f kol-ko chah-sa eh ...
ahf-to-bus?

В колко часа е ...
автобус?

next	**slehd**-vah-shti-ya	следващият
first	**par**-vi-ya	първият
last	po-**sleh**-dni-ya	последният

Metro

METRO/UNDERGROUND	МЕТРО
CHANGE (for coins)	АВТОМАТ ЗА МОНЕТИ
THIS WAY TO ...	КЪМ ...
WAY OUT	ИЗХОД

Which line takes me to ...?
*s ko-**ya** **li**-ni-ya shteh* **sti**-gnah do ...?
    С коя линия ще стигна до ...?

What is the next station?
*ko-**ya** eh **slehd**-vah-shtah-tah **spir**-kah **stahn**-tsi-ya?*
    Коя е следващата спирка станция?

Train

DINING CAR	ВАГОН-РЕСТОРАНТ
EXPRESS	ЕКСПРЕС/БЪРЗ ВЛАК
PLATFORM	ПЕРОН
SLEEPING CAR	СПАЛЕН ВАГОН

Is this the right platform for ...?
*to-**vah** li eh peh-**ro**-na zah ...?*
    Това ли е перонът за ...?

Passengers must ...
    pa-*tni-tsi-teh* **tryab**-*vah dah* ...?
    Пътниците трябва да ...?

change trains
    *smeh-***nyat** *vlah*-*kah*
    сменят влака

change platforms
    *o-ti-daht nah druk peh-***rohn**
    отидат на друг перон

The train leaves from platform ...
    vlah-*kah zah-mi-***nah**-*vah ot peh-***rohn** ...
    Влакът заминава от перон ...

dining car	*vah-***ghon** *rehs-to-***rahnt**	вагон-ресто- рант
express	*ehks-***prehs** *barz vlahk*	експрес бърз влак
local	*krahy-***graht**-*ski vlahk*	крайградски влак
sleeping car	**spah**-*lehn vah-***ghon**	спален вагон
passenger train	**pa**-*tni-chehs-ki vlahk*	пътнически влак

Taxi

Can you take me to ...?
    *mo-zheh-teh li dah meh zah-***kah**-*rah-teh do* ...?
    Можете ли да ме закарате до ...?

Please take me to ...
    *mo-lya zah-***kah**-*rahy-teh meh do* ...
    Моля, закарайте ме до ...

How much does it cost to
go to ...?
   kol-ko stru-vah do ...?   Колко струва до ...?

Instructions

Here is fine, thank you.
   tuk eh do-breh,   Тук е добре,
   blah-gho-dah-rya   благодаря.
The next corner, please.
   nah slehd-vah-shti-ya   На следващия
   a-gal mo-lya   ъгъл, моля.
Continue!
   pro-dal-zhah-vahy-teh!   Продължавайте!
The next street to the left/
right.
   slehd-vah-shtah-tah   Следващата
   u-li-tsah nah-lya-vo   улица наляво/
   nah-dya-sno   надясно.
Stop here!
   spreh-teh tuk!   Спрете тук!
Please slow down.
   mo-lya nah-mah-leh-teh   Моля, намалете.
Please wait here.
   mo-lya chah-kahy-teh tuk   Моля, чакайте тук.

Some Useful Phrases

The train is delayed/
cancelled.
   vlah-kat i-mah   Влакът има
   zah-ka-sneh-ni-eh/   закъснение/
   eh o-tmeh-nehn.   е отменен.

How long will it be
delayed?
   kol-ko *vreh*-meh
   zah-ka-*sneh*-ni-eh
   i-mah *vlah*-kat?

Колко време
закъснение
има влакът?

There is a delay of ... hours.
   i-mah ... *chah*-sah
   zah-ka -*sneh*-ni-eh

Има ... часа
закъснение.

Can I reserve a place?
   mo-ghah li dah si
   zah-*pah*-zya *myas*-to?

Мога ли да си
запазя място?

How long does the trip
take?
   kol-ko *vreh*-meh *trah*-eh
   pa-*tu*-vah-neh-to?

Колко време трае
пътуването?

Is it a direct route?
   pryak pa t li eh?

Пряк път ли е?

Is that seat taken?
   to-*vah myas*-to
   zah-eh-to li eh?

Това място
заето ли е?

I want to get off at ...
   is-kahm dah *slya*-zah
   nah ...

Искам да сляза на ...

Excuse me.
   iz-vi-*neh*-teh

Извинете.

Where can I hire a bicycle?
   ka-*deh* dah-vaht veh-lo-
   si-*peh*-di pot nah-ehm?

Къде дават вело
сипеди под наем?

Car

DETOUR	ОТКЛОНЕНИЕ
FREEWAY	МАГИСТРАЛА
GARAGE	ГАРАЖ
GIVE WAY	ДАЙ ПРЕДИМСТВО
MECHANIC	МОНТЬОР
NO ENTRY	ВХОД ЗАБРАНЕН
NO PARKING	ЗАБРАНЕНО ПАРКИРАНЕТО
NORMAL	ОБИКНОВЕН
ONE WAY	ЕДНОПОСОЧНО ДВИЖЕНИЕ
REPAIRS	СЕРВИЗ
SELF SERVICE	НА САМООБ-СЛУЖВАНЕ
STOP	СПРИ
SUPER	СУПЕР
UNLEADED	БЕЗОЛОВЕН
DIESEL	ДИЗЕЛОВО ГОРИВО

Where can I rent a car?
*ka-**deh** mo-ghah dah nah-**eh**-mah ko-**lah?***

Къде мога да наема кола?

How much is it ...?
kol-ko stru-vah ...?

Колко струва ...?

daily/weekly
nah dehn/nah seh-dmi-tsah

на ден/на седмица

Does that include insurance/
mileage?

> *to-**vah** **fklyuch**-vah li
> zah-strah-**khof**-kah-tah/
> **pro**-beh-ghah?*

Това включва ли
застраховката
пробега?

Where's the next petrol
station?

> *ka-**deh** seh nah-**mi**-rah
> **slehd**-vah-shtah-tah
> behn-zi-no-**stahn**-tsi-ya?*

Къде се намира
следващата
бензиностанция?

Please fill the tank.

> *mo-lya nah-pal-**neh**-teh
> reh-zehr-vo-**ah**-rah*

Моля, напълнете
резервоара.

I want ... litres of petrol (gas).

> *is-kahm ... **lit**-rah
> behn-**zin***

Искам ... литра бензин.

Please check the oil and
water.

> *mo-lya pro-veh-**reh**-teh
> mah-**slo**-to i vo-**dah**-tah*

Моля, проверете
маслото и водата.

How long can I park here?

> *zah **kol**-ko **vreh**-meh
> **mo**-ghah dah
> pahr-**ki**-rahm tuk?*

За колко време
мога да
паркирам тук?

Does this road lead to ...?

> *to-zi pat vo-di li do ...?*

Този път води ли
до ...?

air (for tyres)	*vaz-dukh pot*	въздух под
	*nah-**lya**-ghah-neh*	налягане
battery	*a-ku-mu-**lah**-tor*	акумулатор

brakes	spi-**rahch**-ki	спирачки
clutch	ahm-bri-**ahsh**	амбриаж
driver's licence	sho-**fyor**-skah	шофьорска
	knish-kah	книжка
engine	dvi-**ghah**-tel	двигател
lights	sveh-tli-**ni**	светлини
oil	mah-**slo**	масло
puncture	**spuk**-vah-neh	спукване на
	nah **ghu**-mah	гума
radiator	rah-di-**ah**-tor	радиатор
road map	**pa**-tnah **kahr**-tah	пътна карта
tyres	**van**-shni **ghu**-mi	външни гуми
windscreen	**preh**-dno sta-**klo**	предно стъкло

Car Problems

I need a mechanic.
tryab-vah mi mon-**tyor**
Трябва ми монтьор.

What make is it?
kahk-**vah mahr**-kah eh
ko-**lah**-tah?
Каква марка е
колата?

The battery is flat.
ah-ku-mu-**lah**-to-rah eh
is-to-**stehn**
Акумулаторът е
изтощен.

The radiator is leaking.
rah-di-**ah**-to-rah
teh-**cheh**
Радиаторът тече.

I have a flat tyre.
i-mahm **spu**-kah-nah
ghu-mah
Имам спукана
гума.

It's overheating.
*preh-**ghrya**-vah*   Прегрява.
It's not working.
*neh rah-**bo**-ti*   Не работи.

Accommodation

CAMPING GROUND	КЪМПИНГ
GUEST HOUSE	ПАНСИОН
HOTEL	ХОТЕЛ
MOTEL	МОТЕЛ
YOUTH HOSTEL	ОБЩЕЖИТИЕ

Where is a ...?
*ka-**deh** i-mah ...?*   Къде има ...?
cheap hotel   *ehf-tin kho-**tehl***   евтин хотел
good hotel   *khu-**bahf** kho-**tehl***   хубав хотел
nearby hotel *kho-**tehl** bnah-**bli**-zo*   хотел наблизо
clean hotel   *chis kho-**tehl***   чист хотел

What is the address?
*kah-**kaf** eh ah-**dreh**-sat?*   Какъв е адресът?
Could you write the address,
please?
*bikh-teh li mo-**ghli**,*   Бихте ли могли
*dah mi nah-**pi**-sheh-teh*   да ми напишете
*ah-**dreh**-sah?*   адреса?

At the Hotel

Do you have any rooms
available?
> *i*-mah-teh li
> svo-**bo**-dni **stah**-i?

Имате ли
свободни стаи?

I would like ...
> bikh zheh-**lahl** ...

Бих желал ...

a single room	**stah**-ya s eh-**dno** leh-**ghlo**	стая с едно легло
a double room	**stah**-ya s dveh leh-**ghlah**	стая с две легла
a room with a bathroom	**stah**-ya z bah-nya	стая с баня
to share a dorm	leh-**ghlo** f op-shtah **spahl**-nya	легло в обща спалня
a bed	leh-**ghlo**	легло

I want a room with a ...
> is-kahm **stah**-ya sas ...

Искам стая с ...

bathroom	**bah**-nya	баня
shower	dush	душ
television	teh-leh-**vi**-zor	телевизор
window	pro-**zo**-rehts	прозорец

I'm going to stay for ...
> shteh os-**tah**-nah ...

Ще остана ...

one day	eh-**din** dehn	един ден
two days	dvah **deh**-nah	два дена
one week	eh-**dnah** seh-dmi-tsah	една седмица

Do you have identification?
> *i-mah-teh li do-ku-mehnt
> zah sah-mo-lich-nos?*

Имате ли документ
за самоличност?

Your membership card,
please.
> *vah-shah-tah chlehn-
> skah kahr-tah mo-lya*

Вашат членска
карта, моля.

Sorry, we're full.
> *sa-zhah-lya-vahm
> fsich-ko eh zah-eh-to*

Съжалявам,
всичко е заето.

How long will you be
staying?
> *kol-ko vreh-meh shteh
> os-tah-neh-teh?*

Колко време ще
останете?

How many nights?
> *kol-ko no-shti?*

Колко нощи?

It's ... per day/per person.
> *tryab-vah dah
> plah-ti-teh po ... nah
> dehn/nah cho-vehk*

Трябва да
платите по ... на
ден/на човек.

How much is it per night/
per person?
> *kol-ko eh nah veh-chehr/
> nah cho-vehk?*

Колко е на вечер/
на човек?

Can I see it?
> *mo-ghah li dah ya vi-dya?*

Мога ли да видя?

Are there any others?
> *i-mah-li dru-ghi?*

Има ли други?

Are there any cheaper
rooms?
   i-mah li **po ehf**-ti-ni
   stah-i?

Има ли по-евтини
стаи?

Can I see the bathroom?
   mo-ghah li dah **vi**-dya
   bah-nya-tah?

Мога ли да видя
банята?

Is there a reduction for
students/children?
   i-mah li nah-mah-**leh**-
   nieh zah stu-**dehn**-ti/
   deh-**tsah**?

Има ли намаление
за студенти/деца?

Does it include breakfast?
   zah-**kus**-kah-tah
   fklyu-cheh-nah li eh?

Закуската включена
ли е?

It's fine, I'll take it.
   do-**breh**, shteh ya
   vzeh-mah

Добре, ще я взема.

I'm not sure how long I'm
staying.
   neh znahm zah **kol**-ko
   vreh-meh shteh o
   stah-nah

Не знам за колко
време ще остана.

Is there a lift?
   i-mah li ah-sahn-**syor**?

Има ли асансьор?

Where is the bathroom?
   ka-**deh** eh **bah**-nya-tah?

Къде е банята?

Is there hot water all day?
   i-mah-li **to**-plah vo-**dah**
   prehs **tseh**-li-ya dehn?

Има ли топла вода
през целия ден?

Is there somewhere to wash
clothes?

*i-*mah li **myas**-to zah
prah-**neh** nah **dreh**-khi?

Има ли място за
пране на дрехи?

Can I use the kitchen?

mo-ghah li dah
pol-zvahm
ku-khnya-tah?

Мога ли да
ползувам
кухнята?

Can I use the telephone?

mo-ghah li dah
pol-zvahm
teh-leh-**fo**-nah?

Мога ли да
ползувам
телефона?

Requests & Complaints

Please wake me up at ...

mo-lya sa-bu-**deh**-teh
meh f ...

Моля, събудете ме в ...

The room needs to be
cleaned.

stah-ya-tah **tryab**-vah
dah seh po-**chis**-ti

Стаята трябва
да се почисти.

Please change the
sheets.

mo-lya smeh-**neh**-teh
chahr-**shah**-fi-teh

Моля, сменете
чаршафите.

I can't open/close the
window.

neh **mo**-ghah dah
zah-**tvo**-rya ot-**vo**-rya
pro-**zo**-reh-tsah

Не мога да отворя
затворя прозореца.

I've locked myself out of
my room.

    *vrah-**tah**-tah nah*
    ***stah**-ya-tah mi*
    *seh-czah-**klyu**hi i neh*
    ***mo**-ghah dah **flya**-zah*

Вратата на
стаята ми
се заключи и не.
мога да вляза.

The toilet won't flush.

    *vo-**dah**-tah f to-ah-**leh**-*
    *tnah-tah neh seh **pus**-ka*

Водата в тоалетната
не се пуска.

I don't like this room.

    *neh mi khah-**rehs**-vah*
    *tah-zi **stah**-ya*

Не ми харесва
тази стая.

It's too small.

    ***mno**-gho eh **mahl**-kah*

Много е малка.

It's noisy.

    ***shum**-nah eh*

Шумна е.

It's too dark.

    ***mno**-go eh ta **m**-nah*

Много е тъмна.

It's expensive.

    ***ska**-pah eh*

Скъпа е.

Some Useful Words & Phrases

I am/We are leaving now.

    *zah-mi-**nah**-vahm si/*
    *zah-mi-**nah**-vah-meh si*
    seh-ghah

Заминавам си/
Заминаваме си
сега.

I would like to pay the bill.

    *bikh **is**-kahl dah plah-**ta***
    ***smeht**-kah-tah*

Бих искал да платя
сметката.

name	*i-meh*	име
surname	*fah-**mil**-no i-meh*	фамилно име
room number	*no-mehr nah*	номер на
	***stah**-ya-tah*	стаята
address	*ah-**drehs***	адрес
air-conditioned	*s kli-mah-**tich**-nah*	с климатична
	*in-stah-**lah**-tsi-ya*	инсталация
balcony	*bahl-**kon***	балкон
bathroom	*bah-nya*	баня
bed	*leh-**ghlo***	легло
bill	*smeht-kah*	сметка
blanket	*o-deh-**ya**-lo*	одеяло
candle	*svehsh*	свещ
clean	*chis* (m)	чист
	chis-tah (f)	чиста
	chis-to (neut)	чисто
cupboard	*shkahf*	шкаф
dark	*ta-mehn* (m)	тъмен
	tam-nah (f)	тъмна
	tam-no (neut)	тъмно
dirty	*mra-sehn* (m)	мръсен
	mra-snah (f)	мръсна
	mra-sno (neut)	мръсно
double bed	*dvoy-no leh-**ghlo***	двойно легло
electricity	*eh-lehk-tro-eh-**nehr**-ghi-ya*	електроенер-гия
excluded	*neh eh **fklyu**-chehn*	не е включен
fan	*vehn-ti-**lah**-tor*	вентилатор
included	***fklyu**-chehn*	включен
	klyuch	ключ

lift (elevator)	*lift*	лифт
light bulb	*eh-lehk-**tri**-chehs-kah*	електрическа
	***krush**-kah*	крушка
lock (n)	*brah-**vah***	брава
	*klyu-**cahl**-kah*	ключалка
mattress	*dyu-**shehk***	дюшек
	*pru-**zhi**-nah*	пружина
mirror	*o-ghleh-**dah**-lo*	огледало
padlock	*kah-ti-**nahr***	катинар
pillow	*vaz-**ghlah**-vni-tsah*	възглавница
quiet	*tikh* (m)	тих
	ti-khah (f)	тиха
	ti-kho (neut)	тихо
room (in hotel)	*kho-**tehl**-skah **stah**-ya*	хотелска стая
safe	*sehyf*	сейф
sheet	*chahr-**shahf***	чаршав
shower	*dush*	душ
soap	*sah-**pun***	сапун
suitcase	***ku**-far*	куфар
swimming pool	*bah-**sehyn***	басейн
table	***mah**-sah*	маса
toilet	*to-ah-**leh**-tnah*	тоалетна
toilet paper	*to-ah-**leh**-tnah*	тоалетна
	*khahr-**ti**-ya*	хартия
towel	***kar**-pah*	кърпа
water	*vo-**dah***	вода
cold water	*stu-**deh**-nah vo-**dah***	студена вода
hot water	*gho-**reh**-shtah vo-**dah***	гореща вода
window	*pro-**zo**-rehts*	прозорец

Around Town

What time does it open?
kol-ko chah-**sa** gho
ot-**vah**-ryat?
В колко часа го
отварят?

What time does it close?
f **kol**-ko chah-**sa** gho
zaht-**vah**-ryat?
В колко часа го
затварят?

What street is this?
ko-**ya** eh **tah**-zi **u**-li-tsah? Коя е тази улица?

What suburb is this?
koy eh **to**-zi kvahr-**tahl**? Кой е този квартал?

For directions, see the Getting Around section, page 27.

I'm looking for ...
tar-sya ... Търся ...

the art gallery	khu-**do**-zheh-stveh-nah-tah ghah-**leh**-ri-ya	художестве-ната галерия
a bank	**bahn**-kah	банка
the church	**tsar**-kvah-tah	църквата
the city centre	**tsehn**-ta -rah nah grah-**dah**	центъра на града
the ... embassy	po-**sol**-stvo-to nah ...	посолството на ...
my hotel	lkho-**teh**-lah si	хотела си
the market	pah-**zah**-rah	пазара
the museum	mu-**zeh**-ya	музея
the police	po-**li**-tsi-ya-tah	полицията
the post office	**po**-shtah-tah	пощата

a public toilet	*ghraht-skah*	градска
	to-ah-leh-tnah	тоалетна
the telephone	*teh-leh-fon-nah-tah*	телефонната
centre	*tsehn-trah-lah*	централа
the tourist	*byu-ro-to zah*	бюрото за
information	*tu-ri-sti-chehs-kah*	туристическа
office	*in-for-mah-tsi-ya*	информация

At the Post Office

I would like some stamps.
dahy-teh mi po-shtehn-ski mahr-ki, mo-lya

Дайте ми пощенски марки, моля.

How much is the postage?
kol-ko stru-vah praht-kah-tah?

Колко струва пратката?

How much does it cost to send ... to England?
kol-ko stru-vah dah is-prah-tya ... do ahn-ghli-ya?

Колко струва да изпратя ... до Анлия?

I would like to send ...
is-kahm dah is-prah-tya ... Искам да изпратя ...

a letter	*pis-mo*	писмо
a postcard	*po-shtehn-skah*	пощенска
	kahr-tich-kah	картичка
a parcel	*ko-leht*	колет
a telegram	*teh-leh-ghrah-mah*	телеграма

an aerogram	*pi-smo z*	писмо с
	vaz-du-shnah	въздушна
	po-shtah	поща
air mail	*vaz-du-shnah*	въздушна
	po-shtah	поща
envelope	*plik zah pi-smo*	плик за писмо
mail box	*po-shtehn-skah*	пощенска
	ku-ti-ya	кутия
parcel	*ko-leht*	колет
registered mail	*preh-po-ra-chah-nah*	препоръчана
	po-shtah	поща
surface mail	*o-bil-no-veh-nah*	обикновена
	po-shtah	поща

Telephone

I want to ring ...		
	zheh-lah-ya dah se	желая да се
	o-bah-dya nah ...	обадя на ...
The number is ...		
	no-meh-rat eh ...	Номерът е ...
I want to speak for three minutes.		
	is-kahm dah gho-vo-rya	Искам да говоря
	tri mi-nu-ti	три минути.
How much does a three-minute call cost?		
	kol-ko	Колко
	stru-vahtri-minu-tehn	струватриминутен
	rahz-gho-vor?	разговор?

How much does each extra
minute cost?

> *kol*-ko **stru**-vah **vsya**-
> kah do-pal-**ni**-tehl-nah
> mi-**nu**-tah **rahz**-gho-vor?

Колко струва всяка
допълнителна
минута разговор?

I would like to speak to
Mr Perez.

> bikh **is**-kahl dah
> gho-**vo**-rya z ghos-po-**din**
> **peh**-rehs

Бих искал да
говоря с господин
Перес.

I want to make a reverse-
charges phone call.

> **is**-kahm dah seh
> o-**bah**-dya zah **tya**-khnah
> **smeht**-kah

Искам да се
обадя за тяхна
сметка.

It's engaged.

> **dah**-vah zah-**eh**-to

Дава заето.

I've been cut off.

> preh-**ka**-snah-khah meh

Прекъснаха ме.

At the Bank

I want to exchange
some money/travellers'
cheques.

> **is**-kahm dah o-bmeh-**nya**
> pah-**ri**/**pa**-tni-chehs-ki
> **cheh**-ko-veh

Искам да обменя
пари/пътнически
чекове.

What is the exchange rate?

> kah-**kaf** eh o-**bmehn**-
> ni-ya kurs?

Какъв е обменният
курс?

How many leva per dollar?
 kol-ko **leh**-vah zah
 do-lah?

Колко лева за долар?

Can I have money transferred
here from my bank?
 ot **mo**-ya-tah **bahn**-kah
 mo-ghaht li dah mi preh-
 veh-**dat** pah-**ri** tuk?

От моята банка
могат ли да ми
преведат пари тук?

How long will it take to
arrive?
 zah **kol**-ko **vreh**-meh
 shteh pri-**sti**-ghneh
 preh-vo-da t?

За колко време
ще пристигне
преводът?

Has my money arrived yet?
 pah-**ri**-teh mí pri-**sti**-
 ghnah-khah li **veh**-cheh?

Парите ми присти-
гнаха ли вече?

bankdraft	***bahn***-kov	банков
	preh-vodzah-pis	преводзапис
bank notes	bahn-**kno**-ti	банкноти
cashier	kah-si-**ehr** (m)	касиер
	kah-si-**ehr**-kah (f)	касиерка
coins	mo-**neh**-ti	монети
credit card	***kreh***-di-tnah	кредитна
	kahr-tah	карта
exchange	vah-**lu**-tnah	валутна
	o-**bmya**-nah	обмяна
loose change	pah-**ri** nah	пари на
	dreh-bno	дребно
signature	***pod***-pis	подпис

Sightseeing

Do you have a guidebook/
local map?

i-mah-teh li
tu-ris-*ti*-cheh-ski
pa-teh-vo-*di*-tehl
kahr-tah?

Имате ли
туристически
пътеводител карта?

What are the main attractions?

ko-*i* sah **ghlah-**vni-teh
zah-beh-leh-**zhi**-tehl-
nos-ti?

Кои са главните
забележителности?

What is that?

kahk-*vo* eh o-no-*vah*?

Какво е онова?

How old is it?

ot **kol**-ko gho-**di**-ni eh?

От колко години е?

Can I take photographs?

mo-ghah li dah **prah**-vya
snim-ki?

Мога ли да правя
снимки?

What time does it open/close?

ko-**ghah** gho o-*tvah*-ryat/
zah-**tvah**-ryat?

Кога го отварят/
затварят?

ancient	**dreh**-vehn	древен
archaeological	ahr-kheh-o-lo-**gi**-chehs-ki	археологи чески
beach	**mor**-ski bryak plahsh	морски бряг плаж
building	**zghrah**-dah	сграда
castle	**zah**-mak	замък
cathedral	kah-teh-**drah**-lah	катедрала
church	**tsark**-vah	църква

concert hall	kon-**tsehr**-tnah **zah**-lah	концертна зала
library	bi-bli-o-**teh**-kah	библиотека
main square	tsehn-**trah**-lehn plo-**shtaht**	централен площад
market	pah-**zahr**	пазар
monastery	mah-nahs-**tir**	манастир
monument	**pah**-meh-tnik	паметник
mosque	dzhah-**mi**-ya	джамия
old city	**stah**-ri-ya ghraht	старият град
opera house	o-**peh**-rah	опера
palace	dvo-**rehts** pah-**laht**	дворец палат
ruins	rahz-vah-li-**ni** o-stahn-ki	развалини останки
stadium	stah-di-**on**	стадион
statues	**stah**-tu-i	статуи
synagogue	si-nah-**gho**-ghah	синагога
temple	khrahm	храм
university	du-ni-vahr-si-**taht**	университет

Entertainment

What's there to do in the evenings?

   *kahk-**vi** rahz-vleh-**cheh**-ni-ya **i**-mah **veh**-chehr?*

Какви развлечения има вечер?

Are there any discos?

   *i-mah li dis-ko-**teh**-ki?*

Има ли дискотеки?

Are there places where you
can hear local folk music?
  *mo-zheh li **nya**-ka-deh
  dah seh **slu**-shah **bal**-
  gahr-skah nah-**rod**-nah
  nah-**rod**-nah **mu**-zi-kah?*

Може ли някъде
да се слуша
българска народна
музика?

How much does it cost to
get in?
  ***kol**-ko **stru**-vah
  vkho-dah?*

Колко струва входът?

cinema	*ki-no*	кино
concert	*kon-**tsehrt***	концерт
discotheque	*dis-ko-**teh**-kah*	дискотека
theatre	*teh-**ah**-tar*	театър

In the Country
Weather

What's the weather like?
  *kahk-**vo** eh **vreh**-meh-to?* Какво е времето?
The weather is ... today.
  ***vreh**-meh-to dnehs eh ...* Времето днес е ...
Will it be ... tomorrow?
  *shteh **ba**-deh li ... **u**-treh?* Ще бъде ли ... утре?

cloudy	*o-blah-chno*	облачно
cold	*stu-**deh**-no*	студено
foggy	*ma -**ghli**-vo*	мъгливо
frosty	*mrah-zo-**vi**-to*	мразовито
hot	*gho-**reh**-shto*	горещо

raining	*da zh-do-vi-to*	дъждовно
snowing	*sneh-gho-vi-to*	снеговито
sunny	***slan**-cheh-vo*	слънчево
windy	*veh-tro-vi-to*	ветровито

Camping

Am I allowed to camp here?
* **mo**-ghah li dah
   lah-gheh-**ru**-vahm tuk?

Мога ли да
лагерувам тук?

Is there a campsite nearby?
* **i**-mah li **kam**-pink
   nah-**bli**-zo?

Има ли къмпинг
наблизо?

backpack	*tu-ris-**ti**-chehs-kah*	туристическа
	***rah**-ni-tsah*	раница
can opener	*ot-vah-**rahch**-kah*	отварачка
	zah kon-sehr -vi	за консерви
compass	*kom-**pas***	компас
crampons	***kot**-ki*	котки
firewood	*dar-**vah** zah o-gan-ya*	дърва за огъня
gas cartridge	*pa l-**ni**-tehl z ghas*	пълнител с газ
hammock	*khah-**mahk***	хамак
ice axe	***pi**-kehl*	пикел
mattress	*dyu-**shehk***	дюшек
penknife	***nosh**-cheh*	ножче
rope	*va-**zheh***	въже
tent	*pah-**laht**-kah*	палатка
tent pegs	***kol**-cheh-tah zah*	колчета за
	*pah-**laht**-kah*	палатка
torch (flashlight)	*feh-**nehr**-cheh*	фенерче

sleeping bag	*spah-lehn chu-vahl*	спален чувал
stove	*pehch-kah*	печка
water bottle	*mah-nehr-kah*	манерка

Food

breakfast	*zah-kus-kah*	закуска
lunch	*o-beht*	обед
dinner	*veh-cheh-rya*	вечеря

Table for ..., please.
  mah-sah zah ..., mo-lya   Маса за ..., моля.
Can I see the menu please?
  mo-ghah li dah vi-dya   Мога ли да видя
  meh-nyu-to mo-lya?   менюто, моля?
I would like the set lunch,
please.
  bikh zheh-lahl   Бих желал
  kom-plehk-tu-vah-ni-ya   комплектувания
  o-byat mo-lya   обяд, моля.
What does it include?
  kahk-vo fklyuch-vah?   Какво включва?
Is service included in
the bill?
  op-sluzh-vah-neh-to   Обслужването
  fklyu-cheh-no li eh f   включено ли е в
  smeht-kah-tah?   сметката?
Not too spicy please.
  s po mahl-ko   С по-малко
  pot-prahf-ki mo-lya   подправки, моля.

BULGARIAN

ashtray	*peh-pehl-**nik***	пепелник
the bill	***smeht**-kah-tah*	сметката
a cup	***chahsh**-kah*	чашка
dessert	*deh-**sehrt***	десерт
a drink	*nah-**pit**-kah*	напитка
a fork	***vi**-li-tsah*	вилица
fresh	***preh**-sehn* (m)	пресен
	***prya**-snah* (f)	прясна
	***prya**-sno* (neut)	прясно
a glass	*sta-**kleh**-nah*	стъклена
	***chah**-shah*	чаша
a knife	*nosh*	нож
a plate	*chi-**ni**-ya*	чиния
spicy	*pi-**kahn**-tehn* (m)	пикантен
	*pi-**kahn**-tnah* (f)	пикантна
	*pi-**kahn**-tno* (neut)	пикантно
a spoon	*la-**zhi**-tsah*	лъжица
stale	*bah-**yat***	баят
sweet	***slah**-dak*	сладък
	***slahd**-kah*	сладка
	***slahd**-ko*	сладко
teaspoon	***chah**-eh-nah*	чаена
	*la-**zhich**-kah*	лъжичка
toothpick	***klehch**-kah zah **za**-bi*	клечка за зъби

Vegetarian Meals

I don't eat chicken, fish
or ham.

*neh yam **pi**-leh **ri**-bah i*   Не ям пиле, риба и
***shun**-kah*   шунка.

I am a vegetarian.
> *ahs sa m veh-gheh-tah-ri-ah-nehts* (m)/
> *veh-gheh-tah-ri-ahn-kah* (f)

Аз съм
вегетарианец/
вегетарианка.

I don't eat meat.
> *neh yam meh-so*

Не ям месо.

Баница
bah-ni-tsah

Made of very thin flaky pastry rolls stuffed with white cheese, yoghurt and eggs, baked in the oven.

Бъркани яйца с печени чушки
bar-kah-ni yay-tsah s peh-cheh-ni chush-ki

Scrambled eggs, fried together with diced roast peppers and grated white cheese. Served hot with finely chopped parsley on top.

Градинарска чорба
grah-di-nahr-skah chor-bah

Soup of celery, carrots, parsley, cabbage, potatoes with white cheese and milk added. Served seasoned with ground black pepper.

Гювеч
gyu-vehch

Made of peppers, tomatoes, eggplants, vegetable marrow, okra, onions, potatoes, green peas, parsley, etc, and cooked in the oven. It can also be prepared with pieces of meat.

Зрял фасул
zryal fah-sul

Boiled kidney beans with onions, carrots, celery, dried red pepper (hot or sweet) and mint. Served sprinkled with parsley.

Кьопоолу
kyop-o-o-lu

Aubergine purée with added crushed garlic, salt, vinegar and chopped parsley; garnished with slices of tomato or hard-boiled egg and parsley.

Спанак Загора
*spah-**nahk** zah-**go**-rah*

Spinach cooked, drained and baked on a buttered baking dish with a mixture of minced garlic cloves, sour cream, coarsely chopped walnuts, parmesan cheese, chopped onion, pepper and salt to taste.

Сирене по шопски
*si-reh-neh po **shop**-ski*

White cheese covered with chopped tomatoes, butter and paprika in an earthenware bowl and roasted in the oven. Served with thick egg topping and a small hot pepper.

Таратор
*tah-rah-**tor***

Finely chopped cucumber, crushed walnuts, garlic, oil, dill and salt, all mixed thoroughly in yoghurt. Served with finely chopped parsley and dill on top.

Чорба от зрял фасул
*chor-**bah** ot zryal fah-**sul***

Boiled haricot beans with tomato purée, paprika, mint, salt to taste, oil and lightly fried flour added. Served with chopped parsley, small hot peppers and vinegar to taste.

Шопска салата
*shop-skah sah-**lah**-tah*

Salad made of fresh tomatoes, cucumbers, sweet peppers and grated white cheese.

Main Dishes

Агнешка курбан-чорба
*ah-ghneh-shkah kur-**bahn** chor-**bah***

Boiled lamb cut into cubes with chopped onion, paprika, rice, salt to taste, parsley, and stirred eggs added.

Агнешка шкембе-чорба
*ah-ghneh-shkah shkehm-**beh** chor-**bah***

Soup of lamb's intestines with eggs added. Served seasoned with vinegar and garlic or with ground peppercorns and finely chopped parsley.

Дробсарма
drop-sar-mah

Boiled lamb's liver and intestines with rice and onions wrapped in caul fat and baked in the oven. Served with a thick egg sauce.

Друсан кебап
*dru-sahn keh-**bahp***

Large cubes of meat (usually lamb)first fried in fat and then boiled until tender, with salt, pepper, onions and parsley added. Served hot with fried potatoes, spring onions, gherkins and green salad.

Кебапчета на скара
*keh-**bahp**-cheh-tah nah **skah**-rah*

Oblong rissoles prepared from equal parts of lamb and veal, mixed together with finely chopped onion, cinnamon and salt to taste and grilled at high temperatures until a thin crust is formed, sealing in the meat's juices.

кюфтета на скара
*kyuf-**teh**-tah nah **skah**-rah*

Grilled meatballs prepared and served in much the same way as the rissoles above. Served immediately with finely chopped onions, parsley, small hot peppers, tomatoes, haricot beans and pepper relish.

Кисело мляко
ki-seh-lo mlya-ko

A unique Bulgarian yoghurt culture 'bacillus bulgaricus' which has acquired legendary status as a means of longevity.

Луканка
lu-kahn-kah

Traditional Bulgarian flat sausage usually made from dried pork, beef and spices.

Мусака от телешко месо
mu-sah-kah ot teh-lehsh-ko meh-so

Minced beef, sliced aubergines and tomatoes, finely chopped onion and parsley, black peppercorns and salt to taste — all covered with sauce made of flour, fat, eggs, milk and salt to taste, and baked in the oven.

Овнешко-пилаф
oy-nehsh-ko pi-lahf

Cubed mutton browned in its own fat or oil, with onions, seasonings, rice and tomatoes; cooked until tender.

Печено пиле с домати
peh-cheh-no pi-leh z do-mah-ti

Chicken rubbed with salt and oil and roasted in the oven with halved fresh tomatoes arranged around it; seasoned with salt and plenty of black pepper and served with cooked rice.

Пълнена риба-на фурна
pal-neh-nah ri-bah nah fur-nah

Special stuffed fish, usually made at Christmas. Carp, sea bass or pike is combined with cooked rice, sautéed onion, coarsely ground hazelnuts, basil and rosemary, with plenty of olive oil and lemon around the baked fish. Served cold.

Пълнени пиперки с месо
***pal**-neh-ni pi-**pehr**-ki s meh-so*

Peppers stuffed with minced veal or pork, paprika, rice, peeled and chopped tomatoes, chopped red pepper and parsley, and cooked in a deep saucepan in the oven. Served with sauce prepared from yoghurt, flour and eggs.

Пълнено агне-печено
***pal**-neh-no **ah**-ghneh peh-cheh-no*

Whole lamb stuffed with the finely chopped pluck and spring onions, rice, parsley, mint and salt to taste, and baked in the oven. Served with fried potatoes and green salad.

Пържено месо с праз-лук
***par**-zheh-no meh-**so** s prahz luk*

Pork cut into cubes and fried in a mixture of butter, diced peppers, finely chopped leeks and beaten eggs, and sprinkled with salt and paprika.

Пържоли на скара
*par-**zho**-li nah **skah**-rah*

Grilled veal or pork chops served hot with fried potatoes, roast skinned peppers, relish and pickles.

Риба в плик
***ri**-bah f plik*

Fish (ideally chub) salted, covered with a soft dough and cooked between sheets of greased paper in a parcel.

Риба-плакия
***ri**-bah plah-**ki**-ya*

One of the best known Bulgarian fish dishes, usually made with carp, baked (covered with slices of lemon) with a mixture of sautéed onion in oil and garlic, salt, pepper, paprika, sugar, water and tomato paste.

Свинско с кисело зеле
svin-sko s ki-seh-lo zeh-leh

Pieces of pork and chopped sauerkraut boiled in water and sauerkraut juice with pepper added.

Сърми със зелеви листа
sar-mi sas zeh-leh-vi li-stah

Cabbage leaves stuffed with a mixture of pork (sliced into small rectangular pieces), finely chopped fried onion, peppercorns and salt, and boiled until the meat inside the leaves is soft. Served on a bed of rice.

Сърми с лозови листа
sar-mi s lo-zo-vi li-stah

Vine leaves stuffed with a mixture of minced lean lamb or veal, white bread, finely chopped onion, rice, chopped herbs, salt and pepper, and cooked in a sauce of blanched and blended tomatoes or purée, with added sour cream or yoghurt. Served with red cabbage and salad.

Тюрлюгювеч
tyur-lyu-ghyu-vehch

Stew with diced mutton placed in an earthenware pan together with large pieces of tomatoes, peppers and potatoes, with onions, paprika, salt, carrots, butter, spring beans, sour grapes and beaten eggs added on top.

Чорба от пиле
chor-bah ot pi-leh

Soup made by cooking rice in chicken stock, seasoned with black pepper and salt to taste, and with an added mix of yoghurt, flour and beaten egg yolks; garnished with fresh mint and butter.

Шаран с орехов пълнеж
shah-rahn s o-reh-khof pal-nehsh

Carp stuffed with a mixture of cooked rice, tomatoes and peppers, fried onions, ground walnuts and cinnamon, placed on a baking dish with slices of lemon around the fish, and baked in the oven.

Шиш-кебап от агнешко
shish keh-bahp ot ah-ghneh-shko

Lamb meat cubes (salted in advance and marinaded in a mix of finely chopped onions and garlic), stuck on small skewers and cooked on a hot grill until the meat becomes dark red and soft.

Desserts

Баклава
bah-klah-vah

Thin flaky pastry, butter, walnuts, cinnamon and sugar syrup; baked in the oven.

Бисквити с орехи
bi-skvi-ti s o-reh-khi

Biscuit shapes cut out of soft dough (well-kneaded flour with melted butter, sugar, ground walnuts and grated lemon rind), dipped one side only into beaten egg white and mixture of crushed walnuts and sugar, and baked on a lightly buttered baking tray.

Халва
khahl-vah

Dessert usually made of melted butter, sugar and water. Served with crushed walnut kernels and cinnamon.

BULGARIAN

Nonalcoholic Drinks

buttermilk	*ahy-**ryan***	айрян
coffee	*kah-**feh***	кафе
black coffee	*shvahrts*	шварц
white coffee	*s **mlya**-ko*	с мляко
Turkish coffee	***tur**-sko*	турско
extract-coffee, espresso	*kah-**feh** eks-**preh**-so*	кафе-експресо
instant/soluble coffee	*nehs*	нес
fruit juice	***plo**-dof sok*	плодов сок
lemonade	*li-mo-**nah**-dah*	лимонада
nectar	*nehk-**tahr***	нектар
syrup	*si-**rop***	сироп
tea	*chahy*	чай
with milk	*s **mlya**-ko*	с мляко
with lemon	*s li-**mon***	с лимон
water	*vo-**dah***	вода
mineral water	*mi-neh-**rahl**-nah*	минерална
soda water	*ghah-**zi**-rah-nah*	газирана вода

Alcoholic Drinks

beer	***bi**-rah*	бира
bottled	*bu-ti-**li**-rah-nah*	бутилирана
on tap	*nah-**liy**-nah*	наливна
boza, millet-ale	*bo-**zah***	боза
brandy	*rah-**ki**-ya*	ракия
fruit brandy	*plo-**do**-vah*	плодова
grape brandy	***ghroz**-do-vah*	гроздова
plum brandy	***sli**-vo-vah*	сливова

cognac	ko-**nyak**	коняк
vodka	**vot**-kah	водка
whisky	**uy**-ski	уйски
wine	**vi**-no	вино
bottled wine	bu-ti-li-**rah**-no	бутилирано
broached wine	nah-**liv**-no	наливно
a dessert wine	**slaht**-ko	сладко
dry	**su**-kho	сухо
red/white	chehr-**veh**-no/**bya**-lo	червено/бяло
sparkling/	shu-**myash**-to	шумящо/
champagne	shahm-**pahn**-sko	шампанско

Shopping

How much is it?
   kol-ko **stru**-vah?   Колко струва?

bookshop	kni-**zhahr**-ni-tsah	книжарница
camera shop	mah-ghah-**zin** zah	магазин за
	fo-to-ah-pah-**rah**-ti	фотоапарати
clothing store	mah-ghah-**zin**	магазин
	zah o-bleh-**klo**	за облекло
delicatessen	deh-li-kah-**teh**-sehn	деликатесен
	mah-ghah-**zin**	магазин
general store	u-ni-vehr-**sah**-lehn,	универсален
shop	mah-ghah-**zin**	магазин
laundry	op-**shtehst**-veh-nah	обществена
	peh-**rahl**-nah	перална
market	pah-**zahr**	пазар
newsagency	rehp	РП
pharmacy	ahp-**teh**-kah	аптека

shoeshop	*mah ghah-zin*	магазин
	zah o-buf-ki	за обувки
souvenir shop	*mah-ghah-zin*	магазин
	zah su-veh-ni-ri	за сувенири
supermarket	*su-pehr-mahr-keht*	супермаркет
vegetable shop	*mah-ghah-zin zah*	магазин за
	plo-do-veh i	плодове и
	zeh-lehn-chu-tsi	зеленчуци

I would like to buy ...
   bikh is-kahl dah ku-pya ...   Бих искал да купя ...

Do you have others?
   i-mah-teh li dru-ghi?   Имате ли други?

I don't like it.
   neh mi khah-rehs-vah   Не ми харесва.

Can I look at it?
   mo-ghah li dah gho (m)/   Мога ли да го/я
   ya (f) *vi-dya?*   видя?

I'm just looking.
   sah-mo rahz-ghlehzh-   Само разглеждам.
   dahm

Can you write down the price?
   mo-zheh-teh li dah nah-   Можете ли да на
   pi-sheh-teh tseh-nah-tah?   пишете цената?

Do you accept credit cards?
   pri-eh-mah-teh li   Приемате ли
   kreh-di-tni kahr-ti?   кредитни карти?

Could you lower the price?
bikh-teh li mo-**ghli** dah
nah-mah-**li**-teh
tseh-**nah**-tah?

Бихте ли могли да
намалите цената?

Can I help you?
zheh-**lah**-eh-teh li
neh-shto?

Желаете ли нещо?

Will that be all?
to-**vah** li eh **fsich**-ko?

Това ли е всичко?

Would you like it
wrapped?
dah vi gho
o-pah-**ko**-vah-meh li?

Да Ви го
опаковаме ли?

How much/many do you
want?
kol-ko zheh-**lah**-eh-teh?

Колко желаете?

Souvenirs

earrings	o-beh-**tsi**	обеци
handicraft	**rach**-no iz-rah-**bo**-teh-ni iz-**deh**-li-ya	ръчно израбо-тени изделия
necklace	ghehr-**dahn**	гердан
pottery	keh-**rah**-mi-kah	керамика
ring	**pra**-stehn	пръстен
rug	ki-lim	килим

Clothing

clothing	o-bleh-**klo**	облекло
coat	pahla-**o**	палто

dress	*ro*-klya	рокля
jacket	*ya-keh sah-ko*	яке сако
jumper (sweater)	*pu-lo-vehr*	пуловер
shirt	*ri*-zah	риза
shoes	*o-buf-ki*	обувки
skirt	*po-lah*	пола
trousers	*pahn-tah-lo-ni*	панталони

It doesn't fit.
    *neh **mi stah**-vah*   Не ми става.

It is too ...
    ***mno**-gho eh ...*   Много е ...

big	*gho-**lyam*** (m)	голям
	*gho-**lya**-mah* (f)	голяма
	*gho-**lya**-mo* (neut)	голямо
small	***mah**-lak* (m)	малък
	***mahl**-kah* (f)	малка
	***mahl**-ko* (neut)	малко
short	***mno**-gho eh kas* (m)	Много е къс
	ka**-sah* (f)/ka**-so* (neut)	къса/късо
long	***mno**-gho **da**-lak* (m)	Много дълъг
	***dal**-ghah* (f)	дълга
	***dal**-gho* (neut)	дълго

Materials

cotton	*pah-**muk***	памук
handmade	*rach-nah*	ръчна
	*iz-rah-**bot**-kah*	изработка
leather	*ko-zhah*	кожа
of brass	*ot **meh**-sink*	от месинг

of gold	*ot zlah-to*	от злато
of silver	*ot sreh-bro*	от сребро
silk	*ko-pri-nah*	коприна
wool	*val-nah*	вълна

Colours

black	**cheh**-*rehn* (m)	черен
	chehr-*nah* (f)	черна
	chehr-*no* (neut)	черно
blue	*sin* (m)/**si**-*nya* (f)	син/синя
	si-*nyo* (neut)	синьо
brown	*ka-**fyaf** (m)	къфяв
	*ka-**fya**-vah* (f)	къфява
	*ka-**fya**-vo* (neut)	къфяво
green	*zeh-**lehn*** (m)	зелен
	*zeh-**leh**-nah* (f)	зелена
	*zeh-**leh**-no* (neut)	зелено
orange	*o-**rahn**-zhehf* (m)	оранжев
	*o-**rahn**-zheh-vah* (f)	оранжева
	*o-**rahn**-zheh-vo* (neut)	оранжево
red	*chehr-**vehn*** (m)	червен
	*chehr-**veh**-nah* (f)	червена
	*chehr-**veh**-no* (neut)	червено
white	*byal* (m)/**bya**-*lah* (f)	бял/бяла
	bya-*lo* (neut)	бяло
yellow	*zhalt* (m)/**zhal**-*tah* (f)	жълт/жълта
	zhal-*to* (neut)	жълто

Toiletries

| comb | **ghreh**-*behn* | гребен |
| condoms | *preh-zehr-vah-**ti**-vi* | презервативи |

deodorant	*deh-zo-do-**rahnt***	дезодорант
hairbrush	***cheht**-kah zah ko-**sah***	четка за коса
moisturising cream	*khi-drah-tahn-**tehn** krehm*	хидратантен крем
shaving razor	***nosh**-cheh zah bra-sneh-neh*	ножче за бръснене
sanitary napkins	***dahm**-ski preh-vras-ki*	дамски превръзки
shampoo	*shahm-po-**ahn***	шампоан
shaving cream	*krehm zah **bra**-sneh-neh*	крем за бръснене
soap	*sah-pun*	сапун
sunblock cream	*krehm protif **slan**-cheh-vo iz-**ghah**-rya-neh*	крем против слънчево изгаряне
tampons	*tahm-**po**-ni*	тампони
tissues	*knij-ni **kar**-pi-chki*	книжни кърпички
toilet paper	*leh-tnah khahr-**tiya***	тоалетна хартия
toothbrush	***cheht**-kah zah **za**-bi*	четка за зъби
toothpaste	***pah**-stah zah **za**-bi*	паста за зъби

Stationery & Publications

map	***kahr**-tah*	карта
newspaper	*veh-**snik***	вестник
newspaper in English	*veh-**snik** nah ahn-**ghliy**-ski*	вестник на английски
novels in English	*ro-**mah**-ni nah ahn-**ghliy**-ski*	романи на английски

paper	khahr-**ti**-ya	хартия
pen (ballpoint)	pi-**sahl**-kah	писалка
	khi-mi-**khahl**-kah	химикалка
scissors	**no**-zhi-tsi	ножици

Photography

How much is it to process
this film?
   kol-ko **stru**-vah
   pro-ya-**vya**-vah-neh-to
   nah **to**-zi film?

Колко струва
проявяването
на този филм?

When will it be ready?
   ko-**ghah** shteh
   ba -deh gho-**tof**?

Кога ще бъде готов?

I'd like a film for this
camera.
   zheh-**lah**-ya film zah
   to-zi ah-pah-**raht**

Желая филм за
този апарат.

B&W (film)	cher-no-byal	черно-бял
camera	fo-to-ah-pah-**raht**	фотоапарат
colour (film)	**tsveh**-tehn film	цветен филм
film	film	филм
flash	sveht-**kah**-vi-tsah	светкавица
lens	o-behk-**tif**	обектив
light meter	sveh-tlo-**mehr**	светломер

BULGARIAN

Smoking

A packet of cigarettes,
please.

*pah-**keht** tsi-**ghah**-ri,
mo-lya*

Пакет цигари, моля.

Are these cigarettes mild?

***teh**-zi tsi-**ghah**-ri
meh-ki li sah?*

Тези цигари
меки ли са?

Do you have a light?

*i-mah-teh li
o-**ghan**-cheh?*

Имате ли огънче?

cigarette papers	*khahr-**tiy**-ki zah tsi-**ghah**-ri*	хартийки за цигари
cigarettes	*tsi-**ghah**-ri*	цигари
filtered	*s **fil**-ta r*	с филтър
lighter	*zah-**pahl**-kah*	запалка
matches	*ki-**brit***	кибрит
menthol	*mehn-**tol***	ментол
pipe	*lu-**lah***	лула
tobacco (pipe)	*tyu-**tyun** za lu-**lah***	тютюн за лула

Sizes & Comparisons

small	***mah**-lak (m)	малък
	***mahl**-kah (f)	малка
	***mahl**-ko (neut)	малко
big	*gho-**lyam** (m)	голям
	*gho-**lya**-mah (f)	голяма
	*gho-**lya**-mo (neut)	голямо

heavy	*teh*-zhak (m)	тежък
	tehzh-kah (f)	тежка
	tehzh-ko (neut)	тежко
light	lehk (m)/*leh*-kah (f)	лек/лека
	leh-ko (neut)	леко
more	po-*veh*-cheh	повече
less	po *mahl*-ko	по-малко
too much/many	tvar-deh *mno*-gho	твърде много
many	*mno*-gho	много
enough	do-*stah*-tach-no	достатъчно
also	*sa*-shto	също
a little bit	*mahl*-ko	малко

Health

Where is the ...?
| *ka-deh* seh *nah-mi-rah* ...? | Къде се намира ...? |

doctor	*leh*-kahr-yat (m)	лекарят
	leh-kahr-kah-tah (f)	лекарката
hospital	*bol*-ni-tsah-tah	болницата
chemist	ahp-*teh*-kah-ryat (m)	аптекарят
	ahp-*teh*-kahr-kah-tah (f)	аптекарката
dentist	za-bo-*leh*-kahr-yat (m)	зъболекарят
	za-bo-*leh*-kahr-kah-tah (f)	зъболекарка-та

I am sick.
| *bo*-lehn sam (m) | Болен съм. |
| *bol*-nah sam (f) | болна съм. |

My friend is sick.
   pri-ya-teh-lyat
   mi eh bo-lehn (m)   Приятелят
   pri-ya-tehl-kah-tah   ми е болен.
   mi eh bol-nah (f)   Приятелката
                      ми е болна.
Could I see a female doctor?
   bikh li mo-ghlah dah   Бих ли могла да
   seh kon-sul-ti-rahm s се консултирам с
   leh-kahr-kah?   лекарка?
What's the matter?
   ot kahk-vo seh   От какво се
   o-plahk-vah-teh?   оплаквате?
Where does it hurt?
   ka-deh vi bo-li?   Къде Ви боли?

It hurts here.
   tuk meh bo-li   Тук ме боли.
My ... hurts.
   bo-li meh ...   Боли ме ...

Parts of the Body

ankle	***ghleh***-*zeh-nat*	глезенът
arm	*ra-**kah**-tah*	ръката
back	*ghar-**bay***	гърбът
chest	***ghra***-*dni-yat kosh*	гръдният кош
ear	*u-**kho**-to*	ухото
eye	*o-**ko**-to*	окото
finger	***pras***-*tat*	пръстът
foot	*sta-**pah**-lo-to*	стъпалото
hand	*ra-**kah**-tah*	ръката

head	*ghlah-**vah**-tah*	главата
heart	*sar-**tseh**-to*	сърцето
leg	*krah-**kat***	кракът
mouth	*u-**stah**-tah*	устата
nose	*no-**sat***	носът
skin	***ko**-zhah-tah*	кожата
spine	*ghra-**bnah**-kat*	гръбнакът
stomach	*sto-**mah**-khat*	стомахът
throat	***ghar**-lo-to*	гърлото

Ailments

I have ...		
*i-**mahm** ...*		Имам ...
an allergy	*ah-**lehr**-ghi-ya*	алергия
anaemia	*ah-**neh**-mi-ya*	анемия
a burn	*iz-**ghah**-rya-neh*	изгаряне
a cold	*pros-tu-**dil***	Простудил
	sam seh (m)	съм се.
	*pros-tu-**di**-lah*	Простудила
	sam seh (f)	съм се.
constipation	***zah**-pehk*	запек
a cough	***dkah**-shli-tsah*	кашлица
diarrhoea	*di-**ah**-ri-ya*	диария
fever	*tehm-peh-rah-**tu**-rah*	температура
	***trehs**-kah*	треска
a headache	*ghlah-vo-**bo**-li-eh*	главоболие
hepatitis	*kheh-pah-**tit***	хепатит
indigestion	*sto-**mah**-shno*	стомашно
	*rahs-**stroy**-stvo*	разстройство
an infection	*in-**fehk**-tsi-ya*	инфекция

influenza	*ghrip*	грип
lice	**vash**-*ki*	вършки
low/high blood pressure	*nis-ko /vi-so-ko* **kra**-*vno* *nah-***lya**-*ghah-neh*	ниско/високо крьвно- налягане
a pain	**bol**-*kah*	болка
sore throat	*vas-pah-***leh**-*no* **ghar**-*lo*	възпалено гърло
sprain	*nah-***vyakh**-*vah-neh*	навяхване
sunburn	**slan**-*cheh-vo* *iz-***ghah**-*rya-neh*	слънчево изгаряне
a venereal disease	*veh-neh-***ri**-*chnah* **bo**-*les*	венерична болест
worms	**ghli**-*sti*	глисти

Some Useful Words & Phrases

I'm ...
  ahs sam ...   Аз съм ...

diabetic	*di-ah-beh-***tik**	диабетик
epileptic	*eh-pi-lehp-***tik**	епилептик
asthmatic	*ah-smah-***tik**	астматик

I'm allergic to ...
  *ah-lehr-***ghi**-*chehn sam* ...(m)   Алергичен съм ...
  *ah-lehr-***ghi**-*chnah sam* ...(f) Алергична съм ...

antibiotics	*kam ahn-ti-bi-***o**-*ti-tsi*	към антибио- тици
penicillin	*peh-ni-tsi-***lin**	пеницилин

I'm pregnant.
  breh-mehn-nah sam   Бременна съм.
I'm on the pill.
  vzeh-mahm pro-ti-vo-   Вземам
  zah-chah-ta-chni   противозачатъчни
  khahp-cheh-tah   хапчета.
I haven't had my period
for ... months.
  neh sam i-mah-lah   Не съм имала
  mehn-stru-ah-tsi-ya ot ...   менструация от ...
I have been vaccinated.
  vahk-si-ni-rahn sam (m)   Ваксиниран съм.
  vahk-si-ni-rah-nah   ваксинирана съм.
  sam (f)
I have my own syringe.
  i-mahm sob-stveh-nah   Имам собствена
  i-ghlah   игла.
I feel better/worse.
  chuf-stvahm seh   Чувствувам се
  po-do-breh/po-zleh   по-добре/по-зле.

accident	*zlo-po-lu-kah*	злополука
addiction	*nahr-ko-mah-ni-ya*	наркомания
antibiotics	*ahn-ti-bi-o-ti-tsi*	антибиотици
antiseptic	*ahn-ti-sehp-ti-chno*	антисептично
	srehd-stvo	средство
aspirin	*ahs-pi-rin*	аспирин
bandage	*bint*	бинт
blood pressure	*kra-vno nah-lya-*	кръвно наля-
	ghah-neh	гане

blood test	is-**slehd**-vah-neh nah kraf-**tah**	изследване на кръвта
contraceptive	pro-ti-vo-zah-**chah**-ta-chno **sreht**-stvo	противозача-тъчно средство
injection	in-**zhehk**-tsi-ya	инжекция
medicine	leh-**kahr**-stvo	лекарство
menstruation	mehn-stru-**ah**-tsi-ya	менструация
nausea	**mor**-skah **bo**-lehs **ghah**-deh-neh	морска болест гадене
oxygen	ki-slo-**rot**	кислород
vitamins	vi-tah-**mi**-ni	витамини

At the Chemist

I need medication for ...
   nuzh-**dah**-ya seh ot
   leh-**kahr**-stveh-no
   leh-**cheh**-ni-eh zah ...
I have a prescription.
   i-mahm reh-**tsehp**-tah

Нуждая се от лекарствено лечение за ...

Имам рецепта.

At the Dentist

I have a toothache.
   bo-**li** meh zap
I've lost a filling.
   pah-dnah mi **plom**-bah
I've broken a tooth.
   schu-pikh si za p
My gums hurt.
   bo-**lyat** meh vehn-**tsi**-teh

Боли ме зъб.

Падна ми пломба.

Счупих си зъб.

Болят ме венците.

I don't want it extracted.
> *neh **is**-kahm dah gho*
> ***vah**-di-teh*

Не искам да го
вадите.

Please give me an anaesthetic.
> *mo-lya **dahy**-teh mi*
> *o-behz-bo-**lya**-vah-shto*

Моля, дайте ми
обезболяващо.

Time & Dates

What time is it?
> ***kol**-ko eh chah-**sat**?*

Колко е часът?

It is ... am/pm.
> *chah-**sat** eh ... preh-**di***
> *o-**beht**/sleht o-**beht***

Часът е ... преди обед/
след обед.

What date is it today?
> *ko-**ya** **dah**-tah eh dnehs?*

Коя дата е днес?

in the morning	*su-trin*	сутрин
in the afternoon	*sleh-**do**-beht*	следобед
in the evening	*veh-chehr*	вечер

Days of the Week

Monday	*po-neh-**dehl**-nik*	понеделник
Tuesday	*ftor-nik*	вторник
Wednesday	*srya-dah*	сряда
Thursday	*cheht-**var**-tak*	четвъртък
Friday	*peh-tak*	петък
Saturday	*sa-bo-tah*	събота
Sunday	*neh-**deh**-lya*	неделя

Months

January	*ya-nu-**ah**-ri*	януари
February	*feh-vru-**ah**-ri*	февруари
March	*mart*	март
April	*ah-**pril***	април
May	*mahy*	май
June	***yu**-ni*	юни
July	***yu**-li*	юли
August	*ahv-**ghus***	август
September	*sehp-**tehm**-vri*	септември
October	*ok-**tom**-vri*	октомври
November	*no-**ehm**-vri*	ноември
December	*deh-**kehm**-vri*	декември

Seasons

summer	***lya**-to*	лято
autumn	***eh**-sehn*	есен
winter	***zi**-mah*	зима
spring	***pro**-leht*	пролет

Present

today	*dnehs*	днес
this morning	***tah**-zi **su**-trin*	тази сутрин
tonight	*do-**veh**-cheh-rah*	довечера
this week/year	***tah**-zi **seh**-dmi-tsah*	тази седмица
	*gho-**di**-nah*	година
now	*seh-**ghah***	сега

Past

yesterday	*fcheh*-rah	вчера
yesterday morning	*fcheh*-rah su-trin-**tah**	вчера сутринта
last night	**mi**-nah-lah-tah nosh	миналата нощ
	veh-chehr	вечер
last week/year	**mi**-nah-lah-tah	миналата
	gho-**di**-nah	година

Future

tomorrow	*utreh*	утре
day after tomorrow	*vdru-ghi dehn*	другиден
next year	**slehd**-vah-shtah-tah	ледващата
	gho-**di**-nah	година

During the Day

afternoon	slehd-**o**-beht	следобед
dawn, very early morning	**u**-tro	утро
day	*dehn*	ден
early	**rah**-no	рано
midnight	sreh-**dnosh**	среднощ
morning	**su**-trin	сутрин
night	*nosh*	нощ
noon	*o-beht*	обед
sunset	**zah**-lehs	залез
sunrise	**iz**-ghrehf	изгрев

Numbers & Amounts

0	*nu-lah*	нула
1	*eh-din* (m)	един
	eh-dnah (f)	една
	eh-dno (neut)	едно
2	*dvah* (m)/*dveh* (f/neut)	два/две
3	*tri*	три
4	*cheh-ti-ri*	четири
5	*peht*	пет
6	*shehs*	шест
7	*seh-dehm*	седем
8	*o-sehm*	осем
9	*deh-veht*	девет
10	*deh-seht*	десет
20	*dvahy-seht*	двайсет
30	*triy-seht*	трийсет
40	*cheh-ti-riy-seht*	четирийсет
50	*pehd-deh-seht*	петдесет
60	*shehz-deh-seht*	шестдесет
70	*seh-dehm-deh-seht*	седемдесет
80	*o-sehm-deh-seht*	осемдесет
90	*deh-vehd-deh-seht*	деветдесет
100	*sto*	сто
1000	*khi-lya-dah*	хиляда
one million	*eh-din mi-li-on*	един милион
1st	*par-vil-vah/-vo*	първи/-ва/-во
2nd	*fto-ril-rah/-ro*	втори/-ра/-ро
3rd	*treh-til-tah/-to*	трети/-та/-то

1/4	eh-**dnah cheht**-vart	една четвърт
1/3	eh-**dnah treh**-tah	една трета
1/2	eh-**dnah fto**-rah	една втора
3/4	tri **cheht**-var-ti	три четвърти

Some Useful Words

a little (amount)	**mahl**-ko	малко
	ko-**li**-cheh-stvo	количество
double	**dvoy**-no	двойно
a dozen	du-**zi**-nah	дузина
Enough!	do-**stah**-ta-chno/	Достатъчно/
	sti-ghah	стига.
few	**mahl**-ko **nya**-kol-ko	малко няколко
less	po **mahl**-ko	по-малко
many	**mno**-gho	много
more	**po**-veh-cheh	повече
once	veh-**dnash**/	веднъж/
	eh-**din** pat	един път
a pair	chif	чифт
percent	pro-**tsehnt**	процент
some	**nya**-kol-ko/	няколко/
	mahl-ko	малко
too much	tvar-deh **mno**-gho	твърде много
twice	dvah **pa**-ti	два пъти

Abbreviations

БДЖ	Bulgarian Railways
БТА	Bulgarian Telegraph Agency
ВУЗ	Institute of Higher Education/University
г/кг	gm/kg
г-н/г-жа/ г-ца	Mr/Mrs/Ms
ДЕТМАГ	Children's World (store)
д-р	Dr
ЕИО	EEC
и др.	et al.
и т.н.	etc
КАТ	Traffic Police
ЮНЕСКО	UNESCO
от н.е./ от ст.е.	AD/BC
СПИН	AIDS
см/м/км	cm/m/km
СОС	SOS
САЩ	USA
ООН	UN
ул./бул./ пл.	St/Rd/Sq
ЦУМ	'Central Universal Store' (major department store)
ч/мин/сек	h/min/sec

Czech

Introduction

The Czech language belongs to the Slavonic group of Indo-European languages, which is subdivided into East, West and South Slavonic groups. Czech, together with Slovak, Polish and Lusatian, is part of the West Slavonic group. It is the main language of the Czech Republic and is spoken by 10 million people.

Although Czech has several dialects, this phrasebook uses a standardised form of the language, literary Czech (*spisovná čeština*), which is based on the central Bohemian dialect. However, this is no longer associated with a particular social group or territory, and functions as a common language understood by all Czechs. Therefore, you won't have trouble communicating wherever you are in the country.

Some Czech sentences will be phrased differently depending on whether you are male or female, so both forms are given when applicable.

Pronunciation

Czech is spelt as it is spoken, and once you become familiar with the sounds, it can be read easily.

Vowels

An accent over a vowel indicates that it is lengthened.

a	as the 'ah' sound in 'cut'
á	as the 'a' in 'father'
e	as the 'eh' sound in 'bet'
é	as 'air'
ě	as the 'ye' in 'yet'
i/y	as the 'i' in 'bit'
í/ý	as the 'ee' in 'see'
o	as the 'o' in 'pot'
ó	as the 'aw' in 'saw'
u	as the 'u' in 'pull'
ú/ů	as the 'oo' in 'zoo'

Diphthongs

aj	as the 'i' in 'ice'
áj	like 'eye'
au	an 'ow' sound as in 'out'
ej	as the 'ay' in 'day'
ij/yj	a short 'eey' sound
íj/ýj	a long 'eey' sound
oj	as the 'oi' in 'void'
ou	as the 'o' in 'note', but both the 'o' and 'u' are more strongly pronounced than in English
uj	a short 'u' sound as in 'pull', followed by 'y'
ůj	a long 'oo' sound as in 'zoo', followed by 'y'

Consonants

c	as the 'ts' in 'lets'
č	as the 'ch' in 'chew'
ch	a 'kh' sound, as in the Scottish 'loch', or German 'Buch'

g	a hard sound like the 'g' in 'get'
h	always pronounced, as the 'h' in 'hand'
j	as the 'y' in 'year'
r	a rolled 'r', made with the tip of the tongue
ř	'rzh'. It's the sound in the composer's name Dvořák – a rolled 'r' followed by the 's' in 'treasure'.
s	as the 's' in 'sit', not as in 'rose'
š	as the 'sh' in 'ship'
ž	a 'zh' sound, as the 's' in 'treasure'
ď, ň & ť	are very soft palatal sounds. There is a momentary contact between the tongue and the hard palate, as if a 'y' sound is added, as in the 'ny' in canyon. The same sound occurs with **d**, **n** and **t** followed by **i**, **í** & **ě**.

All other consonants are similar to English, apart from **k**, **p** and **t**, which are pronounced with no puff of breath after them.

Stress

In Czech the first syllable is usually stressed. Vowels are pronounced the same whether they are stressed or not – say each syllable clearly and distinctly.

Greetings & Civilities
Top 10 Useful Phrases
Hello./Goodbye.

dob-ree-dehn/
nah-skhleh-dah-noh

Dobrý den./
Na shledanou.

Yes./No.
   ah-*no*/*neh*   Ano./Ne.
Yes. (colloquial)
   yo   Jo.
Excuse me.
   zdo-*vo*-*leh*-*nyeem*   S dovolením.
May I? Do you mind?
   do-*vol*-*teh*-*mi?*   Dovolte mi?
Sorry. (excuse me,
   forgive me)
   pro-*miny*-*teh*   Promiňte.
Please.
   pro-*seem*   Prosím.
Thank you.
   dyeh-*ku*-*yi*   Děkuji.
Many thanks.
   mots-*kraat* *dyeh*-*ku*-*yi*   Mockrát děkuji.
That's fine. You're welcome.
   neh-*nyee* *zahch.* *pro*-   Není zač. Prosím.
   seem

Greetings

Good morning!
   dob-*rair* *yit*-*ro* (*raa*-*no*)!   Dobré jitro (ráno)!
Good afternoon!
   dob-*rair* *ot*-*po*-*lehd*-*neh*!   Dobré odpoledne!
Good evening/night!
   dob-*ree* *veh*-*chehr*!   Dobrý večer!
   dob-*roh* *nots*!   Dobrou noc!

How are you?
   *yahk-seh **maa**-teh?*   Jak se máte?
Well, thanks.
   *dyeh-ku-yi, **dob**-rzheh*   Děkuji, dobře.

Forms of Address

Madam/Mrs	***pah**-nyee*	Paní
Sir/Mr	*pahn*	Pan
Miss	***slehch**-nah*	Slečna
companion,	***przhee**-tehl* (m)	přítel
friend	***przhee**-tehl-ki-nyeh* (f)	přítelkyně

Small Talk
Meeting People

What is your name?
   *yahk-seh **ymeh**-nu-yeh-teh?* Jak se jmenujete?
My name is ...
   ymeh-nu-yi-seh ...   Jmenuji se ...
I'd like to introduce you
to ...
   *mo-hu vaas **przheht**-* Mohu vás představit ...
   stah-vit ...
I'm pleased to meet you.
   tye-shee mnyeh, zheh Těší mně, že vás poznávám.
   *vaas **po**-znaa-vaam*

I like ...
   *mnyeh **seh**-to lee-bee ...* Mně se to líbí ...

I don't like ...
  *mnyeh **seh**-to*
  neh-lee-bee ...   Mně se to nelíbí ...
How old are you?
  ***ko**-lik yeh vaam leht?*   Kolik je vám let?
I am ... years old.
  yeh mi ... let   Je mi ... let.

Nationalities
Where are you from?
  ***od**-kud **po**-khaa-zee-teh?*   Odkud pocházíte?

I am from ...
  ysehm ...   Jsem ...

Australia	*sow-straa-li-yeh*	z Austrálie
Canada	*skah-nah-di*	z Kanady
England	*sahn-gli-yeh*	z Anglie
Ireland	*sir-skah*	z Irska
New Zealand	*sno-vair-ho* *zair-lahn-du*	z Nového Zélandu
Scotland	*zeh **skot**-skah*	ze Skotska
the USA	*zeh **spo**-yeh-neekh* *staa-too*	ze Spojených států
Wales	*zvah-leh-su*	z Walesu

Occupations
What do you do?
  *tso **dyeh**-laa-teh?*   Co děláte?
I am a/an ...
  ysehm ...   Jsem ...

artist	*u*-*myeh-lehts* (m)	umělec
	u-*myehl-ki-nyeh* (f)	umělkyně
business person	*op*-*kho-dnyeek* (m)	obchodník
	op-*kho-dnyi-tseh* (f)	obchodnice
doctor	*lair*-*kahrzh* (m)	lékař
	lair-*kahrzh-kah* (f)	lékařka
engineer	*in*-*zheh-neer* (m)	inženýr
	in-*zheh-neer-kah* (f)	inženýrka
farmer	*zeh*-*myeh-dyeh-lehts* (m)	zemědělec
	zeh-*myeh-dyehl-ki-nyeh* (f)	zemědělkyně
journalist	*no*-*vi-naarzh* (m)	novinár
	no-*vi-naarzh-kah* (f)	novinářka
lawyer	*praa*-*vnyeek* (m)	právník
	praa-*vnyi-chkah* (f)	právnička
manual worker	*dyehl*-*nyeek* (m)	dělník
	dyehl-*nyi-tseh* (f)	dělnice
mechanic	*ow*-*to-meh-khah-nik* (m)	automechanik
	ow-*to-meh-khah-nich-kah* (f)	automechanička
nurse	*o*-*sheh-trzho-vah-tehl* (m)	ošetřovatel
	o-*sheh-trzho-vah-tehl-kah* (f)	ošetřovatelka
office worker	*oo*-*rzheh-dnyeek* (m)	úředník
	oo-*rzheh-dnyi-tseh* (f)	úřednice
scientist	*vyeh*-*dehts* (m)	vědec
	vyeht-*ki-nyeh* (f)	vědkyně
student	*stu*-*dehnt* (m)	student
	stu-*dehnt-kah* (f)	studentka

teacher	*u*-chi-tehl (m)	učitel
	u-chi-tehl-kah (f)	učitelka
waiter	*chee*-shnyeek (m)	číšník
	chee-shnyi-tseh	číšnice
	(*sehr*-veer-kah) (f)	(servírka)
writer	*spi*-so-vah-tehl (m)	spisovatel
	spi-so-vah-tehl-kah (f)	spisovatelka

Religion

What is your religion?

yah-kair-ho ysteh	Jakého jste náboženského
naa-bo-zhehn-skair-ho	vyznání?
vi-znaa-nyee?	

I am not religious.

ysehm behz *vi*-znaa-nyee	Jsem bez vyznání.

I am ...

ysehm ...	Jsem ...
Buddhist	*bu*-dhi-stah (m)	buddhista
	bu-dhist-kah (f)	budhistka
Catholic	*kah*-to-leek (m)	katolík
	kah-to-li-chkah (f)	katolička
Christian	*krzheh*-styahny (m)	křesťan
	krzheh-styahny-kah (f)	křesťanka
Hindu	*hin*-du	hindu
Jewish	zhid (m)	žid
	zhi-dof-kah (f)	židovka
Muslim	*mu*-slim (m)	muslim
	mu-slim-kah (f)	muslimka

CZECH

Family

Are you married?
   *ysteh **zheh**-nah-tee?* (m)   Jste ženatý?
   *ysteh **vdah**-naa?* (f)   Jste vdaná?

I am single.
   *ysehm **svo**-bo-dnee* (m)   Jsem svobodný.
   *ysehm **svo**-bo-dnaa* (f)   Jsem svobodná.

I am married.
   *ysehm **zheh**-nah-tee* (m)   Jsem ženatý.
   *ysehm **fdah**-naa* (f)   Jsem vdaná.

How many children do you have?
   *ko-lik **maa**-teh **dyeh**-tyee?*   Kolik máte dětí?

I don't have any children.
   ***neh**-maam **dyeh**-tyi*   Nemám děti.

I have a daughter/a son.
   ***maam** si-nah/**tseh**-ru*   Mám syna/dceru.

How many brothers/sisters do you have?
   *ko-lik **maa**-teh*   Kolik máte bratrů/sester?
   ***brah**-troo/**sehs**-tehr?*

Is your husband here?
   *yeh zdeh **vaash***   Je zde váš manžel?
   ***mahn**-zhehl?*

Is your wife here?
   *yeh zdeh **vah**-sheh***   Je zde vaše manželka?
   ***mahn**-zhehl-kah?*

Do you have a boyfriend/
girlfriend?
> **maa**-teh **znaa**-most?   Máte známost?

brother	**brah**-tr	bratr
children	**dyeh**-tyi	děti
daughter	**tseh**-rah	dcera
family	**ro**-dyi-nah	rodina
father	**o**-tehts	otec
grandfather	**dyeh**-deh-chehk	dědeček
grandmother	**bah**-bi-chkah	babička
husband	**mahn**-zhehl	manžel
mother	**maht**-kah	matka
sister	**sehs**-trah	sestra
son	sin	syn
wife	**mahn**-zhehl-kah	manželka

Feelings
(I am ...)

angry	hnyeh-vaam-seh	Hněvám se.
cold	yeh mi **zi**-mah	Je mi zima.
happy	ysehm **shtyahst**-nee (m)	Jsem šťastný.
	ysehm **shtyahst**-naa (f)	Jsem šťastná.
hot	yeh mi **hor**-ko	Je mi horko.
hungry/thirsty	maam hlaht/ **zhee**-zehny	Mám hlad/žízeň.
in a hurry	spyeh-khaam	Spěchám.
right	maam **prahf**-du	Mám pravdu.

CZECH

sad	*ysehm* **smut**-*nee* (m)	Jsem smutný.
	ysehm **smut**-*naa* (f)	Jsem smutná.
tired	*ysehm* **u**-*nah-veh-nee* (m)	Jsem unavený.
	ysehm **u**-*nah-veh-naa* (f)	Jsem unavená.
well	**mnyeh**-*yeh* **dob**-*rzheh*	Mně je dobře.
worried	*maahm* **stah**-*rost*	Mám starost.

I am sorry. (condolence)
   u-przhee-mnoh **soh**-*strahst* Upřímnou soustrast.
I am grateful.
   ysehm vaam **vdyehch**-*nee* (m) Jsem vám vděčný.
   ysehm vam **vdyehch**-*naa* (f) Jsem vám vděčná.

Language Problems

Do you speak English?
   mlu-*vee-teh* **ahn**-*glits-ki?* Mluvíte anglicky?
Does anyone speak English?
   mlu-*vee* **nyeh**-*gdo* **ahn**-*glits-ki?* Mluví někdo anglicky?
I speak a little ...
   mlu-*veem* **tro**-*khu* ... Mluvím trochu ...
I don't speak ...
   neh-*mlu-veem* ... Nemluvím ...
I understand.
   ro-zu-meem Rozumím.

I don't understand.
  neh-roh-zu-meem   Nerozumím.
Could you speak more
slowly please?
  moo-zheh-teh mlu-vit Můžete mluvit pomaleji?
  po-mah-leh-yi?
Could you repeat that?
  moo-zheh-teh to   Můžete to opakovat?
  o-pah-ko-vaht?
How do you say ...?
  yahk-seh rzheh-kneh ...? Jak se řekne ...?
What does ... mean?
  tso znah-meh-naa ...? Co znamená ...?

I speak ...
  mlu-veem ...   Mluvím ...
Dutch   *ho-lahn-ski*   holandsky
English   *ahn-glits-ki*   anglicky
French   *frahn-tsoh-ski*   francouzsky
German   *nye-mehts-ki*   německy
Hungarian   *mah-dyahrs-ki*   maďarsky
Italian   *i-tahl-ski*   italsky
Russian   *rus-ki*   rusky
Spanish   *shpah-nyehl-ski* španělsky

Some Useful Phrases
Sure.
  yi-styeh!   Jistě!
Just a minute.
  poch-kehy-teh khvee-li Počkejte chvíli.

It's important.
toh-yeh **doo**-le-zhi-tair — To je důležité.

It's not important.
toh **neh**-nyi **doo**-leh-zhi-tair — To neni důležité.

It's possible.
to-yeh **mo**-zhnair. — To je možné.

It's not possible.
to **neh**-nyi **mo**-zhnair — To neni možné.

Wait!
poch-kehy-teh! — Počkejte!

Good luck!
przheh-yu vaam **mno**-ho **shtyeh**-styee! — Přeju vám mnoho štěstí!

Signs

BAGGAGE COUNTER	PODEJ ZAVAZADEL
CHECK-IN COUNTER	ODBAVENÍ
CUSTOMS	CELNICE
EMERGENCY EXIT	NOUZOVÝ VÝCHOD
ENTRANCE	VCHOD
EXIT	VÝCHOD
FREE ADMISSION	VSTUP VOLNÝ
HOT/COLD	TEPLÁ/STUDENÁ
INFORMATION	INFORMACE
NO ENTRY	VSTUP ZAKÁZÁN
NO SMOKING	ZÁKAZ KOUŘENÍ
OPEN/CLOSED	OTEVŘENO/ZAVŘENO
PROHIBITED	ZAKÁZÁNO

RESERVED	ZADÁNO/RESERVOVÁNO
TELEPHONE	TELEFON
TOILETS	ZÁCHODY/WC/TOALETY

Emergencies

POLICE	POLICIE
POLICE STATION	POLICEJNÍ STANICE

Help!
  po-mots

Pomoc!

It's an emergency!
  to-yeh **nah**-lair-hah-vee
  przhee-paht!

To je naléhavý případ!

There's been an accident!
  do-shlo **kneh**-ho-dyeh

Došlo k nehodě!

Call a doctor/ambulance/
police!
  zah-vo-lehy-teh **do**-kto-
  rah/**sah**-nit-ku/**po**-li-tsi-yi!

Zavolejte doktora/sanitku/
policii!

Where is the police station?
  gdeh-yeh **po**-li-tsehy-
  nyee **stah**-nyi-tseh?

Kde je policejní stanice?

I've been raped.
  bi-lah ysehm **znaa**-sil-
  nyeh-naa

Byla jsem znásilněná.

I've been robbed.
bil ysehm o-krah-dehn (m) Byl jsem okraden.
bi-lah ysehm o-krah-deh-naa (f) Byla jsem okradená.
Go away!
byezh-teh prich! Běžte pryč!
I'll call the police!
zah-vo-laam po-li-tsi-yi! Zavolám policii!
Thief!
zlo-dyehy! Zloděj!

I am ill.
ysehm neh-mo-tsnee (m) Jsem nemocný.
ysehm neh-mo-tsnaa (f) Jsem nemocná.
I am lost.
zah-bloh-dyil-sem (m) Zabloudil jsem.
zah-bloh-dyi-lah-sem (f) Zabloudila jsem.
Where are the toilets?
gdeh-ysoh zaa-kho-di? Kde jsou záchody?
Could you help me please?
pro-seem, moo-zheh-teh mi po-mo-tsi? Prosím, můžete mi pomoci?
Could I please use the
telephone?
do-vo-lee-teh, ah-bikh-si ah-teh-leh-fo-no-vahl? (m) Dovolíte, abych si zatelefonoval?
do-vo-lee-teh, ah-bikh-si zah-teh-leh-fo-no-vah-lah? (f) Dovolíte, abych si zatelefonovala?

I'm sorry. I apologise.
   ***pro**-miny-teh.*
   ***o**-mloh-vaam-seh.*

Promiňte.
Omlouvám se.

I didn't realise I was doing
anything wrong.
   ***neh**-u-vyeh-do-mil*
   ***ysehm**-si zheh ysehm*
   *u-dyeh-lahl **nyeh**-tso*
   ***shpaht**-nair-ho* (m)
   ***neh**-u-vyeh-do-mi-lah*
   ***ysehm**-si zheh ysehm*
   *u-dyeh-lah-lah **nyeh**-tso*
   ***shpaht**-nair-ho* (f)

Neuvědomil jsem si
že jsem udělal něco
špatného.

Neuvědomila jsem si
že jsem udělala něco
špatného.

I didn't do it.
   ***neh**-u-dye-lahl*
   ***ysehm**-to* (m)
   ***neh**-u-dye-lahl-lah*
   ***ysehm**-to* (f)

Neudělal jsem to.

Neudělala jsem to.

I wish to contact my
embassy/consulate.
   ***przheh**-yu-si **mlu**-vit*
   *zmeem **vehl**-vi-slah-*
   nehts-tveem/
   ***kon**-zu-laa-tehm*

Přeju si mluvit s mým
velvyslanectvím/konzulátem.

I have medical insurance.
   *maam **neh**-mo-tsehns-koh*
   po-yist-ku

Mám nemocenskou pojistku.

My possessions are insured.
   ***mo**-yeh **zah**-vah-zah-dlah*
   *ysou **po**-yi-shtyeh-naa*

Moje zavazadla
jsou pojištěná.

My ... was stolen.
   u-krah-dli myeh ...   Ukradli mě ...
I've lost ...
   strah-tyil ysehm ... (m)   Ztratil jsem ...
   strah-tyi-lah ysehm ... (f)   Ztratila jsem ...

my bags	*mo-yeh zah-vah-zah-dlah*	moje zavazadla
my handbag	*mo-yee kah-behl-ku*	mojí kabelku
my money	*mo-yeh peh-nyee-zeh*	moje peníze
my travellers' cheques	*mo-yeh tsehs-to-vnyee sheh-ki*	moje cestovní šeky
my passport	*mooy pahs*	můj pas

Forms

name	*ymair-no*	Jméno
address	*ah-dreh-sah*	Adresa
date of birth	*dah-tum nah-ro-zeh-nyee*	Datum narození
place of birth	*mees-to nah-ro-zeh-nyee*	Místo narození
age	*vyehk*	Věk
sex	*po-hlah-vee*	Pohlaví
nationality	*staa-tynyee przhee-slush-nost*	Státní příslušnost
next of kin	*nehy-blizh-shee przhee-bu-znee* (m)	Nejbližší příbuzný
	nehy-blizh-shee przhee-bu-znaa (f)	Nejbližší příbuzná

religion	**naa**-bo-zhehn-stvee	Náboženství
reason for travel	**oo**-chehl **tsehs**-ti	Účel cesty
profession	**po**-vo-laa-nyee	Povolání
marital status	**mahn**-zhehl-skee stahf	Manželský stav
passport	**pahs**	Pas
passport number	**chee**-slo **pah**-su	Pas č. (číslo)
visa	**vee**-zum	Vízum
identity card	**proo**-kahz **to**-to-zhno-styi	Průkaz totožnosti
identification	**leh**-gi-ti-mah-tseh	Legitimace
birth certificate	**ro**-dnee list	Rodný list
car registration	**tehkh**-ni-tskee **proo**-kahz	Technický průkaz
driver's licence	**rzhi**-dyich-skee **proo**-kahz	Řidičský průkaz
customs	**tslo**	Clo
border	**hrah**-nyi-tseh	Hranice

Getting Around

ARRIVALS	PŘÍJEZDY
BUS STOP	AUTOBUSOVÁ ZASTÁVKA
DEPARTURES	ODJEZDY
STATION	STANICE
SUBWAY	METRO
TICKET OFFICE	POKLADNA
TIMETABLE	JÍZDNÍ ŘÁD
TRAIN STATION	NÁDRAŽÍ

What time does ... leave/
arrive?

*gdi **ot**-yee-zhdyee/* ***przhi**-yee-zhdyee ...?*		Kdy odjíždí/přijíždí ...?
the boat	*lody*	loď
the bus (city)	(***myehst**-skee)* ***ow**-to-bus*	(městský) autobus
the bus (intercity)	(***meh**-zi-myehst-skee)* ***ow**-to-bus*	(meziměstský) autobus
the train	*vlahk*	vlak
the tram	***trahm**-vahy*	tramvaj

Directions

Where is ...?
  gdeh-yeh ...?   Kde je ...?
How do I get to ...?
  yahk-seh do-stah-nu k ...? Jak se dostanu k ...?
Is it far from/near here?
  *yeh to **dah**-leh-ko/* Je to daleko/blízko?
  ***blees**-ko?*
Can I walk there?
  do-stah-nu-seh Dostanu se tam pěšky?
  *tahm **pyehsh**-ki?*
Can you show me (on
the map)?
  *moo-zheh-teh **mi**-to* Můžete mi to ukázat (na
  *u-**kaa**-zaht (nah* mapě)?
  ***mah**-pyeh)?*

Are there other means of
getting there?
    mo-hu-seh tahm do-staht   Mohu se tam dostat jinak?
    yi-nahk?
I want to go to ...
    khtsi yeet ...   Chci jít ...

Go straight ahead.
    ydyeh-teh przhee-mo   Jděte přímo.
It's two blocks down.
    o dvyeh u-li-tseh daal   O dvě ulice dál.
Turn left ...
    zah-to-chteh vleh-vo ...   Zatočte vlevo ...
Turn right ...
    zah-toch-teh fprah-vo ...   Zatočte vpravo ...
at the next corner
    nah przhee-shtyeem   na příštím rohu
    ro-hu
at the traffic lights
    u seh-mah-for-ru   u semaforu

behind	*zah*	za
in front of	*przhehd*	před
far	*dah-leh-ko*	daleko
near	*blees-ko*	blízko
opposite	*nah-pro-tyi*	naproti

CZECH

Booking Tickets

Excuse me, where is the
ticket office?
   pro-seem, gdeh-yeh   Prosím, kde je pokladna?
   po-klah-dnah?

Where can I buy a ticket?
   gdeh-seh pro-daa-vah-   Kde se prodávají jízdenky?
   yee yeez-dehn-ki?

I want to go to ...
   khtsi yeht do ...   Chci jet do ...

Do I need to book?
   po-trzheh-bu-yi   Potřebuji místenku?
   mees-tehn-ku?

You need to book.
   po-trzheh-bu-yeh-teh   Potřebujete místenku.
   mee-stehn-ku?

I would like to book a seat to ...
   pro-sil bikh mees-tehn-ku Prosil bych místenku do ...
   do ... (m)
   pro-si-lah bikh mees-   Prosila bych místenku do ...
   tehn-ku do ... (f)

It is full.
   yeh o-psah-zeh-no   Je obsazeno.

Is it completely full?
   jeh oo-pl-nyeh   Je úplně obsazeno?
   o-psah-zeh-no?

I would like ...
   raad bikh ... (m)   Rád bych ...
   raa-dah bikh ... (f)   Ráda bych ...

a one-way ticket
  yeh-dno-smyehr-noh jednosměrnou jízdenku
  yeez-dehn-ku
a return ticket
  spaa-teh-chnyee zpáteční jízdenku
  yeez-dehn-ku
two tickets
  dvyeh yee-zdehn-ki dvě jízdenky
tickets for all of us
  yeez-dehn-ki pro jízdenky pro všechny
  vshehkh-ni
a student's fare
  stu-dehnts-koh studentskou jízdenku
  yeez-dehn-ku
a child's fare
  dyets-koh yeez-dehn-ku dětskou jízdenku
1st class
  pr-vnyee trzhee-du první třídu
2nd class
  dru-hoh trzhee-du druhou třídu

Air

CHECKING IN	ODBAVENÍ
LUGGAGE PICKUP	VÝDEJ ZAVAZADEL
REGISTRATION	REGISTRACE

Is there a flight to ...?
  yeh leh-teh-tskair Je letecké spojení do ...?
  spo-yeh-nyee do ...?

CZECH

When is the next flight to ...?
   gdi-yeh **przhee**-*shtyee*   Kdy je příští let do ...?
   leht **do** ... ?

How long does the flight take?
   yahk **dloh**-*ho* **tr**-*vaa leht?*   Jak dlouho trvá let?

What is the flight number?
   yah-kair yeh **chee**-*slo*   Jaké je číslo letu?
   leh-*tu?*

You must check in at ...
   mu-see-teh-seh   Musíte se přihlásit ...
   przhi-hlaa-sit ...

airport tax	*leh-tyish-tnyee po-plah-tehk*	letištní poplatek
boarding pass	*pah-lub-nyee fstu-pehn-kah*	palubní vstupenka
customs	*tsehl-nyi-tseh*	celnice

Bus

BUS/TRAM STOP	AUTOBUSOVÁ/ TRAMVAJOVÁ ZASTÁVKA

Where is the bus/tram stop?
   gdeh-yeh **stah**-*nyi-tseh*   Kde je stanice autobusů/
   *ow-to-bu-soo/**trahm**-vah-yee?* tramvají?

CZECH

Which bus goes to ...?
   kteh-ree ow-to-bus
   yeh-deh do ...?

Který autobus jede do ...?

Does this bus go to ...?
   yeh-deh tehn-hleh
   ow-to-bus do ...?

Jede tenhle autobus do ...?

How often do buses pass by?
   yahk chahs-to tu-di
   yehz-dyee ow-to-bus?

Jak často tudy jezdí autobus?

Could you let me know when
we get to ...?
   mohl bi-steh-mi pro-seem
   rzhee-tsi, gdi przhi-yeh-
   deh-meh do ...? (m)

Mohl byste mi prosím říci,
kdy přijedeme do ...?

   moh-lah bi-steh-mi pro-
   seem rzhee-tsi, gdi przhi-
   yeh-deh-meh do ...? (f)

Mohla byste mi prosím říci,
kdy přijedeme do ...?

I want to get off!
   khtsi vi-stoh-pit!

Chci vystoupit!

What time is the ... bus?
   gdi yeh-deh ... ow-to-bus?

Kdy jede ... autobus?

next	*przheesh-tyee*	příští
first	*pr-vnyee*	první
last	*po-sleh-dnyee*	poslední

Metro

METRO/UNDERGROUND	METRO
THIS WAY TO	PŘÍCHOD
WAY OUT/WAY IN	VÝCHOD/VCHOD

CZECH

Which line takes me to ...?
*kteh-raa **trah**-sah
veh-deh **do** ...?*   Která trasa vede do ...?
What is the next station?
*yahk-seh ymeh-nu-yeh
przhee-shtyee **stah**-
nyi-tseh?*   Jak se jmenuje příští stanice?

Train

PLATFORM NO	NÁSTUPIŠTĚ

Is this the right platform
for ...?
*yeh-deh vlahk **do** ...
sto-ho-to
naa-stu-pi-shtyeh?*   Jede vlak do ... z tohoto nástupiště?
Passengers must change
trains to ...
*tsehs-tu-yee-tsee do ...
mu-see **przheh**-stoh-pit f ...*   Cestující do ... musí přestoupit v ...
The train leaves from
platform ...
*vlahk **ot**-yeezh-dyee
znaas-tu-pi-shtyeh ...*   Vlak odjíždí z nástupiště ...

dining car	*yee-dehl-nyee vooz*	jídelní vůz
express	*ri-khleek*	rychlík
local	*mees-tnyee*	místní
sleeping car	*spah-tsee vooz*	spací vůz

CZECH

Taxi

Can you take me to ...?
  moo-zheh-teh mnyeh
  do-vairst do ...?
Můžete mě dovést do ...?

Please take me to ...
  pro-seem, *od*-vehs-teh
  mnyeh *do* ...?
Prosím, odvezte mě do ...?

How much does it cost to go to ...?
  ko-lik *sto*-yee *tsehs*-tah *do* ...?
Kolik stojí cesta do ...?

Instructions

Here is fine, thank you.
  zahs-tahf-teh zdeh,
  pro-seem
Zastavte zde, prosím.

The next corner, please.
  nah *przheesh*-tyeem
  ro-hu, *pro*-seem
Na příštím rohu, prosím.

Continue!
  po-krah-chuy-teh!
Pokračujte!

The next street to the left/right.
  przhee-shtyee *u*-li-tsi
  vleh-vo/*fprah*-vo
Příští ulici vlevo/vpravo.

Stop here!
  zah-stahf-teh zdeh!
Zastavte zde!

Please slow down.
  yehty-teh po-mah-leh-yi,
  pro-seem.
Jeďte pomaleji, prosím.

Please wait here.
poch-*kehy-teh zdeh,*
pro-*seem*

Počkejte zde, prosím.

Some Useful Phrases

The train is cancelled.
vlahk yeh **zru**-*sheh-nee*

Vlak je zrušený.

The train is delayed.
vlahk maa **spozh**-*dyeh-nyee*

Vlak má zpoždění.

How long will it be delayed?
yah-*kair maa* **spozh**-*dyeh-nyee?*

Jaké má zpoždění?

There is a delay of ... hours.
maa ... **ho**-*dyi-no-vair* **spozh**-*dyeh-nyee?*

Má ... -hodinové zpoždění?

Can I reserve a place?
mo-*hu-si* **reh**-*zehr-vo-vaht* **mee**-*stehn-ku?*

Mohu si reservovat místenku?

How long does the trip take?
yahk **dloh**-*ho* **trvaa** *tsehs-tah?*

Jak dlouho trvá cesta?

Is it a direct route?
yeh-to **przhee**-*maa* *tsehs-tah?*

Je to přímá cesta?

Is that seat taken?
yeh **to**-*to* **mees**-*to* *op-sah-zeh-no?*

Je toto místo obsazeno?

I want to get off at ...
*khtsi **vis**-toh-pit f ...*

Chci vystoupit v ...

Excuse me.
zdo-vo-leh-nyeem

S dovolením.

Where can I hire a bicycle?
***gdeh**-si mo-hu **pooy**-chit **ko**-lo?*

Kde si mohu půjčit kolo?

Car

DETOUR	OBJÍŽĎKA
FREEWAY	DÁLNICE
GARAGE	BENZÍNOVÁ PUMPA
GIVE WAY	DEJ PŘEDNOST V JÍZDĚ
MECHANIC	AUTOMECHANIK
NO ENTRY	ZÁKAZ VJEZDU
NO PARKING	ZÁKAZ PARKOVÁNÍ
NORMAL	STANDART
ONE WAY	JEDNOSMĚRNÝ PROVOZ
REPAIRS	AUTOOPRAVNA
SELF SERVICE	SAMOOBSLUHA
STOP	ZASTAVTE/STOP
SUPER	SUPER
UNLEADED	NATURAL

Where can I rent a car?
***gdeh**-si **mo**-hu pro-nahy-moht **ow**-to?*

Kde si mohu pronajmout auto?

How much is it ...?
ko-lik **sto**-yee ...?   Kolik stojí ...?

daily/weekly
deh-nyeh/**tee**-dnyeh   denně/týdně

Does that include insurance/
mileage?
yeh **zah**-hr-nu-tah **ftseh**-
nyeh po-yist-kah/**po**-plah-   Je zahrnuta v ceně pojistka/
tehk zah **nah**-yeh-tair   poplatek za najeté kilometry?
ki-lo-meh-tri?

Where's the next petrol
station?
gdeh-yeh **przheesh**-tyee   Kde je přští benzínová
behn-zee-no-vaa   pumpa?
pum-pah?

Please fill the tank.
pl-**noh naa**-drzh,   Plnou nádrž, prosím.
pro-seem

I want ... litres of petrol (gas).
po-**trzheh**-bu-yi ... **li**-troo   Potřebuji ... litrů benzínu.
behn-zee-nu

Please check the oil and water.
pro-seem-vaas,   Prosím vás zkontrolujte
skon-tro-luy-teh   ole ja vodu.
o-lehy ah **vo**-du

How long can I park here?
yahk **dloh-ho** zdeh   Jak dlouho zde mohu
mo-hu **pahr**-ko-vaht?   parkovat?

Does this road lead to ...?
veh-**deh tah**-to   Vede tato cesta do ...?
tsehs-tah do ...?

What make is it?
yah-kee yeh-to mo-dehl?   Jaký je to model?

air (for tyres)	*vzdukh*	vzduch
battery	*bah-teh-ri-yeh*	baterie
brakes	*brz-di*	brzdy
clutch	*spoy-kah*	spojka
driver's licence	*rzhi-dyich-skee*	řidičský průkaz
	proo-kahz	
engine	*mo-tor*	motor
lights	*svyeh-tlah*	světla
oil	*o-lehy*	olej
puncture	*pee-khlaa*	píchlá pneumatika
	pneh-u-mah-ti-kah	
radiator	*khlah-dyich*	chladič
road map	*ow-to-mah-pah*	automapa
tyres	*pneh-u-mah-ti-ki*	pneumatiky
windscreen	*przheh-dnyee sklo*	přední sklo

Car Problems

I need a mechanic.
po-trzheh-bu-yi   Potřebuji automechanika.
ow-to-meh-khah-ni-kah
The battery is flat.
bah-tair-ri-eh yeh   Baterie je vybitá.
vi-bi-taa
The radiator is leaking.
khlah-dyich teh-cheh   Chladič teče.
I have a flat tyre.
maam pee-khloh   Mám píchlou pneumatiku.
pneh-u-mah-ti-ku

CZECH

It's overheating.
   mo-tor-seh
   przheh-hrzhee-vaa   Motor se přehřívá.
It's not working.
   neh-fun-gu-yeh-to   Nefunguje to.

Accommodation

CAMPING GROUND	STANOVÝ TÁBOR/ AUTOKEMP
GUEST HOUSE	PENZIÓN
HOTEL	HOTEL
MOTEL	MOTEL
PRIVATE ACCOMMODATION	ZIMMER FREI/PRIVÁT
STUDENT HOSTEL	STUDENTSKÁ NOCLEHÁRNA
YOUTH HOSTEL	MLÁDEŽNICKÁ UBYTOVNA/TURISTICKÁ UBYTOVNA

I am looking for ...
   hleh-daam ...   Hledám ...
Where is a ...?
   gdeh-yeh ...?   Kde je ...?

cheap hotel	*leh-vnee ho-tehl*	levný hotel
good hotel	*do-bree ho-tehl*	dobrý hotel

| nearby hotel | **bleez**-kee **ho**-tehl | blízký hotel |
| clean hotel | **chis**-tee **ho**-tehl | čistý hotel |

What is the address?
yah-kaa yeh **zdehy**-shee **ah**-dreh-sah?   Jaká je zdejší adresa?

Could you write the address, please?
moo-zheh-teh mi **nah**-psaht **ah**-dreh-su, **pro**-seem?   Můžete mi napsat adresu, prosím?

At the Hotel

Do you have any rooms available?
maa-teh **vol**-nair po-ko-yeh?   Máte volné pokoje?

I would like ...
przhaal bikh-si ... (m)   Přál bych si ...
przhaa-lah bikh-si ... (f)   Přála bych si ...

a single room	**yeh**-dno-loozh-ko-vee **po**-koy	jednolůžkový pokoj
a double room	**dvoh**-loozh-ko-vee **po**-koy	dvoulůžkový pok
a room with a bathroom	**po**-koy skoh-pehl-noh	pokoj s koupelnou
a bed	**loozh**-ko	lůžko

I want a room ...
mo-hu meet po-koy ...   Mohu mít pokoj ...
with a bathroom   **skoh-**pehl-noh   s koupelnou
with a shower   **seh-**spr-khoh   se sprchou
with a television **steh-**leh-vi-zee   s televizí
with a window   **so-**knehm   s oknem

I'm going to stay for ...
zoo-stah-nu ...   Zůstanu ...
one day   **yeh-**dehn dehn   jeden den
two days   dvah dni   dva dny
one week   **yeh-**dehn **tee-**dehn   jeden týden

Do you have passport/
identification?
maa-teh pahs/   Máte pas/osobní průkaz?
o-so-bnyee **proo-**kahz?
Your membership card,
please.
maa-teh **chlehn-**skoh   Máte členskou legitimaci,
leh-gi-ti-ma-tsi, pro-seem   prosím.
Sorry, we're full.
pro-miny-teh, **neh-**maa-   Promiňte, nemáme volné
meh **vol-**nair po-ko-yeh   pokoje.
How long will you be
staying?
yah-kaa **bu-**deh **dairl-**   Jaká bude délka vašeho
kah vah-sheh-ho po-bi-tu?   pobytu?

How many nights?
ko-lik no-tsee? — Kolik nocí?

It's ... per day/per person.
*sto-yee-to ... dehn-nyeh/
zah o-so-bu* — Stojí to ... denně/za osobu.

How much is it per night?
*ko-lik sto-yee
yeh-dnah nots?* — Kolik stojí jedna noc?

How much is it per person?
*ko-lik to sto-yee zah
o-so-bu?* — Kolik to stojí za osobu?

Can I see it?
*mo-hu-seh nah-nyey
po-dyee-vaht?* — Mohu se na něj podívat?

Are there any others?
*neh-maa-teh yi-nee
po-koj?* — Nemáte jiný pokoj?

Are there any cheaper rooms?
*neh-maa-teh leh-
vnyeh-shee po-ko-yeh?* — Nemáte levnější pokoje?

Can I see the bathroom?
*mo-hu-seh po-dyee-vaht
nah koh-pehl-nu?* — Mohu se podívat na koupelnu?

Is there a reduction for students/children?
*maa-teh sleh-vu pro
stu-dehn-ti/dyeh-tyi?* — Máte slevu pro studenty/děti?

CZECH

Does it include breakfast?
*yeh ftom **zah**-hr-nu-tah
snyee-dah-nyeh?*

Je v tom zahrnuta snídaně?

It's fine, I'll take it.
***to**-yeh **fpo**-rzhaat-ku,
yaa ho **vehz**-mu*

To je v pořádku, já ho vezmu.

I'm not sure how long I'm
staying.
***nehy**-sehm-si yist yahk
dloh-ho zdeh **zoos**-tah-nu*

Nejsem si jist jak dlouho zde
zůstanu.

Is there a lift?
*yeh tu **vee**-tah?*

Je tu výtah?

Where is the bathroom?
***gdeh**-yeh **koh**-pehl-nah?*

Kde je koupelna?

Is there hot water all day?
***maa**-teh-tu **hor**-koh
vo-du **tseh**-lee dehn?*

Máte tu horkou vodu celý
den?

Do you have a safe where I
can leave my valuables?
***maa**-teh-tu **treh**-zor
gde-si mo-hu u-lo-zhit
tseh-no-styi?*

Máte tu trezor kde si mohu
uložit cennosti?

Is there somewhere to wash
clothes?
***gdeh**-si mo-hu **vi**-praht
o-bleh-cheh-nyee?*

Kde si mohu vyprat oblečení?

Can I use the kitchen?
*mo-hu-si **u**-vah-rzhit
fku-khi-nyi?*

Mohu si uvařit v kuchyni?

Can I use the telephone?
mo-hu-si zah-teh-leh-fo-no-vaht?

Mohu si zatelefonovat?

Requests & Complaints

Please wake me up at ...
pro-seem, vzbudy-teh-mnyeh v ...

Prosím, vzbuďte mě v ...

The room needs to be cleaned.
mooy po-koy po-trzheh-bu-yeh u-kli-dyit

Můj pokoj potřebuje uklidit.

Please change the sheets.
pro-seem, przheh-vlair-knyeh-teh-mi lo-zhnyee praa-dlo

Prosím, převlékněte mi ložní prádlo.

I can't open/close the window.
neh-mo-hu o-teh-vrzheet/ zah-vrzheet o-kno

Nemohu otevřít/zavřít okno.

I've locked myself out of my room.
zah-klahp-nul (m)/
zah-klahp-nu-lah (f)
ysehm-si klee-cheh fmairm po-ko-yi

Zaklapnul/Zaplapnulá jsem si klíče v mém pokoji.

The toilet won't flush.
zaa-khod neh-splah-khu-yeh

Záchod nesplachuje.

I don't like this room.
> *po*-koy seh mi *neh*-lee-bee — Pokoj se mi nelíbí.

It's too small.
> yeh *przhee-lish* **mah**-lee — Je příliš malý.

It's noisy.
> *po*-koy yeh **hlu**-chnee — Pokoj je hlučný.

It's too dark.
> yeh *przhee-lish* **tmah**-vee — Je příliš tmavý.

It's expensive.
> yeh *przhee-lish* **drah**-hee — Je příliš drahý.

Some Useful Words & Phrases

I am/We are leaving ...
> *od*-yeezh-dyeem ... — Odjíždím ...
> *od*-yeezh-dyee-meh ... — Odjíždíme ...

now/tomorrow
> *tehdy/zee-trah* — teď/zítra

I would like to pay the bill.
> *raad bikh* **zah**-plah-tyil
> **oo**-cheht (m) — Rád bych zaplatil účet.
> *raa*-dah bikh **zah**-plah-t
> tyi-lah **oo**-cheht (f) — Ráda bych zaplatila účet.

name	*ymai -no*	jméno
surname	*przheey*-myeh-nyee	příjmění
room number	*chee*-slo *po*-ko-yeh	číslo pokoje
address	*ah*-dreh-sah	adresa
air-conditioned	*kli*-mah-ti-zah-tseh	klimatizace

balcony	**bahl**-kawn	balkón
bathroom	koh-pehl-nah	koupelna
bed	**loozh**-ko	lůžko
bill	oo-cheht	účet
blanket	po-kreef-kah	pokrývka
candle	**sveech**-kah	svíčka
chair	zhi-dleh	židle
clean	chis-tee	čistý
cupboard	**kreh**-dehnts	kredenc
dark	tmah-vee	tmavý
dirty	**shpi**-nah-vee	špinavý
double bed	dvoh-loozh-ko-vaa	dvoulůžková
	po-stehl	postel
electricity	eh-lehk-trzhi-nah	elektřina
excluded	neh-nyi	neni zahrnuta
	zahhr-nu-tah	
fan	vyeh-traak	větrák
included	zah-hr-nu-tair	zahrnuté
key	kleech	klíč
lift (elevator)	vee-tah	výtah
light bulb	zhaa-rof-kah	žárovka
lock (n)	zaa-mehk	zámek
mattress	mah-trah-tseh	matrace
mirror	zr-tsah-dlo	zrcadlo
padlock	vi-sah-tsee **zaa**-mehk	visací zámek
pillow	pol-shtaarzh	polštář
quiet	tyi-kho	ticho
room (in hotel)	po-koy	pokoj
sheet	pro-styeh-rah-dlo	prostěradlo
shower	spr-khah	sprcha
soap	mee-dlo	mýdlo

CZECH

suitcase	**ku**-fr	kufr
swimming pool	**bah**-zairn	bazén
table	stool	stůl
toilet	**zaa**-khod/**vair**-tsair	záchod/WC
toilet paper	**toah**-leh-tynyee **pah**-peer	toaletní papír
towel	**ru**-chnyeek	ručník
water	**vo**-dah	voda
cold water	stu-deh-naa **vo**-dah	studená voda
hot water	teh-plaa **vo**-dah	teplá voda
window	**o**-kno	okno

Around Town

I'm looking for ...
hleh-daam ...   Hledám ...

the art gallery	**u**-myeh-lehts-koh gah-**lair**-ri-i	uměleckou galérii
a bank	**bahn**-ku	banku
the church	**ko**-stehl	kostel
the city centre	strzhehd **myehs**-tah (**tsehn**-trum)	střed města (centrum)
the ... embassy	**vehl**-vi-slah-nehts-vee ...	velvyslanectví ...
my hotel	muy **ho**-tehl	muj hotel
the market	**tr**-zhi-shtyeh	tržiště
the museum	**mu**-seh-um	museum
the police	po-**li**-tsi-yi	policii
the post office	**posh**-tu	poštu
a public toilet	veh-**rzhehy**-nair **zaa**-kho-di	veřejné záchody

| the telephone centre | *teh-leh-fo-nyee oo-strzheh-dnu* | telefonní ústřednu |
| the tourist information office | *in-for-mah-chnyee* *kahn-tse-laarzh* *pro tu-ri-sti* | informační kancelář pro turisty |

What time does it open?
 fko-lik ho-dyin o-teh-vee-rah-yee? V kolik hodin otevírají?

What time does it close?
 fko-lik ho-dyin zah-vee-rah-yee? V kolik hodin zavírají?

What ... is this?
 yahk-seh ymeh-nu-yeh tah-hleh ...? Jak se jmenuje tahle ...?

| street | *u-li-tseh* | ulice |
| suburb | *chtvrty* | čtvrť |

For directions, see the Getting Around section, page 106.

At the Post Office

I would like some stamps.
 raad (m)/*raa-dah* (f) *bikh* Rád/Ráda bych
 nyeh-yah-kair znaam-ki nějaké známky.

How much is the postage?
 ko-lik sto-yee posh-to-vnair? Kolik stojí poštovné?

How much does it cost to
send ... to ...?

   ko-lik **sto**-*yee* **po**-*slaht* ...   Kolik stojí poslat ... do ...?
   do ...?

I would like to send ...

   khtyehl bikh **pos**-*laht* ... (m) Chtěl bych poslat ...
   khtyeh-*lah bikh*   Chtěla bych poslat ...
   pos-*laht* ... (f)

a letter	***do***-*pis*	dopis
a postcard	***po***-*hlehd*	pohled
a telegram	***teh***-*leh-grahm*	telegram

an aerogram	***ah***-*eh-ro-grahm*	aerogram
air mail	***leh***-*teh-tski*	letecky
envelope	*o*-***baal***-*kah*	obálka
mail box	*po*-***shto***-*vnyee*	poštovní schránka
	skhraan-*kah*	
parcel	***bah***-*leek*	balík
registered mail	***do***-*po-ru-cheh-nyeh*	doporučeně
surface mail	*o*-***bi***-*chehy-noh*	obyčejnou poštou
	posh-*toh*	

Telephone

I want to ring ...

   raad **bikh**-*si* **zah**-*teh-leh-*   Rád bych si zatelefonoval ...
   fo-no-vahl ... (m)
   raa-*dah* **bikh**-*si* **zah**-*teh-*
   leh-fo-no-vah-lah ... (f)   Ráda bych si zatelefonovala ...

The number is ...
   chees-lo yeh ...   Číslo je ...
I want to speak for three
minutes.
   *raad bikh **mlu**-vil*   Rád bych mluvil tři minuty.
   *trzhi **mi**-nu-ti* (m)
   ***raa**-dah bikh **mlu**-vi-lah* Ráda bykh mluvila tři minuty.
   *trzhi **mi**-nu-ti* (f)
How much does a three-
minute call cost?
   *ko-lik **sto**-yee trzhee*   Kolik stojí tří minutový
   *mi-nu-to-vee **roz**-ho-vor?* rozhovor?
How much does each extra
minute cost?
   *ko-lik **sto**-yee **kazh**-daa* Kolik stojí každá další
   ***dahl**-shee mi-nu-tah?*   minuta?
I would like to speak to
Mr Perez.
   *khtyehl bikh **mlu**-vit*   Chtěl bych mluvit s panem
   *spah-nehm **Peh**-rehz* (m) Perez.
   ***khtyeh**-lah bikh **mlu**-vit* Chtěla bych mluvit s panem
   *spah-nehm **Peh**-rehz* (f) Perez.
I want to make a reverse-
charges phone call.
   *raad bikh **zah**-vo-lal nah* Rád bych zavolal
   ***oo**-cheht vo-lah-nair-*   na účet volaného.
   ho (m)
   ***raa**-dah bikh **zah**-vo-la-* Ráda bykh zavolala
   *lah nah **oo**-cheht vo-lah-* na účet volaného.
   nair-ho (f)
It's engaged.
   *yeh **op**-sah-zeh-no*   Je obsazeno.

CZECH

I've been cut off.
bil ysehm przheh-ru-   Byl jsem přerušen.
shehn (m)
bi-lah ysehm przheh-ru-   Byla jsem přerušena.
sheh-nah (f)

At the Bank

I want to exchange some
money/travellers' cheques.
khtyehl bikh vi-mnyeh-nyit Chtěl bych vyměnit peníze/
peh-nyee-zeh/tsehs-tov- cestovní šeky.
nyee sheh-ki (m)
khtyeh-lah bikh vi-mnyeh- Chtěla bych vyměnit peníze/
nyit peh-nyee-zeh/tsehs- cestovní šeky.
tov-nyee sheh-ki (f)

What is the exchange rate?
yah-kee yeh vee-mnyeh- Jaký je výměnný kurs?
nee kurs?

How many crowns are there
per US dollar?
ko-lik ko-run do-stah-nu Kolik korun dostanu za jeden
zah yeh-dehn ah-meh- americký dolar?
ri-tskee do-lahr?

Can I have money transferred
here from my bank?
mo-hoh mair peh- Mohou mé peníze být
nyee-zeh beet przheh- převedeny z mého konta
veh-deh-ni smair-ho ... (name of bank)
kon-tah ... bahn-ki do banky do zdejší banky?
zdehy-shee bahn-ki?

How long will it take to
arrive?

yahk **dloh**-*ho* **bu**-*deh* **tr**-
vaht nehzh **zdeh** *bu***-doh?**

Jak dlouho bude
trvat než zde budou?

Has my money arrived yet?

przhi-*shli-mi mo-yeh*
peh-*nyee-zeh?*

Přišly mi moje peníze?

bankdraft	**bahn**-*ko-vnyee* **smnyehn**-*kah*	bankovní směnka
bank notes	**bahn**-*kof-ki*	bankovky
cashier	*po*-**klah**-*dnyeek*	pokladník
coins	**min**-*tseh*	mince
credit card	*oo*-*vyeh*-*ro*-*vaa* **kahr**-*tah*	úvěrová karta
exchange	**smyeh**-*naar-nah*	směnárna
signature	**pot**-*pis*	podpis

Sightseeing

Do you have a guidebook/
local map?

maa-*teh* **proo**-*vot-tseh/*
mah-*pu o-ko-lee?*

Máte průvodce/mapu okolí?

What are the main attractions?

yah-*kair ysoh* **zdehy**-*shee*
po-*zo*-*ru*-*ho*-*dno-styi?*

Jaké jsou zdejší
pozoruhodnosti?

What is that?

tso-*yeh to?*

Co je to?

How old is it? *

yahk-*yeh to* **stah**-*rair?*

Jak je to staré?

Can I take photographs?
*yeh zdeh **po**-vo-leh-no
fo-to-grah-fo-vaht?*   Je zde povoleno fotografovat?

What time does it open/
close?
*f**ko**-lik **ho**-dyin o-teh-vee-
rah-yee/**za**-vee-rah-yee?*   V kolik hodin otevírají/
zavírají?

ancient	**stah**-ro-vyeh-kee	starověký
archaeological	**ahr**-kheh-o-lo-gits-kair	archeologické
beach	*plaazh*	pláž
building	**bu**-do-vah	budova
castle	*hrahd/**zaa**-mehk*	hrad/zámek
cathedral	**kah**-teh-draa-lah	katedrála
church	**ko**-stehl	kostel
concert hall	**kon**-tsehrt-nyee seeny	koncertní síň
library	**knyi**-ho-vnah	knihovna
main square	**hla**-vnyee **naa**-myeh-styee	hlavní náměstí
market	*trh*	trh
monastery	**klaash**-tehr	klášter
monument	**pah**-maa-tyneek/**po**-mnyeek	památník/pomník
mosque	**meh**-shi-tah	mešita
old city	**stah**-rair **myehs**-to	staré město
palace	**pah**-laats	palác
opera house	*o-**peh**-rah*	opera
ruins	**zrzhee**-tseh-nyi-ni	zříceniny

stadium	*stah*-di-awn	stadión
statues	*so*-khi	sochy
synagogue	*si*-nah-gaw-gah	synagóga
temple	*khraam*	chrám
university	*u*-ni-vehr-si-tah	universita

Entertainment

What's there to do in the evenings?
  kahm-seh-tu daa *veh*-chehr yeet?   Kam se tu dá večer jít?

Are there any discos?
  ysoh zdeh dis-ko-tair-ki?   Jsou zde diskotéky?

Are there places where you can hear local folk music?
  hrah-yee *nyeh*-gdeh *li*-do-voh *hud*-bu?   Hraji někde lidovou hudbu?

How much is it to get in?
  ko-lik yeh *fstu*-pnair?   Kolik je vstupné?

cinema	*ki*-no	kino
concert	*kon*-tsehrt	koncert
discotheque	*dis*-ko-tair-kah	diskotéka
theatre	*dyi*-vah-dlo	divadlo

In the Country

Weather

What's the weather like?
  yah-kair yeh *po*-chah-see?   Jaké je počasí?

Will it be ... tomorrow?
>   ***bu**-deh zee-trah ...?*   Bude zítra ...?

cloudy	***zah**-tah-zheh-no*	zataženo
cold	***khlah**-dno*	chladno
foggy	***ml**-hah-vo*	mlhavo
frosty	*mraaz*	mráz
hot	***hor**-ko*	horko
sunny	***slu**-neh-chno*	slunečno
windy	***vyeh**-tr-no*	větrno
It's raining.	***pr**-shee*	Prší.
It's snowing.	***snyeh**-zhe*	Sněží.

Camping

Am I allowed to camp here?
>   ***mo**-hu zdeh **stah**-no-vaht?*   Mohu zde stanovat?

Is there a campsite nearby?
>   *yeh **fo**-ko-lee*   Je v okolí tábořiště?
>   ***taa**-bo-rzhi-shtyeh?*

backpack	***bah**-tyoh*	baťoh
can opener	*o-**tvee**-rahch*	otvírač konzerv
	*kon-**zehrf***	
compass	***kom**-pahs*	kompas
crampons	***mah**-chki*	mačky
firewood	***drzheh**-vo*	dřevo
gas cartridge	***pli**-no-vaa*	plynová bombička
	***bom**-bi-chkah*	
hammock	***ha**-mahk*	hamak
ice axe	***tseh**-peen*	cepín
mattress	***mah**-trah-tseh*	matrace

penknife	*kah*-peh-snyee noozh	kapesní nůž
rope	*pro*-vahz	provaz
tent	*stahn*	stan
tent pegs	*stah*-no-vair *ko*-lee-ki	stanové kolíky
torch (flashlight)	*bah*-tehr-kah	baterka
sleeping bag	*spah*-tsee pi-tehl	spací pytel
stove	*vah*-rzhich	vařič
water bottle	*pol*-nyee *laa*-hehf	polní láhev

Food

breakfast	*snyee*-dah-nyeh	snídaně
lunch	*o*-byehd	oběd
dinner	*veh*-cheh-rzheh	večeře

Table for ..., please.
  stool pro ..., pro-seem   Stůl pro ..., prosím.
May I have the menu please?
  yee-dehl-nyee lee-stehk,   Jídelní lístek, prosím.
  pro-seem
I would like today's special.
  mo-hu-si o-byeh-dnaht   Mohu si objednat
  speh-tsi-ah-li-tu dneh   specialitu dne.
What is today's special?
  yah-kaa yeh *speh*-tsi-   Jaká je specialita dne?
  ah-li-tah **dneh**?
Is service included in the
bill?
  *yeh to **fcheh**-tnyeh*   Je to včetně obsluhy?
  op-slu-hi?

CZECH

Not too spicy.
*neh **przhee**-lish*   Ne příliš kořeněné.
ko-rzheh-nyeh-nair

ashtray	*po-pehl-nyeek*	popelník
the bill	*oo-cheht*	účet
Bon appétit.	*do-broh khuty*	Dobrou chuť.
Cheers!	*nah-zdrah-vee*	Na zdraví!
a cup	*shaa-lehk*	šálek
dessert	*moh-chnyeek*	moučník
a drink	*pi-tyee*	pití
a fork	*vi-dli-chkah*	vidlička
fresh	*chehr-stvee*	čerstvý
a glass	*skleh-nyi-tseh*	sklenice
a knife	*noozh*	nůž
off/spoiled	*skah-zheh-nee*	zkažený
a plate	*tah-leerzh*	talíř
spicy	*ko-rzheh-nyeh-nee*	kořeněný
a spoon	*lzhee-tseh*	lžíce
stale	*o-ko-rah-lee*	okoralý
sweet	*slaht-kee*	sladký
teaspoon	*lzhi-chkah*	lžička
toothpick	*paa-raat-ko*	párátko

Vegetarian Meals

I am a vegetarian.
*ysehm **veh**-geh-tah-ri-aan* (m)   Jsem vegetarián.

*ysehm **veh**-geh-tah-ri-aan-kah* (f)   Jsem vegetariánka.

I don't eat meat.
   *neh-yeem **mah**-so*   Nejím maso.
I don't eat chicken/fish/ham.
   *neh-yeem **ku**-rzheh/*   Nejím kuře/rybu/šunku.
   *ri-bu/**shun**-ku*

CZECH

Staple Foods & Condiments

à la carte	*Jídla na objednávku*
bread	*Chléb*
butter	*Máslo*
cabbage, similar to saurkraut	*Zelí*
cheese	*Sýr*
chips	*Hranolky*
(bread) dumplings	*Houskové knedlíky*
(potato) dumplings	*Bramborové knedlíky*
eggs	*Vejce*
fish	*Ryba*
fruit	*Ovoce*
ham	*Šunka*
honey	*Med*
horseradish	*Křen*
kidneys	*Ledvinky*
liver	*Játra*
long roll	*Rohlík*
meat	*Maso*
mustard	*Hořčice*
pastry	*Pečivo*
pepper	*Pepř*
pickled cabbage/vegetables	*Sterilizované zelí/zelenina*
potatoes	*Brambory*

rice	*Rýže*
roll	*Houska*
salt	*Sůl*
sugar	*Cukr*
tartare sauce	*Tatarská omáčka*
vegetable	*Zelenina*
vinegar	*Ocet*
water	*Voda*

Breakfast Menu

eggs	*Vejce*
bacon and eggs	*Vejce se slaninou*
boiled eggs	*Vařená vejce*
fried eggs	*Smažená vejce*
ham and eggs	*Vejce se šunkou*
omelette	*Omeleta*
scrambled eggs	*Míchaná vejce*
soft/hard-boiled eggs	*Vejce na měkko/tvrdo*
jam	*Džem/Marmeláda*
type of croissant	*Loupáček*

Starters & Buffet Meals

Klobásy
   Mild or spicy sausages.
Langoše
   A Hungarian snack made of fried pastry coated in garlic,
   cheese, butter or jam.
Obložené chlebíčky
   Open sandwiches.

Párky
  Frankfurt or wiener-type sausages.
Pražská šunka s okurkou
  Prague ham with gherkins.
Ruská vejce
  Hard boiled egg with mayonnaise, potato salad and sometimes a slice of salami.
Sýrový nářez
  A serve of two or three cheeses.
Tlačenka s octem a cibulí
  Seasoned jellied meat loaf with vinegar and fresh onion.
Uherský salám s okurkou
  Hungarian salami with gherkin.
Vuřt/Buřt
  Thick sausage.
Zavináče
  Rollmops – herring fillets rolled around onion and/or gherkin, and pickled.

Soups

beef	*Hovězí*
beef chunks with spices	*Gulašová*
broth with egg	*Bujón*
mushroom	*Houbová*
pea	*Hrachová*
potato	*Bramborová*
tomato with a little rice	*Rajská*
tripe and spices	*Drštková*
vegetable	*Zeleninová*

Main Meals

Dušená roštěnka
Braised slices of beef in sauce.

Hovězí guláš
Beef chunks in a brown sauce.

Hovězí karbanátky
A type of beef hamburger with bread crumbs, egg and onion.

Meruňkové knedlíky
Apricots wrapped in pastry and topped with cottage cheese, melted butter and sugar.

Okurkový salát
Cucumber salad.

Pečená husa/kachna/kuře
Roast goose/duck/chicken.

Plněné papriky
Capsicum stuffed with a mixture of minced meat and rice, served with tomato sauce.

Přírodní řízek
Pork or veal schnitzel without the breadcrumbs.

Řízek (telecí nebo vepřový)
Veal or pork schnitzel.

Segedínský guláš
A goulash with three types of meat and saurkraut in sauce.

Sekaná pečeně
Roast minced meat.

Svíčková
Roasted beef served with a sour cream sauce and spices.

Švestkové knedlíky
Plums wrapped in pastry and topped with crushed poppy seeds, melted butter and sugar.

Telecí pečeně
  Roast veal.
Vepřová pečeně
  Roasted pork with caraway seed.
Zajíc na smetaně
  Hare in a cream sauce.
Znojemská pečeně
  Slices of roast beef in a gherkin sauce.

Desserts

pineapple	*Ananas*
blueberries	*Borůvky*
pears	*Hrušky*
apple strudel	*Jablkový závin*
strawberries	*Jahody*
preserved and canned fruit	*Kompot*
raspberries	*Maliny*
apricots	*Meruňky*
plums	*Švestky*
cherries/sour cherries	*Třešně/višně*
poppy-seed cake	*Makový koláč*
fruit slices	*Ovocné koláče*
pancakes with canned fruit/ ice cream	*Palačinky s kompotem/ zmrzlinou*
meringue with whipped cream	*Rakvičky*
ice cream	*Zmrzlina*
chocolate	*Čokoládová*
coffee	*Kávová*
fruit punch	*Punčová*

CZECH

| nut | Oříšková |
| vanilla | Vanilková |

Nonalcoholic Drinks

coffee	Káva
black coffee	Černá káva
espresso	Espreso
Vienna coffee with whipped cream	Vídeňská káva
white coffee	Bílá káva
fruit juice	Ovocná šťáva/Džus
hot chocolate	Kakao
ice	Led
lemonade, but it quite often refers to all soft drinks.	Limonáda
mineral water	Minerálka
milk	Mléko
sugar	S cukrem
tea (with sugar/milk)	Čaj (s cukrem/mlékem)
water	Voda

Alcoholic Drinks

beer	Pivo
spirits	Lihoviny
wine	Víno

Shopping

How much is it?
ko-lik-to **sto**-yee?   Kolik to stojí?

bookshop	*knyih-ku-pets-tvee*	knihkupectví
camera shop	*fo-to po-trzheh-bi*	foto potřeby
clothing store	*o-dyeh-vi*	oděvy
delicatessen	*lah-hoot-ki*	lahůdky
general store, shop	*smee-sheh-nair*	smíšené zboží/
	zbo-zhee/po-trah-vi-ni, o-pkhod	potraviny, obchod
laundry	*praa-dehl-nah*	prádelna
market	*trh*	trh
newsagency	*no-vi-no-vee staa-nehk/tah-baak*	novinový stánek/ tabák
pharmacy	*lair-kaar-nah*	lékárna
shoeshop	*o-buv*	obuv
souvenir shop	*su-veh-nee-ri*	suvenýry
stationers	*pah-peer-nyits-tvee*	papírnictví
supermarket	*sah-mo-op-slu-hah*	samoobsluha
vegetable shop	*zeh-leh-nyi-nah ah o-vo-tseh*	zelenina a ovoce

I would like to buy ...
   *raad **bikh**-si **koh**-pil* ... (m) Rád bych si koupil ...
   *raa-dah **bikh**-si **koh**-pi-lah* ...(f) Ráda bych si koupila ...
Do you have other ...?
   maa-teh yi-nair ...? Máte jiné ...?
I don't like it.
   to-seh mi neh-lee-bee To se mi nelíbí.
Can I look at it?
   *mo-hu-seh **nah**-to po-dyee-vaht?* Mohu se na to podívat?

I'm just looking.
   yehn-seh **dyee**-*vaam* Jen se dívám.

Can you write down the price?
   moo-zheh-teh-mi
   nah-psaht **tseh**-nu? Můžete mi napsat cenu?

Do you accept credit cards?
   przhi-yee-maa-teh
   oo-vyeh-ro-vair **kahr**-ti? Přijímáte úvěrové karty?

Could you lower the price?
   neh-moo-zheh-teh-
   mi *nyeh*-tso **sleh**-vit? Nemůžete mi něco slevit?

I don't have much money.
   neh-maam mots
   peh-nyehs Nemám moc peněz.

Can I help you?
   tso-si **przheh**-yeh-teh? Co si přejete?

Will that be all?
   bu-deh-to fsheh? Bude to vše?

Would you like it wrapped?
   przheh-yeh-teh **si**-to
   zah-bah-lit? Přejete si to zabalit?

Sorry, this is the only one.
   pro-miny-teh **to**-hleh yeh
   po-sleh-dnyee kus Promiňte, tohle je poslední kus.

How much/many do you want?
   ko-lik **ku**-soo si
   prveh-yeh-teh? Kolik kusů si přejete?

CZECH

Souvenirs

earrings	*naa-u-shnyi-tseh*	náušnice
handicraft	*li-do-vair u-myeh-nyee*	lidové umění
necklace	*naa-hr-dehl-nyeek*	náhrdelník
pottery	*keh-rah-mi-kah*	keramika
ring	*pr-stehn*	prsten
rug	*ko-beh-rehts*	koberec

Clothing

clothing	*o-dyehv*	oděv
coat	*kah-baat*	kabát
dress	*shah-ti*	šaty
jacket	*sah-ko*	sako
jumper (sweater)	*sveh-tr*	svetr
shirt	*ko-shi-leh*	košile
shoes	*bo-ti*	boty
skirt	*su-knyeh*	sukně
trousers	*kahl-ho-ti*	kalhoty

It is too ...
   ysoh mi mots ...   Jsou mi moc ...

big	*veh-li-kair*	veliké
small	*mah-lair*	malé
short	*kraat-kair*	krátké
long	*dloh-hair*	dlouhé
tight	*tyehs-nair*	těsné
loose	*vol-nair*	volné

It doesn't fit.
   neh-seh-dyee mi to   Nesedí mi to.

Materials

cotton	*bah-vl-nah*	bavlna
handmade	*ru-chnyeh vi-ro-beh-nair*	ručně vyrobené
leather	*koo-zheh*	kůže
brass	*mo-sahz*	mosaz
gold	*zlah-to*	zlato
silver	*strzhree-bro*	stříbro
pure alpaca	*chis-taa ahl-pah-ko-vaa vl-nah*	čistá alpaková vlna
silk	*hehd-vaa-bee*	hedvábí
wool	*vl-nah*	vlna

Colours

black	*chehr-nee*	černý
blue	*mo-dree*	modrý
brown	*hnyeh-dee*	hnědý
green	*zeh-leh-nee*	zelený
orange	*o-rahn-zho-vee*	oranžový
pink	*roo-zho-vee*	růžový
red	*chehr-veh-nee*	červený
white	*bee-lee*	bílý
yellow	*zhlu-tee*	žlutý

Toiletries

comb	*hrzheh-behn*	hřeben
condoms	*preh-zehr-vah-ti-vi*	prezervativy

deodorant	*deh*-o-do-rant	deodorant
hairbrush	*kahr*-taach *nah*-vlah-si	kartáč na vlasy
moisturising cream	*pleh*-tyo-vee krairm	pleťový krém
razor	*brzhi*-tvah	břitva
sanitary napkins	*vlozh*-ki	vložky
shampoo	*shahm*-pawn	šampón
shaving cream	*ho*-li-tsee krairm	holicí krém
soap	*mee*-dlo	mýdlo
sunblock cream	krairm nah o-pah-lo-vaa-nyee	krém na opalování
tampons	*tahm*-paw-ni	tampóny
tissues	*pah*-pee-ro-vair *kah*-pehs-nyee-ki	papírové kapesníky
toilet paper	*to*-ah-leh-tnyee *pah*-peer	toaletní papír
toothbrush	*kahr*-taa-chehk nah *zu*-bi	kartáček na zuby
toothpaste	*pahs*-tah nah *zu*-bi	pasta na zuby

Stationery & Publications

map	*mah*-pah	mapa
newspaper	*no*-vi-ni	noviny
newspaper in English	*no*-vi-ni *fahn*-glich-tyi-nye	noviny v angličtině
novels in English	*knyi*-hi *fahn*-gli-chtyi-nyeh	knihy v angličtině
paper	*pah*-peer	papír
pen (ballpoint)	*pro*-pi-so-vach-ka	propisovačka
scissors	*noozh*-ki	nůžky

Photography

How much is it to process
this film?
    *ko-lik **sto**-yee*
    *vi-vo-laa-nyee **fil**-mu?*   Kolik stojí vyvolání filmu?
When will it be ready?
    *gdi **bu**-deh ho-to-vee?*   Kdy bude hotový?
I'd like a film for this camera.
    ***maa**-teh film do **to**-ho-to*   Máte film do tohoto
    ***fo**-to-ah-pah-raa-tu?*   fotoaparátu?

B&W (film)	*chehr-no-bee-lee*	černobílý
camera	*fo-to-ah-pah-raat*	fotoaparát
colour (film)	*bah-reh-vnee*	barevný
film	*film*	film
flash	*blehsk*	blesk
lens	*ob-yehk-tif*	objektiv
light meter	*ehks-po-zi-meh-tr*	expozimeter

Smoking

A packet of cigarettes, please.
    ***pro**-sil bikh **kra**-bich-ku*   Prosil bych krabičku cigaret.
    ***tsi**-gah-reht* (m)
    ***pro**-si-lah bikh **kra**-bich-*   Prosila bych krabičku cigaret.
    *ku **tsi**-gah-reht* (f)

Are these cigarettes strong/ mild?
ysoh-ti **tsi**-gah-reh-ti **przhee**-lish **sil**-nair/ **yehm**-nair?

Jsou ty cigarety příliš silné/ jemné?

Do you have a light?
maa-teh **zaa**-pahl-ki/ **zah**-pah-lo-vahch?

Máte zápalky/zapalovač?

cigarette papers	**tsi**-gah-reh-to-vair **pah**-peer-ki	cigaretové papírky
cigarettes	**tsi**-gah-reh-ti	cigarety
filtered	**sfil**-trehm	s filtrem
lighter	**zah**-pah-lo-vahch	zapalovač
matches	**zaa**-pahl-ki/**sir**-ki	zápalky/sirky
menthol	**mehn**-tol-ki	mentolky
pipe	**deem**-kah	dýmka
tobacco (pipe)	**tah**-baak (pro **deem**-ku)	tabák (pro dýmku)

Sizes & Comparisons

small	**mah**-lair	malé
big	**veh**-li-kair	veliké
heavy	**tyezh**-kair	těžké
light	**leh**-kair	lehké
more	**vee**-tseh	více
less	**mair**-nyeh	méně
too much/many	**przhee**-lish **ho**-dnyeh/**mno**-ho	Příliš hodně/ mnoho
many	**mno**-ho	mnoho

CZECH

enough	*dost*	dost
also	*tah-kair*	také
a little bit	*tro-khu*	trochu

Health

Where is the ...?
gde-yeh ...?   Kde je ...?

chemist	*lair-kaar-nah*	lékárna
dentist	*zub-nyee lair-kahrzh/zu-bahrzh*	zubní lékař/zubař
doctor	*dok-tor*	doktor
hospital	*neh-mo-tsnyi-tseh*	nemocnice

I am sick.
   ysehm neh-mo-tsnee (m)   Jsem nemocný.
   ysehm neh-mo-tsnaa (f)   Jsem nemocná.
My friend is sick.
   mooy przhee-tehl yeh neh-mo-tsnee (m)   Můj přítel je nemocný.
   mo-yeh przhee-tehl-ki-nyeh yeh neh-mots-naa (f)   Moje přítelkyně je nemocná.
Could I see a female doctor?
   przhaa-la bikh-si nahf-shtyee-vit dok-tor-ku?   Přála bych si navštívit doktorku?
What's the matter?
   tso-yeh vaam?   Co je vám?
Where does it hurt?
   gdeh vaas-to bo-lee?   Kde vás to bolí?

It hurts here.
bo-lee-myeh zdeh   Bolí mě zde.
My ... hurts.
bo-lee-myeh ...   Bolí mě ...

Parts of the Body

ankle	*kot-nyeek*	kotník
arm	*pah-zheh*	paže
back	*zaa-dah*	záda
chest	*nah pr-soh*	na prsou
ear	*u-kho*	ucho
eye	*o-ko*	oko
finger	*prst*	prst
foot	*kho-dyi-dlo*	chodidlo
hand	*ru-kah*	ruka
head	*hlah-vah*	hlava
heart	*u srd-tseh*	u srdce
leg	*no-hah*	noha
mouth	*foo-stehkh*	v ústech
nose	*nos*	nos
skin	*koo-zheh*	kůže
spine	*paa-tehrzh*	páteř
stomach	*zhah-lu-dehk*	žaludek
teeth	*zu-bi*	zuby
throat	*hr-dlo*	hrdlo

Ailments

I have ...
maam ...   Mám ...
constipation   *zaats-pu*   zácpu

CZECH

a cough	*kah*-shehl	kašel
diarrhoea	*proo*-yehm	průjem
fever	*ho*-rehch-ku	horečku
hepatitis	*zhloh*-tehn-ku	žloutenku
an infection	*in*-fehk-tsi	infekci
influenza	*khrzhip*-ku	chřipku
lice	*fshi*	vši
low/high blood	*nyeez*-kee/*vi*-so-kee	nízký/vysoký
pressure	*kreh*-vnyee tlak	krevní tlak
sprain	*pod*-vr-tnu-tyee	podvrtnutí
sunburn	*oo*-zheh	úžeh
a venereal	*po*-hlah-vnyee	pohlavní nemoc
disease	*neh*-mots	
worms	*chehr*-vi	červy

I have ...
   ysehm ...   Jsem ...

anaemia.	*khu*-do-kreh-vnee	chudokrevný
a burn	*po-paa*-leh-nee	popálený
a cold	*nah*-khlah-zeh-nee	nachlazený

I have ...
   bo-lee-myeh ...   Bolí mě ...

a headache	*hlah*-vah	hlava
a sore throat	*fkr*-ku	v krku
a stomachache	*brzhi*-kho	břicho

Some Useful Words & Phrases

I'm ...
maam ...   Mám ...
diabetic   *tsu-krof-ku*   cukrovku
epileptic   *eh-pi-leh-psi-i*   epilepsii
asthmatic   *ahst-mah*   astma

I'm allergic to antibiotics/
penicillin
    *ysehm **ah**-lehr-gits-kee*   Jsem alergický
    *nah **ahn**-ti-bio-ti-kah/*   na antibiotika/
    peh-ni-tsi-lin*   penicilin.
I'm pregnant.
    *ysehm **tyeh**-ho-tnaa*   Jsem těhotná.
I'm on the pill.
    *u-zhee-vaam **ahn**-ti-*   Užívám antikoncepční prášky
    kon-tsehp-chnyee
    praash-ki*
I haven't had my period
for ... months.
    neh-mehn-stru-o-vah-*   Nemenstruovala jsem
    lah ysehm uzh ...   už ... měsíce.
    myeh-see-tseh*
I have been vaccinated.
    *bil ysehm **o**-chko-*   Byl jsem očkovaný.
    vah-nee (m)
    bi-lah ysehm **o**-chko-*   Byla jsem očkovaná.
    vah-naa (f)
I have my own syringe.
    *maam **svo**-yee **i**-nyeh-*   Mám svojí injekční stříkačku.
    *kchnyee **strzhee**-kach-ku*

CZECH

I feel better/worse.
tsee-*tyem-seh* **lair**-*peh/*   Cítím se lépe/hůře.
hoo-*rzheh*

accident	**neh**-*ho-dah*	nehoda
addiction	**nahr**-*ko-mah-nieh*	narkomanie
antibiotics	**ahn**-*ti-bio-ti-kah*	antibiotika
antiseptic	**ahn**-*ti-sehp-tits-kee/*	antiseptický/
	deh-*zin-fehk-chnyee*	dezinfekční
aspirin	**ahs**-*pi-rin*	aspirin
bandage	**ob**-*vahz*	obvaz
blood pressure	**kreh**-*vnyee tlahk*	krevní tlak
blood test	**kreh**-*vnyee skoh-*	krevní zkouška
	shkah	
contraceptives	**ahn***ti-kon-tsehp-*	antikoncepční
	chnyee **pro**-*strzhed-ki*	prostředky
injection	**i**-*nyehk-tseh*	injekce
injury	**zrah**-*nyeh-nyee*	zranění
medicine	**lair**-*kahrzh-stvee*	lékařství
menstruation	**mehn**-*stru-ah-tseh*	menstruace
nausea	**zveh**-*daa-nyee*	zvedání žaludku
	zhah-*lud-ku*	
oxygen	**ki**-*sleek*	kyslík
vitamins	**vi**-*tah-mee-ni*	vitamíny
wound	**raa**-*nah*	rána

At the Chemist
I need medication for ...
po-*trzheh-bu-yi* **lair**-*ki* ...   Potřebuji léky ...

I have a prescription.
maam przhehd-pis   Mám předpis.

At the Dentist

I have a toothache.
bo-lee-myeh zub   Bolí mě zub.
I've lost a filling.
vi-pah-dlah-mi plom-bah   Vypadla mi plomba.
I've broken a tooth.
maam zlo-meh-nee zub   Mám zlomený zub.
My gums hurt.
bo-lee-myeh daa-snyeh   Bolí mě dásně.
I don't want it extracted.
neh-tr-hehy-teh-mi   Netrhejte mi tento zub.
tehn-to zub
Please give me an
anaesthetic.
pro-seem, umr-tvyeh-teh   Prosím, umrtvěte mi to.
mi-to

Time & Dates

Telling the time in Czech is difficult to explain in the short space
of this chapter. Ask for specific times to be written down.

What time is it?
ko-lik-yeh ho-dyin?   Kolik je hodin?
What date is it today?
ko-li-kaa-tair-ho yeh   Kolikátého je dnes?
dnehs?

CZECH

Could you write that down?
nah-pi-shteh mi-to,   Napište mi to, prosím!
pro-seem!

in the morning	**raa**-no	ráno
in the afternoon	**ot**-po-leh-dneh	odpoledne
in the evening	**veh**-chehr	večer

Days of the Week

Monday	**pon**-dyeh-lee	Pondělí
Tuesday	**oo**-teh-ree	Úterý
Wednesday	**strzheh**-dah	Středa
Thursday	**chtvr**-tehk	Čtvrtek
Friday	**paa**-tehk	Pátek
Saturday	**so**-bo-tah	Sobota
Sunday	**neh**-dyeh-leh	Neděle

Months

January	**leh**-dehn	Leden
February	**oo**-nor	Únor
March	**brzheh**-zehn	Březen
April	**du**-behn	Duben
May	**kvyeh**-tehn	Květen
June	**chehr**-vehn	Červen
July	**chehr**-veh-nehts	Červenec
August	**sr**-pehn	Srpen
September	**zaa**-rzhee	Září
October	**rzhee**-yehn	Říjen
November	**lis**-to-pahd	Listopad
December	**pro**-si-nehtz	Prosinec

Seasons

summer	*lair-to*	léto
autumn	*pod-zim*	podzim
winter	*zi-mah*	zima
spring	*yah-ro*	jaro

Present

today	*dnehs*	dnes
this morning	*dnehs raa-no*	dnes ráno
tonight	*dnehs veh-chehr/*	dnes večer/
	dnehs vno-tsi	dnes v noci
this week	*tehn-to tee-dehn*	tento týden
this year	*leh-tos/vleh-tosh-nyeem ro-tseh*	letos/v letoš-ním roce
now	*tehdy*	teď

Past

yesterday	*fcheh-rah*	včera
day before yesterday	*przheh-dehf-chee-rehm*	předevčírem
last night	*fcheh-rah veh-chehr*	včera večer
last week/year	*mi-nu-lee tee-dehn/ rok*	minulý týden/rok

Future

tomorrow	*zee-trah*	zítra
day after tomorrow	*po-zee-trzhee*	pozítří
tomorrow afternoon	*zee-trah ot-po-leh-dneh/veh-chehr*	zítra odpoledne/večer

CZECH

| next week | **przheesh**-tyee **tee**-dehn | příští týden |
| next year | **przheesh**-tyee rok | příští rok |

During the Day

afternoon	*ot*-po-leh-dneh	odpoledne
dawn, very early morning	svee-taa-nyee/ **vehl**-mi **br**-zo **raa**-no	svítání/ velmy brzo ráno
day	dehn	den
early	**br**-zo	brzo
midnight	**pool**-nots	půlnoc
morning (between 9 am and midday)	**raa**-no/ *do*-po-leh-dneh	ráno/ dopoledne
night	nots	noc
noon	po-leh-dneh	poledne
sundown	**zaa**-pahd **slun**-tseh	západ slunce
sunrise	vee-khod **slun**-tseh	východ slunce

Numbers & Amounts

0	**nu**-lah	nula
1	**yeh**-dnah	jedna
2	dvah	dva
3	trzhi	tři
4	**chti**-rzhi	čtyři
5	pyeht	pět
6	shehst	šest
7	**seh**-dum	sedm
8	*o*-sum	osm

9	*deh-vyeht*	devět
10	*deh-seht*	deset
11	*yeh-deh-naatst*	jedenáct
12	*dvah-naatst*	dvanáct
13	*trzhi-naatst*	třináct
14	*chtr-naatst*	čtrnáct
15	*pah-tnaatst*	patnáct
16	*shehst-naatst*	šestnáct
17	*seh-dum-naatst*	sedmnáct
18	*o-sum-naatst*	osmnáct
19	*deh-vah-teh-naatst*	devatenáct
20	*dvah-tseht*	dvacet
21	*dva-tseht yeh-dnah/*	dvacet jedna/
	yeh-dna-dvah-tseht	jednadvacet
30	*trzhi-tseht*	třicet
40	*chti-rzhi-tseht*	čtyřicet
50	*pah-deh-saat*	padesát
60	*sheh-deh-saat*	šedesát
70	*seh-dum-deh-saat*	sedmdesát
80	*o-sum-deh-saat*	osmdesát
90	*deh-vah-deh-saat*	devadesát
100	*sto*	sto
1000	*tyi-seets*	tisíc
one million	*mi-li-yawn*	milión
1st	*pr-vnyee*	první
2nd	*dru-hee*	druhý
3rd	*trzheh-tyee*	třetí
1/4	*chtvr-tyi-nah*	čtvrtina
1/3	*trzheh-tyi-nah*	třetina

CZECH

1/2	*po-lo-vi-nah*	polovina
3/4	*trzhi-chtvr-tyi-nah*	třičtvrtina

Some Useful Words

a little (amount)	*tro-khu*	trochu
double	*dvoh-yi-tee*	dvojitý
a dozen	*tu-tseht*	tucet
Enough!	*dost!*	Dost!
few	*nyeh-ko-lik*	několik
less	*mair-nyeh*	méně
many	*mno-ho*	mnoho
more	*vee-tseh*	více
once	*yeh-dnoh*	jednou
a pair	*paar*	pár
percent	*pro-tsehn-to*	procento
some	*nyeh-kteh-ree*	některý
too much	*przhee-lish ho-dnyeh*	příliš hodně
twice	*dvah-kraat*	dvakrát

CZECH

Abbreviations

AMU	Academy of Performing Arts
ATS	Austrian schilling
cm/m/km	cm/m/km
č./čís.	number/s
ČAD	Czech Coachline
ČČK	Czech Red Cross
ČD	Czech Railway
ČEDOK	Czech Travel Agency
ČR	Czech Republic
ČSA	Czechoslovak Airlines
ČSFR	Czech & Slovak Federal Republic
ČTK	Czech Press Agency
DEM	Deutschmark
EU	EU
atd.	etc
FRF	French franc
GBP	British pound
h or hod	hour, or halíř (h), small unit of currency
hl. m.	capital city
JZD	State Farming Cooperative
Kč	Czech crown
KU or UK	Charles University – Prague
nám.	town square
OSN	United Nations
p/pí/sl	Mr/Mrs/Ms
SBČ	Czech State Bank
ul	street
USD	American dollar

Hungarian

Introduction

Hungarian, or Magyar as it is known to the Magyars (who constitute 95% of the population in Hungary), is a unique language in Europe. The roots of this Finno-Ugric tongue and its people lie in the lands east of the Ural mountain chain, from where, in around 2000 BC, there was a major migration west. In the process, the group split, some moving north to Finland and Estonia, and the others, the Ugric people, moving through to Hungary. The original language was also split along with the two groups. In the two and a half millennia from 'departure' to the conquest of Hungary in 896, when seven Magyar tribes occupied the Danube basin and the foundations of modern Hungary were laid, the Ugric language evolved. While it picked up certain Persian, Turkish and Bulgar words along the way, it developed into modern Hungarian which is now only spoken in Hungary. Finnish is the nearest European relative, bearing some resemblances in form and structure, but the two languages are mutually incomprehensible.

There is a Hungarian-speaking population of 10.6 million in Hungary, and a sizable ethnic Hungarian-speaking community around the borders: nearly two million in Romania, mostly in Transylvania (and making up one of the largest ethnic minorities in Europe), some 600,000 in the Slovak Republic, half a million in Vojvodina and Croatia, and 200,000 in Ukraine.

However daunting it may appear at first sight, there is a certain regularity and code to the language which, once grasped, can help enormously. Word formation is agglutinative, meaning that you start with a 'root' and build on it.

Here are a few basics. The suffix 't' is added in the accusative case. Verb conjugations have two forms, definite and indefinite, and the whole language rests on a complex set of vowel-harmony rules which dictate which ending to use. The definite article ('the' in English) has two forms in Hungarian: 'az' before a word starting with a vowel, and 'a' before a consonant.

There is a complicated set of rules governing prepositions, which in Hungarian are actually word endings. In order to simplify this Lonely Planet language guide we generally omitted the wide variety of endings that could be used, which depend on general vowel harmony rules combined with specific cases. Although this makes for some grammatically incorrect sentences, such as 'Which bus goes Buda?', there should be no problems in being understood. For your information, some of the common endings you may see or hear are: -ba, -be, -ra, -re, -hoz, -hez, -höz, -nal, -nál and -nél.

For beginners, good pronunciation will get you further than good grammar, and Hungarians are delighted to hear any of their tongue emerge from a non-Magyar.

Pronunciation

The rules are simple, and the actual pronunciation just takes a little practice. In the vast majority of words there is a slight stress on the first syllable. Each syllable after the first is given equal weight, even in the longest words. There are no diphthongs – each vowel is pronounced. Most double consonants should be lengthened to the point where you can just distinguish the two letters.

HUNGARIAN

Vowels

a	somewhere in between 'a' and 'o', nearly the 'o' in 'hot' or the 'a' in 'was'
á	a longer and more open sound, like the 'a' in 'father'
e	as in 'set'
é	somewhere between 'a' and 'e', as in 'make'
i	short as in 'pit'
í	like a long double 'e', as in 'fleet'
o	rounded and short as in 'solitude', 'orange'
ó	long as in 'door'
ö	short and rounded as in 'worse'
ő	a lengthened **ö** as in 'world'
u	short as in 'group'
ú	long, as in 'blue', 'two'
ü	like a simple **u** but more rounded, as in the French 'rue'. Similar to the 'u' sound in 'few' but shorter. (Rendered as *ü* in our pronunciation guide.)
ű	a lengthened **ü**, similar to 'feud' (Rendered as *üü* in our pronunciation guide.)

Consonants

Only those consonants which differ greatly from the English pronunciation have been listed here.

c	an English 'ts' as in 'hats'
cs	like the 'ch' in 'church'
gy	like a combination of 'd' and 'j' as in 'jury'
j	pronounced as the 'y' in 'yellow'
ly	traditionally used in some words instead of **j**

ny	as in 'new'
r	as in 'red' but a pointed sound
s	'sh' as in 'shower'
sz	an English 's' as in 'see'
ty	like a combination of 't' and 'ch', as in 'statue'
zs	a buzzing sound, as in 'pleasure'

Greetings & Civilities
Top 10 Useful Phrases

Hello.
  yoh nah-pot kee-vaa-nok!   Jó napot kívánok!
Goodbye.
  vi-sont-laa-taash-rah!   Viszontlátásra! (formal, common use)
  si-ah!   Szia! (informal only)
Yes./No.
  i-ghen/nem   Igen./Nem.
Excuse me.
  bo-chaa-naht   Bocsánat.
May I? Do you mind?
  le-het?   Lehet?
Sorry. (excuse me, forgive me)
  bo-chaa-naht   Bocsánat.
Please.
  keh-rem   Kérem.
Thank you.
  ker-ser-nerm   Köszönöm.
Many thanks.
  nah-djon ker-ser-nerm   Nagyon köszönöm.

HUNGARIAN

That's fine. You're welcome.
rend-ben see-ve-shen Rendben. Szívesen.

Greetings
Good morning!
yoh regh-ghelt! Jó reggelt!
Good afternoon!
yoh nah-pot! Jó napot!
Good evening/night!
yoh esh-teht/ehy-sah-kaat! Jó estét/éjszakát!

How are you?
hodj vahn? Hogy van?
Well, thanks.
ker-ser-nerm, yohl Köszönöm, jól.

Forms of Address
Madam/Mrs	*herldj/as-sony*	Hölgy/Asszony
Sir/Mr	*oor*	Úr
Miss	*kish-as-sony*	Kisasszony
companion	*taarsh*	társ
friend	*bah-raat*	barát

Note: Hungarian names start with the family name.

Small Talk
Meeting People
What is your name?
hodj heev-yaak? Hogy hívják?

My name is ...
 ah ne-vem ...

A nevem ...

I'd like to introduce you to ...
 se-ret-nehm ernt
 be-mu-taht-ni ...

Szeretném önt
bemutatni ...

I'm pleased to meet you.
 er-rü-lerk hodj
 meg-ish-mer-he-tem

Örülök, hogy megismerhetem.

I like .../I don't like ...
 ne-kem tet-sik .../
 ne-kem nem tet-sik ...

Nekem tetszik .../
Nekem nem tetszik ...

How old are you?
 ern haany eh-vesh?

Ön hány éves?

I am ... years old.
 ... eh-vesh vah-djok

... éves vagyok.

Nationalities

Where are you from?
 ern hon-nahn yertt?

Ön honnan jött?

Australia	*ah-ust-raa-li-ah*	Ausztrália
Canada	*kah-nah-dah*	Kanada
England	*ahn-ghli-ah*	Anglia
Ireland	*eer-or-saagh*	Irország
New Zealand	*ooy zeh-lahnd*	Új-Zéland
Scotland	*shkoh-tsi-ah*	Skócia
the USA	*ahz edje-shült*	Az Egyesült
	aallahm-ok	Államok
Wales	*vels*	Wales

HUNGARIAN

Occupations

What do you do?

mi ah fogh-lahl-ko-zaa-shah?		Mi a foglalkozása?

I am a/an ...

... *vah-djok*		... vagyok
artist	*müü-vehs*	művész
business person	*üz-let-em-ber* (m)	üzletember
	üz-let-as-sony (f)	üzletasszony
doctor	*or-vosh*	orvos
engineer	*mehr-nerk*	mérnök
farmer	*ghahz-dah*	gazda
journalist	*ooy-shaagh-ee-roh*	újságíró
lawyer	*yo-ghaas*	jogász
manual worker	*fi-zi-kahi mun-kaash*	fizikai munkás
mechanic	*se-re-loer*	szerelő
nurse	*aa-po-loh* (m)	ápoló
	aa-po-loh-noer (f)	ápolónő
office worker	*iro-dah-i dol-gho-zoh*	irodai dolgozó
scientist	*tu-dohsh*	tudós
student	*di-aak*	diák
teacher	*tah-naar* (m)	tanár
	tah-naar-noer (f)	tanárnő
waiter	*pin-tsehr* (m)	pincér
	pin-tsehr-noer (f)	pincérnő
writer	*ee-roh*	író

Religion

What is your religion?
   mi-yen vahl-laa-shoo?   Milyen vallású?
I am not religious.
   nem vah-djok   Nem vagyok vallásos.
   vahl-laa-shosh

I am ...
   ... vah-djok   ... vagyok

Buddhist	*bud-hish-tah*	buddhista
Catholic	*kah-to-li-kush*	katolikus
Christian	*ke-res-tehny*	keresztény
Hindu	*hin-du*	hindu
Jewish	*zhi-doh*	zsidó
Muslim	*mu-zul-maan*	muzulmán

Family

Are you married?
   fehry-nehl vahn ? (f)   Férjnél van?
   noers? (m)   Nős?
I am single.
   hah-yah-don vah-djok (f)   Hajadon vagyok.
   noert-len vah-djok (m)   Nőtlen vagyok.
I am married.
   fehry-nehl vah-djok (f)   Férjnél vagyok
   noersh vah-djok (m)   Nős vagyok.
How many children do you
have?
   haany djer-me-ke vahn?   Hány gyermeke van?

I don't have any children.
ninch djer-me-kem Nincs gyermekem.

I have a daughter/a son.
edj laa-nyom/fi-ahm vahn Egy lányom/fiam van.

How many brothers/sisters
do you have?
haany baaty-ya/ Hány bátyja/nővére van?
noer-veh-re vahn?

Is your husband/wife here?
itt vahn ah fehr-ye/ Itt van a férje/felesége?
fe-le-sheh-ghe?

Do you have a boyfriend/
girlfriend?
vahn bah-raat-yah/ Van barátja/barátnője?
bah-raat-noer-ye?

brother	*fioo-tesht-vehr*	fiútestvér
children	*dje-re-kek*	gyerekek
daughter	*laany*	lány
family	*chah-laad*	család
father	*ah-pah*	apa
grandfather	*nahdj-pah-pah*	nagypapa
grandmother	*nahdj-mah-mah*	nagymama
husband	*fehry*	férj
mother	*ah-nyah*	anya
sister	*le-aany-tesht-vehr*	leánytestvér
son	*fioo*	fiú
wife	*fe-le-shehgh*	feleség

Feelings

I am sorry. (condolence)
shahy-naa-lom   Sajnálom.
I am grateful.
haa-laash vah-djok   Hálás vagyok.

(I am ...)

angry	*mehr-ghesh vah-djok*	Mérges vagyok.
cold	*faa-zom*	Fázom.
hot	*me-le-ghem vahn*	Melegem van.
happy	*bol-dogh vah-djok*	Boldog vagyok.
hungry	*eh-hesh vah-djok*	Éhes vagyok.
thirsty	*som-yahsh vah-djok*	Szomjas vagyok.
in a hurry	*shi-e-tek*	Sietek.
right	*yohl vah-djok*	Jól vagyok.
sad	*so-mo-roo vah-djok*	Szomorú.
sleepy	*aal-mosh vah-djok*	Álmos vagyok.
tired	*faa-rahdt vah-djok*	Fáradt vagyok.
well	*yohl vah-djok*	Jól vagyok.
worried	*ahgh-ghoh-dom*	Aggódom.

HUNGARIAN

Language Problems

Do you speak English?
be-sehl ahn-gho-lul?   Beszél angolul?
Does anyone speak English?
be-sehl vah-lah-ki   Beszél valaki angolul?
ahn-gho-lul?
I speak a little ...
ehn be-seh-lek edj   Én beszélek egy kicsit ... ul/ül.
ki-chit ... ul/ul

I don't speak ...
  nem be-seh-lek ... ul/ül   Nem beszélek ... ul/ül
I (don't) understand.
  (nem) ehr-tem   (Nem) Értem.
Could you speak more
slowly please?
  keh-rem tud-nah lahsh-   Kérem, tudna
  shahb-ban be-sehl-ni?   lassabban beszélni?
Could you repeat that?
  megh-ish-meh-tel-neh?   Megismételné?
How do you say ...?
  hodj kell mon-dah-ni ...?   Hogy kell mondani ...?
What does ... mean?
  mit ye-lent ...?   Mit jelent ...?

Some Useful Phrases
Sure.
  per-se   Persze.
Just a minute.
  edj pil-lah-naht   Egy pillanat.
It's (not) important.
  (nem) fon-tosh   (Nem) Fontos.
It's (not) possible.
  (nem) le-het   (Nem) Lehet.
Wait!
  vaar-yon!   Várjon!
Good luck!
  shok se-ren-cheht!   Sok szerencsét!

Signs

BAGGAGE COUNTER	CSOMAG
CUSTOMS	VÁMKEZELÉS
EMERGENCY EXIT	VÉSZKIJÁRAT
ENTRANCE	BEJÁRAT
EXIT	KIJÁRAT
FREE ADMISSION	SZABAD BELÉPÉS
HOT/COLD	MELEG/HIDEG
INFORMATION	INFORMÁCIÓ
NO ENTRY	TILOS BELÉPNI
NO SMOKING	TILOS A DOHÁNYZÁS
OPEN/CLOSED	NYITVA/ZÁRVA
PROHIBITED	TILOS
RESERVED	FOGLALT
TELEPHONE	TELEFON
TOILETS	WC or TOALETT

HUNGARIAN

Emergencies

POLICE	RENDŐRSÉG
POLICE STATION	RENDŐRŐRSZOBA

Help!
she-gheet-shehgh! Segítség!

It's an emergency!
shüür-ghoersh! Sűrgős!

There's been an accident!
bah-le-shet ter-tehnt!   Baleset történt!
Call a doctor!
heev-yon edj or-vosht!   Hívjon egy orvost!
Call an ambulance!
heev-yah ah men-toer-ket!   Hívja a mentőket!

I've been raped.
megh-eroer-sah-kol-tahk   Megerőszakoltak.
I've been robbed!
ki-rah-bol-tahk!   Kiraboltak!
Call the police!
heev-yah ah ren-doer-sheh-ghet!   Hívja a rendőrséget!
Where is the police station?
hol ah ren-doer-shehgh?   Hol a rendőrség?

Go away!
men-yen el!   Menjen el!
I'll call the police!
hee-vom ah ren-doert!   Hívom a rendőrt!
Thief!
tol-vahy!   Tolvaj!

I am ill.
be-tegh vah-djok   Beteg vagyok.
My friend is ill.
ah bah-raa-tom be-tegh   A barátom beteg.
I am lost.
el-teh-ved-tem   Eltévedtem.

Where are the toilets?
hol vahn ah veh-tseh? Hol van a WC?

Could you help me please?
tud-nah she-ghee-te-ni Tudna segíteni kérem?
keh-rem?

Could I please use the
telephone?
keh-rem hahs-naal-haht Kérem, használhatnám
naam ah te-le-font? a telefont?

I'm sorry. I apologise.
shahy-naa-lom Sajnálom.
el-neh-zehsht keh-rek Elnézést kérek.

I didn't do it.
nem ehn chi-naal-tahm Nem én csináltam.

I didn't realise I was doing
anything wrong.
nem tud-tahm hodj vah- Nem tudtam, hogy valami
lah-mi ros-saht tet-tem rosszat tettem.

I wish to contact my
embassy/consulate.
se-ret-nehk ah ker-vet- Szeretnék a követséggel/
shehgh-ghel/kon-zu-laa- konzulátussal beszélni
tush-shahl be-sehl-ni

I speak English.
be-seh-lek (ahn-gho-lul) Beszélek (angolul).

I have medical insurance.
vahn be-tegh-biz-to-shee- Van betegbiztosításom.
taa-shom

HUNGARIAN

My possessions are insured.
vahn vah-djon-biz-to-   Van vagyonbiztosításom.
shee-taa-shom

I've lost ...
el-ves-tet-tem ...   Elvesztettem ...
My ... was stolen.
el-lop-taak ah/ahz ... m   Ellopták a/az ... m.

my bags	*ah taash-kaa-i-maht*	a táskáimat
my handbag	*ah keh-zi-taash-kaa-maht*	a kézitáskámat
my money	*ah pehn-ze-met*	a pénzemet
my travellers' cheques	*ahz u-tah-zaa-shi chekk-ye-i-met*	az utazási csekkjeimet
my passport	*ahz oot-le-ve-le-met*	az útleve lemet

Forms

name	*nehv*	név
address	*tseem*	cím
date of birth	*sü-le-teh-shi daa-tum*	születési dátum
place of birth	*sü-le-teh-shi hey*	születési hely
age	*kor*	kor
sex	*nem*	nem
nationality	*nem-ze-ti-shehgh*	nemzetiség
next of kin	*ker-ze-li hoz-zaa-tahr-to-zoh*	közeli hozzátartozó
religion	*vahl-laash*	vallás
reason for travel	*ahz u-tah-zaash tsehl-yah*	az utazás célja

profession	*fogh-lahl-ko-zaa-shah*	foglalkozása
marital status	*chah-laa-di aal-lah-pot*	családi állapot
passport	*oot-le-vehl*	útlevél
passport number	*oot-le-vehl-saam*	útlevélszám
visa	*vee-zum*	vízum
tourist card	*tu-rish-tah kaar-tyah*	turista kártya
identification	*se-mehy-ah-zo-nosh-shaagh*	személyazonosság
birth certificate	*sü-le-teh-shi ah-nyah-kerny-vi ki-vo-naht*	születésianyakonyvi kivonat
driver's licence	*yo-gho-sheet-vaany*	jogosítvány
car owner's title	*for-ghahl-mi en-ghe-dehy*	forgalmi engedély
car registration	*gehp-ko-chi rend-saam*	gépkocsi rendszám
customs	*vaam*	vám
immigration	*be-vaan-dor-laash*	bevándorlás
border	*hah-taar*	határ

HUNGARIAN

Getting Around

ARRIVALS	ÉRKEZÉS
BUS STOP	AUTÓBUSZ MEGÁLLÓ
DEPARTURES	INDULÁS
STATION	ÁLLOMÁS

SUBWAY	METRÓ
TICKET OFFICE	JEGYIRODA
TIMETABLE	MENETREND
TRAIN STATION	VASÚTÁLLOMÁS

What time does ... leave/
arrive?
   mi-kor in-dul/   Mikor indul/érkezik a ...?
   ehr-ke-zik ah ...?

airplane	*re-pü-loer-gehp*	repülőgép
boat	*hah-yoh*	hajó
bus (city)	*he-yi ahu-toh-bus*	helyi autóbusz
bus (intercity)	*taa-vol-shaa-ghi*	távolsági autóbusz
	ahu-toh-bus	
train	*vo-naht*	vonat
tram	*vil-lah-mosh*	villamos

Directions

Where is ...?
   hol vahn ah/ahz ...?   Hol van a/az ...?
How do I get to ...?
   hodj yu-tok ah/ahz ...?   Hogy jutok a/az ...?
Is it far from/near here?
   mes-se vahn in-nen/   Messze van innen/
   ker-zel vahn ide?   közel van ide?
Can I walk there?
   me-he-tek odah djah-   Mehetek oda gyalog?
   logh?

Can you show me (on the map)?
megh tud-naa ne-kem mu-taht-ni (ah tehr-keh-pen)? — Meg tudná nekem mutatni (a térképen)?

Are there other means of getting there?
maash-kehp-pen ish el le-het odah yut-ni? — Másképpen is el lehet oda jutni?

I want to go to ...
se-ret-nehk ...men-ni — Szeretnék ... menni

Go straight ahead.
men-yen e-dje-ne-shen e-loere — Menjen egyenesen előre.

It's two blocks down.
keht haaz-termb-re vahn in-nen — Két háztömbre van innen.

Turn left ...
for-dul-yon bahl-rah ... — Forduljon balra ...

Turn right ...
for-dul-yon yobb-rah ... — Forduljon jobbra ...

at the next corner.
ah ker-vet-ke-zoer shah-rok-naal — a következő saroknál

at the traffic lights.
ah kerz-le-ke-deh-shi laam-paa-naal — a közlekedési lámpánál

| behind | *mer-gert* | mögött |
| in front of | *e-loertt* | előtt |

far	*mes-se*	messze
near	*ker-zel*	közel
in front of	*e-loertt*	előtt
opposite	*sem-ben*	szemben

Booking Tickets

Excuse me, where is the ticket office?
   el-neh-zehsht, hol vahn   Elnézést, hol van a jegyiroda?
   ah yedj-i-ro-dah?

Where can I buy a ticket?
   hol ve-he-tem megh ah   Hol vehetem meg a jegyet?
   ye-djet?

I want to go to ...
   se-ret-nehk ... men-ni   Szeretnék ... menni.

Do I need to book?
   sük-sheh-ghesh he-yet   Szükséges helyet foglalnom?
   fog-lahl-nom?

You need to book.
   sük-sheh-ghesh he-yet   Szükséges helyet foglalnia.
   fog-lahl-ni-ah

I would like to book a seat to ...
   se-ret-nehk edj he-yet   Szeretnék egy helyet
   fog-lahl-ni ...   foglalni ...

I would like ...
   se-ret-nehk ...   Szeretnék ...

a one-way ticket
   edj ye-djet chahk odah   egy jegyet csak oda

a return ticket
   edj re-toor-ye-djet   egy retúrjegyet
two tickets
   keht ye-djet   két jegyet
tickets for all of us
   edj-edj ye-djet mind-   egy-egy jegyet
   ahny-nyi-unk-nahk   mindannyiunknak
a student's fare
   edj di-aak-ye-djet   egy diákjegyet
a child's/pensioner's fare
   edj dje-rek-ye-djet/   egy gyerekjegyet/
   nyugh-dee-yash-ye-djet   nyugdíjasjegyet

1st class
   el-shoer os-taay   első osztály
2nd class
   maa-shod-os-taay   másodosztály

It is full.
   te-le vahn   Tele van.
Is it completely full?
   tel-ye-shen te-le vahn?   Teljesen tele van?
Can I get a stand-by ticket?
   kahp-hah-tok edj stand-   Kaphatok egy stand-by jegyet?
   by ye-djet?

Air

CHECKING IN	CHECK-IN
LUGGAGE PICKUP	CSOMAG ÁTVÉTEL
REGISTRATION	REGISZTRÁCIÓ

HUNGARIAN

Is there a flight to ...?
vahn re-püloer-yaa-raht ...? Van repülőjárat ...?

When is the next flight to ...?
mi-kor vahn ah ker-vet-ke-zoer re-püloer-yaa-raht ...? Mikor van a következő repülőjárat ...?

How long does the flight take?
meny-nyi i-de-igh tahrt ah re-püloer-oot? Mennyi ideig tart a repülőút?

What is the flight number?
meny-nyi ah yaa-raht-saam? Mennyi a járatszám?

You must check in at ...
ah ... kell ye-lent-kez-ni-e A ... kell jelentkeznie

airport tax	*re-pü-loer-teh-ri ah-doh*	repülőtéri adó
boarding pass	*be-saal-loh-kaar-tyah*	beszállókártya
customs	*vaam*	vám

Bus

BUS STOP	AUTÓBUSZ MEGÁLLÓ
TRAM STOP	VILLAMOS MEGÁLLÓ

Where is the bus/tram stop?
hol vahn ahz ahu-toh-bus/   Hol van az autóbusz/
ah vil-lah-mosh   a villamos megálló?
megh-aal-loh?

Which bus goes to ...?
me-yik ahu-toh-bus   Melyik autóbusz megy ...?
medj ...?

Does this bus go to ...?
ez ahz ahu-toh-bus   Ez az autóbusz megy ...?
medj ...?

How often do buses pass by?
mi-yen djahk-rahn yaar-   Milyen gyakran járnak az
nahk ahz ahu-toh-busok   autóbuszok?

Could you let me know
when we get to ...?
sohl-nah keh-rem ah-mi-   Szólna kérem, amikor
kor megh-ehr-ke-zünk ...?   megérkezünk ...?

I want to get off!
se-ret-nehk le-saall-ni!   Szeretnék leszállni!

What time is the ... bus?
mi-kor in-dul ah/ahz ...   Mikor indul a/az ... autóbusz?
ahu-toh-bus?

next	*ker-vet-ke-zoer*	következő
first	*el-shoer*	első
last	*u-tol-shoh*	utolsó

HUNGARIAN

Metro

METRO/ UNDERGROUND	METRÓ/FÖLDALATTI
CHANGE (for coins)	VÁLTÁS
WAY OUT	KIJÁRAT

Which line takes me to ...?
me-yik vo-nahl medj ...? Melyik vonal megy...?

What is the next station?
mi ah ker-vet-ke-zoer aal-lo-maash? Mi a következő állomás?

Train

DINING CAR	ÉTKEZŐ KOCSI
EXPRESS	EXPRESSZ
PLATFORM	VÁGÁNY
SLEEPING CAR	HÁLÓKOCSI

Is this the right platform for ...?
er-roerl ah vaa-ghaany-rohl in-dul ah vo-naht ...? Erről a vágányról indul a vonat ...?

Passengers ...
ahz u-tah-shok-nahk ... Az utasoknak ...

must change trains
aat kell saall-ni át kell szállni

must change platforms
maa-shik vaa-ghaany-   másik vágányhoz kell
hoz kell men-ni   menni
The train leaves from
platform ...
ah vo-naht ah ... saa-moo   A vonat a ... számú vágány-ról
vaa-ghaany-rohl in-dul   indul

dining car	*eht-ke-zoer ko-chi*	étkező kocsi
express	*ex-press*	expressz
local	*he-yi*	helyi
sleeping car	*haa-loh-ko-chi*	hálókocsi

HUNGARIAN

Taxi

Can you take me to ...?
el tud-nah vin-ni ...?   El tudna vinni ...?
Please take me to ...
keh-rem vi-djen el ...   Kérem, vigyen el ...
How much does it cost to
go to ...?
meny-nyi-be ke-rül ... ig?   Mennyibe kerül ... ig?

Instructions

Here is fine, thank you.
itt joh les, ker-ser-nerm   Itt jó lesz, köszönöm.
The next corner, please.
ah ker-vet-ke-zoer shah-   A következő saroknál, legyen
rok-naal, le-djen see-vesh   szíves.

The next street to the left/
right.
    ah ker-vet-ke-zoer ut-tsaa-   A következő utcánál balra/
    naal bahl-rah/yobb-rah   jobbra.
Stop here!
    aall-yon meg itt!   Álljon meg itt!
Please slow down.
    keh-rem, lash-sheet-   Kérem, lassítson le.
    shon le
Please wait here.
    keh-rem, vaar-yon itt   Kérem, várjon itt.

Some Useful Phrases
The train is delayed.
    ah vo-naht keh-shik   A vonat késik.
The train is cancelled.
    ah vo-naht nem yaar   A vonat nem jár.
How long will it be delayed?
    meny-nyit fogh kehsh-ni?   Mennyit fog késni?
There is a delay of ... hours.
    ... oh-raat keh-shik   ... órát késik.
Can I reserve a place?
    fogh-lahl-hah-tok edj   Foglalhatok egy helyet?
    he-yet?
How long does the trip take?
    meny-nyi i-de-igh   Mennyi ideig tart az utazás?
    tahrt ahz u-tah-zaash?
Is it a direct route?
    ez edj kerz-vet-len   Ez egy közvetlen útvonal?
    oot-vo-nahl?

Is that seat taken?
fogh-lahlt ahz ah hey?   Foglalt az a hely?
I want to get off at ...
se-ret-nehk le-saall-ni ...   Szeretnék leszállni ...
Where can I hire a bicycle?
hol beh-rel-he-tek edj   Hol bérelhetek egy kerékpárt?
ke-rehk-paart?

Car

DETOUR	KERÜLŐÚT
FREEWAY	SZABADÚT
GARAGE	GARÁZS
MECHANIC	SZERELŐ
NO ENTRY	NEM BEJÁRAT
NO PARKING	TILOS A PARKOLÁS
NORMAL	NORMÁL
ONE WAY	EGYIRÁNYÚ
REPAIRS	JAVÍTÁSOK
SELF SERVICE	ÖNKISZOLGÁLÓ
SUPER	SZUPER
UNLEADED	ÓLOMMENTES

Where can I rent a car?
hol beh-rel-he-tek edj   Hol bérelhetek egy autót?
ahu-toht?
How much is it ...?
meny-nyi-be ke-rül ...?   Mennyibe kerül ...?
daily/weekly
nah-pon-tah/he-ten-te   naponta/hetente

Does that include insurance/
mileage?
*ahz aar tahr-tahl-mahz-
zah ah biz-to-shee-taasht/
ki-loh-meh-tert?*
   Az ár tartalmazza a
biztosítást/kilométert?

What make is it?
*mi-yen djaart-maa-nyoo
ahz ahu-toh?*
   Milyen gyártmányú az autó?

Where's the next petrol
station?
*hol vahn ah legh-ker-ze-
leb-bi ben-zin-koot?*
   Hol van a legközelebbi
ben zinkút?

Please fill the tank.
*keh-rem terl-che megh ah
ben-zin-tahr-taayt*
   Kérem töltse meg a
benzintartályt.

I want ... litres of petrol (gas).
keh-rek ... li-ter ben-zint
   Kérek ... liter benzint.

Please check the oil and
water.
*keh-rem el-le-noer-riz-ze
ahz o-lah-yaht ehsh
ah vi-zet*
   Kérem, ellenőrizze
az olajat és a vizet.

How long can I park here?
*med-digh pahr-kol-hah-
tok itt?*
   Meddig parkolhatok itt?

Does this road lead to...?
ez ahz oot ve-zet ...?
   Ez az út vezet ...?

air (for tyres)	*le-ve-ghoer*	levegő
battery	*ahk-ku-mu-laa-tor*	akkumulátor

brakes	*fehk*	fék
clutch	*kup-lungh*	kuplung
driver's licence	*yo-gho-sheet-vaany*	jogosítvány
engine	*mo-tor*	motor
lights	*vi-laa-ghee-taash*	világítás
oil	*o-lahy*	olaj
puncture	*de-fekt*	defekt
radiator	*hüü-toer*	hűtő
road map	*ahu-tohsh tehr-kehp*	autós térkép
tyres	*ke-rehk-gu-mi*	kerékgumi
windscreen	*sehl-veh-doer*	szélvédő

HUNGARIAN

Car Problems

I need a mechanic.
   sük-sheh-ghem vahn edj   Szükségem van egy szerelőre.
   se-re-loer-re
The battery is flat.
   le-me-rült ahz akku-mu-   Lemerült az akkumulátor.
   laa-tor
The radiator is leaking.
   fo-yik ah hüü-toer   Folyik a hűtő.
I have a flat tyre.
   de-fek-tet kahp-tahm   Defektet kaptam.
It's overheating.
   tool-füüt   Túlfűt.
It's not working.
   nem müü-ker-dik   Nem működik.

Accommodation

CAMPING GROUND	KEMPING
GUEST HOUSE	VENDÉGHÁZ
HOTEL	SZÁLLODA
MOTEL	MOTEL
YOUTH HOSTEL	IFJÚSÁGI SZÁLLÓ

Where is a ...?
hol vahn edj ...?   Hol van egy ...?

cheap hotel	*ol-choh saal-lo-dah*	olcsó szálloda
good hotel	*yoh saal-lo-dah*	jó szálloda
nearby hotel	*ker-ze-li saal-lo-dah*	közeli szálloda
clean hotel	*tis-tah saal-lo-dah*	tiszta szálloda

What is the address?
mi ah tseem?   Mi a cím?
Could you write the address,
please?
le-eer-naa ah tsee-met   Leírná a címet kérem?
keh-rem?

At the Hotel
Do you have any rooms
available?
vahn sah-bahd   Van szabad szobájuk?
so-baa-yuk?

I would like ...
se-ret-nehk edj ... Szeretnék egy ...

a single room	*edj-aa-djahsh so-baat*	egyágyas szobát
a double room	*keht-aa-djahsh so-baat*	kétágyas szobát
a room with a bathroom	*für-doer-so-baash so-baat*	fürdőszobás szobát
to share a dorm	*aa-djaht edj haa-loh-te-rem-ben*	ágyat egy hálóteremben
a bed	*edj aa-djaht*	egy ágyat

I want a room ...
se-ret-nehk edj so-baat ... Szeretnék egy szobát ...

with a bathroom	*für-doer-so-baa-vahl*	fürdőszobával
with a shower	*zu-hah-nyo-zoh-vahl*	zuhanyozóval
with a television	*te-le-vee-zioh-vahl*	televízióval
with a window	*ahb-lahk-kahl*	ablakkal

I'm going to stay for ...
... mah-rah-dok ... maradok

one day	*edj nah-pigh*	egy napig
two days	*keht nah-pigh*	két napig
one week	*edj heh-tigh*	egy hétig

Do you have identification?
vahn vah-lah-mi-yen ah se-mehy-ah-zo-nosh-shaa-ghaat i-ghah-zo-loh pah-peer-yah?

Van valamilyen a személyazonosságát igazoló papírja?

Your membership card,
please.
> *keh-rem ah tahgh-shaa-ghi* Kérem a tagsági igazolványát.
> *i-ghah-zol-vaa-nyaat*

Sorry, we're full.
> *shahy-naa-lom de te-le* Sajnálom, de tele vagyunk.
> *vah-djunk*

How long will you be
staying?
> *med-digh mah-rahd?* Meddig marad?

How many nights?
> *haany ehy-sah-kaat* Hány éjszakát marad?
> *mah-rahd?*

It's ... per day/per person.
> *... ft nah-pon-tah/* ... Ft naponta/személyenként.
> *se-meh-yen-kehnt*

How much is it per night/
per person?
> *meny-nyi-be ke-rül* Mennyibe kerül éjszakánként/
> *ehy-sah-kaan-kehnt/* személyenként?
> *se-meh- yen-kehnt?*

Can I see it?
> *megh-nehz-he-tem ah so-* Megnézhetem a szobát?
> *baat?*

Are there any others?
> *vahn edj maa-shik so-bah?* Van egy másik szoba?

Are there any cheaper
rooms?
> *vahn edj ol-chohbb* Van egy olcsóbb szoba?
> *so-bah?*

Can I see the bathroom?
meg-nehz-he-tem ah
für-doer-so-baat?

Megnézhetem a fürdőszobát?

Is there a reduction for
students/children?
vahn ked-vez-mehny
di-aa-kok-nahk/
dje-re-kek-nek?

Van kedvezmény diákoknak/
gyerekeknek?

Does it include breakfast?
ahz aar tahr-tahl-
mahz-zah ah regh-ghe-lit?

Az ár tartalmazza a reggelit?

It's fine, I'll take it.
ez yoh les

Ez jó lesz.

I don't know how long I'm
staying.
mehgh nem tu-dom
pon-to-shahn hodj
med-digh mah-rah-dok

Még nem tudom pontosan,
hogy meddig maradok.

Is there a lift?
lift vahn?

Lift van?

Where is the bathroom?
hol vahn ah für-doer-
so-bah?

Hol van a fürdőszoba?

Is there hot water all day?
e-ghehs nahp vahn
me-legh veez?

Egész nap van meleg víz?

Do you have a safe where I
can leave my valuables?
vahn er-nerk-nehl sehf,
ah-hol ahz ehr-teh-ke-
i-met hahdj-hah-tom?

Van önöknél széf, ahol az
értékeimet hagyhatom?

Is there somewhere to wash
clothes?

> *vahn vah-lah-hol edj hey,* Van valahol egy hely,
> *ah-hol mosh-hah-tok?* ahol moshatok?

Can I use the kitchen?

> *hahs-naal-hah-tom ah* Használhatom a konyhát?
> *kony-haat?*

Can I use the telephone?

> *hahs-naal-hah-tom ah* Használhatom a telefont?
> *te-le-font?*

Requests & Complaints

Please wake me up at ...

> *keh-rek ehb-res-tehsht ...* Kérek ébresztést ... órakor.
> *oh-rah-kor*

The room needs to be cleaned.

> *ah so-baat ki kell* A szobát ki kell takarítani.
> *tah-kah-ree-tah-ni*

Please change the sheets.

> *keh-rem che-rehl-ye ki* Kérem, cseréljc ki a lepedőt.
> *ah le-pe-doert*

I can't open/close the
window.

> *nem tu-dom ki-nyit-ni/* Nem tudom kinyitni/
> *be-chuk-ni ahz* becsukni az ablakot.
> *ahb-lah-kot*

I've locked myself out of
my room.

> *ki-zaar-tahm mah-ghahm* Kizártam magam a
> *ah so-baam-bohl* szobámból.

The toilet won't flush.
ah veh tseh nem erb-leet   A WC nem öblít.

I don't like this room.
ez ah so-bah nem tet-sik   Ez a szoba nem tetszik.

It's too small.
tool ki-chi   Túl kicsi.

It's noisy.
zah-yosh   Zajos.

It's too dark.
tool sher-teht   Túl sötét.

It's expensive.
draa-ghah   Drága.

Some Useful Words & Phrases

I am/We are leaving ...
... me-djek el/me-djünk el   ... megyek el/megyünk el
now/tomorrow
mosht/hol-nahp   most/holnap

I would like to pay the bill.
se-ret-nehk fi-zet-ni   Szeretnék fizetni.

name	*nehv*	név
surname	*ve-ze-tehk-nehv*	vezetéknév
room number	*so-bah-saam*	szobaszám

address	*tseem*	cím
air-conditioned	*lehgh-kon-di-tsi-o-naalt*	légkondicionált

HUNGARIAN

balcony	*er-kehy*	erkély
bathroom	*für-doer-so-bah*	fürdőszoba
bed	*aadj*	ágy
bill	*saam-lah*	számla
blanket	*tah-kah-roh*	takaró
candle	*djer-tyah*	gyertya
chair	*sehk*	szék
clean	*tis-tah*	tiszta
cupboard	*sek-rehny*	szekrény
dark	*sher-teht*	sötét
dirty	*pis-kosh*	piszkos
double bed	*dup-lah aadj*	dupla ágy
electricity	*e-lekt-ro-mosh-shaagh*	elektromosság
excluded	*ki-veh-te-leh-vel*	kivételével
fan	*ven-til-laa-tor*	ventillátor
included	*be-le-ehrt-ve*	beleértve
key	*kulch*	kulcs
lift (elevator)	*lift*	lift
light bulb	*eh-goer*	égő
lock (n)	*zaar*	zár
mattress	*maht-rats*	matrac
mirror	*tü-ker*	tükör
padlock	*lah-kaht*	lakat
pillow	*paar-nah*	párna
quiet	*chen-desh*	csendes
room (in hotel)	*so-bah*	szoba
sheet	*le-pe-doer*	lepedő
shower	*zu-hah-nyo-zoh*	zuhanyozó
soap	*sahp-pahn*	szappan
suitcase	*boer-rernd*	bőrönd

swimming pool	*u-so-dah*	uszoda
table	*ahs-tahl*	asztal
toilet	*veh tseh*	WC
toilet paper	*veh tseh pah-peer*	WC papír
towel	*ter-rül-ker-zoer*	törülköző
water	*veez*	víz
cold water	*hi-degh veez*	hideg víz
hot water	*me-legh veez*	meleg víz
window	*ahb-lahk*	ablak

Around Town

What time does it open?
  mi-kor nyit ki?   Mikor nyit ki?
What time does it close?
  mi-kor zaar be?   Mikor zár be?

I'm looking for ...
  ke-re-shem ...   Keresem ...

the art gallery	*ah gah-leh-ri-aat*	a galériát
a bank	*edj bahn-kot*	egy bankot
the church	*ah temp-lo-mot*	a templomot
the city centre	*ah vaa-rosh-kerz-pon-tot*	a városközpontot
the ... embassy	*ah/ahz ... ker-vet-sheh-ghet*	a/az ... követséget
my hotel	*ah saal-lo-daa-maht*	a szállodámat
the market	*ah pi-ah-tsot*	a piacot
the museum	*ah moo-ze-u-mot*	a múzeumot
the police	*ah ren-doer-sheh-ghet*	a rendőrséget

the post office	*ah posh-taat*	a postát
a public toilet	*edj nyil-vaa-nosh veh tseht*	egy nyilvános WCt
the telephone centre	*ah te-le-fon-kerz-pon-tot*	a telefonközpontot
the tourist information office	*ah tu-rish-tah in-for-maa-tsi-ohsh i-ro-daat*	a turista információs irodát

What ... is this?

me-yik ... ez?		Melyik ... ez?
street	*ut-tsah*	utca
suburb	*ke-rü-let*	kerület

For directions, see the Getting Around section, page 180.

At the Post Office

I would like some stamps.
beh-ye-ghe-ket se-ret-nehk ven-ni   Bélyegeket szeretnék venni.

How much is the postage?
meny-nyi-be ke-rül ah beh-yegh?   Mennyibe kerül a bélyeg?

How much does it cost to send ... to ...?
meny-nyi-be ke-rül el-kül-de-ni ...?   Mennyibe kerül elküldeni ...?

I would like to send ...
se-ret-nehk el-kül-de-ni ...   Szeretnék elküldeni ...

a letter	*edj le-ve-let*	egy levelet
a postcard	*edj keh-pesh-lah-pot*	egy képeslapot
a parcel	*edj cho-mah-ghot*	egy csomagot
a telegram	*edj taa-vi-rah-tot*	egy táviratot
aerogram	*ern-bo-ree-teh-ko-loh*	önborítékoló
	leh-ghi-posh-tah	légi posta levél
	le-vehl	
air mail	*leh-ghi-posh-tah*	légiposta
envelope	*bo-ree-tehk*	boríték
mail box	*posh-tah-laa-dah*	postaláda
registered mail	*ah-yaan-lott*	ajánlott küldemény
	kül-de-mehny	
surface mail	*shi-mah posh-tah*	síma posta

HUNGARIAN

Telephone

I want to ring ...
  se-ret-nehk ...   Szeretnék ... telefonálni.
  te-le-fo-naal-ni
The number is ...
  ah saam ...   A szám ...
I want to speak for three minutes.
  haa-rom per-tsigh   Három percig
  se-ret-nehk be-sehl-ni   szeretnék beszélni.
How much does a three-minute call cost?
  meny-nyi-be ke-rül   Mennyibe kerül egy három
  edj haa-rom-per-tsesh   perces hívás?
  hee-vaash?

How much does each extra
minute cost?
   meny-nyi-be ke-rül   Mennyibe kerül minden
   min-den to-vaab-bi edj   további egy perc?
   perts?
I would like to speak to
Mr Perez.
   pe-rez oor-rahl   Perez úrral szeretnék beszélni.
   se-ret-nehk be-sehl-ni
I want to make a reverse-
charges phone call.
   er be-sehl-ghe-tehsht   R beszélgetést szeretnék.
   se-ret-nehk
It's engaged.
   fog-lahlt   Foglalt.
I've been cut off.
   meg-sah-kahdt ah vo-nahl   Megszakadt a vonal.

At the Bank
I want to exchange some
money/travellers' cheques.
   se-ret-nehk pehnzt/utah-   Szeretnék pénzt/utazási
   zaa-shi chek-ket vaal-   csekket váltani.
   tah-ni
What is the exchange rate?
   meny-nyi ahz   Mennyi az árfolyam?
   aar-fo-yahm?
How many forints per dollar?
   haany fo-rint edj dol-laar?   Hány forint egy dollár?

Can I have money transferred
here from my bank?

aat-u-tahl-hah-tok pehnzt Átutalhatok pénzt ide
i-de ah bahn-kom-bohl? a bankomból?

How long will it take to
arrive?

meny-nyi idoer ah-lahtt Mennyi idő alatt
ehr-ke-zik megh ah érkezik meg a pénz?
pehnz?

Has my money arrived yet?

megh-ehr-ke-zett maar Megérkezett már a pénzem?
ah pehn-zem?

bankdraft	*bahnk-in-tehz-vehny*	bankintézvény
bank notes	*bahnk-ye-djek*	bankjegyek
cashier	*pehnz-taar*	pénztár
coins	*ehr-mehk*	érmék
credit card	*hi-tel-kaar-tyah*	hitelkártya
exchange	*vaal-taash*	váltás
loose change	*ahp-roh*	apró
signature	*ah-laa-ee-raash*	aláírás

Sightseeing

Do you have a guidebook/
local map?

vahn ooti-kerny-vük/ Van útikönyvük/térképük?
tehr-keh-pük?

What are the main attractions?

me-yek ah foerbb Melyek a főbb látnivalók?
laat-ni-vah-lohk?

What is that?
mi ahz?   Mi az?
How old is it?
mi-yen reh-ghi?   Milyen régi?
Can I take photographs?
fehny-keh-pez-he-tek?   Fényképezhetek?
What time does it open/close?
mi-kor nyit ki/zaar be?   Mikor nyit ki/zár be?

ancient	*oer-shi*	ősi
archaeological	*reh-gheh-se-ti*	régészeti
beach	*shtrahnd*	strand
building	*eh-pü-let*	épület
castle	*vaar*	vár
cathedral	*seh-kesh-edj-haaz*	székesegyház
church	*temp-lom*	templom
concert hall	*hahngh-ver-sheny-te-rem*	hangversenyterem
library	*kernyv-taar*	könyvtár
main square	*foer tehr*	fő tér
market	*pi-ahts*	piac
monastery	*ko-losh-tor*	kolostor
monument	*em-lehk-müü*	emlékmű
mosque	*me-chet*	mecset
old city	*reh-ghi vaa-rosh*	régi város
palace	*pah-lo-tah*	palota
opera house	*o-pe-rah-haaz*	operaház
ruins	*ro-mok*	romok
stadium	*shtah-di-on*	stadion
statues	*sob-rok*	szobrok
synagogue	*zhi-nah-ghoh-ghah*	zsinagóga

| temple | *temp-lom* | templom |
| university | *e-dje-tem* | egyetem |

Entertainment

What is there to do in the evenings?
mit le-het chi-naal-ni esh-tehn-kehnt?   Mit lehet csinálni esténként?

Are there any discos?
vahn-nahk dis-kohk?   Vannak diszkók?

Are there places where you can hear local folk music?
vah-nahk o-yahn he-yek, ah-hol he-yi nehp-ze-neht le-het hahll-ghaht-ni?   Vannak olyan helyek, ahol helyi népzenét lehet hallgatni?

How much does it cost to get in?
meny-nyi-be ke-rül ah be-leh-poer?   Mennyibe kerül a belépő?

cinema	*mo-zi*	mozi
concert	*kon-tsert*	koncert
discotheque	*dis-koh*	diszkó
theatre	*seen-haaz*	színház

In the Country

Weather

What's the weather like?
mi-yen ahz i-doer?   Milyen az idő?

The weather is ... today.
ahz i-doer ... mah   Az idő ... ma.
Will it be ... tomorrow?
... les hol-nahp?   ... lesz holnap?

cloudy	*fel-hoersh*	felhős
cold	*hi-degh*	hideg
foggy	*ker-dersh*	ködös
frosty	*hüü-versh*	hűvös
hot	*me-legh*	meleg
raining	*e-shoer*	esős
snowing	*hah-vah-zaash*	havazás
sunny	*nah-posh*	napos
windy	*se-lesh*	szeles

Camping

Am I allowed to camp here?
itt le-het kem-pin-ghez-ni?   Itt lehet kempingezni?
Is there a campsite nearby?
vahn itt vah-lah-hol ah   Van itt valahol a
ker-zel-ben edj kem-pingh?   közelben egy kemping?

backpack	*haa-ti-zhaak*	hátizsák
can opener	*kon-zerv-nyi-toh*	konzervnyitó
compass	*i-raany-tüü*	iránytű
crampons	*yehgh-segh*	jégszeg
firewood	*tüü-zi-fah*	tűzifa
gas cartridge	*gaaz-paht-ron*	gázpatron
hammock	*fügh-ghoer-aadj*	függőágy
ice axe	*yehgh-chaa-kaany*	jégcsákány
mattress	*maht-rats*	matrac

penknife	*zheb-kehsh*	zsebkés
rope	*ker-tehl*	kötél
tent	*shaa-tor*	sátor
tent pegs	*shaa-tor tser-ler-perk*	sátor cölöpök
torch (flashlight)	*zheb-laam-pah*	zseblámpa
sleeping bag	*haa-loh-zhaak*	hálózsák
stove	*kem-pingh-foer-zoer*	kempingfőző
water bottle	*vi-zesh-pah-lahtsk*	vizespalack

HUNGARIAN

Food

As befits a country that has been at the crossroads of history for centuries, Hungarian cuisine is a special mixture of foods from many cultures, such as Balkan, Czech, German and Austrian. Add to this traditional regional specialities and the visitor will not be disappointed in the wide range of spicy, sweet, sour and smoky flavours. Many dishes contain the famous Hungarian paprika, ranging from biting hot 'csípős' to the sweet 'rose paprika'. Sour cream is also a favourite and accompanies a vast range of dishes. Pork is the most common meat, found in most establishments along with poultry dishes. Fish is often fresh and excellent, particularly around Lake Balaton, the Danube or the Tisza rivers; beef and lamb are not as common. Do not miss the game dishes if you find a restaurant specialising in such. Hungarian wines are famed throughout the world, and some of the local beers are excellent too. It is not a great country for vegetarians who wish to eat out, although things are changing fast in the cities; however in the summer, vegetables and fruit are plentiful and cheap.

The main types of restaurants can be classified as:
Vendéglő – smaller with good food at reasonable prices;
Étterem – wide variety of dishes, wide variations in service;
Csárda – country cooking, limited menu but usually good;
Önkiszolgáló – self service, cheap and filling. No prizes
for *haute cuisine*.

breakfast	regh-ghe-li	reggeli
lunch	e-behd	ebéd
dinner	vah-cho-rah	vacsora

Table for ..., please.
   se-ret-nehk edj   Szeretnék egy asztalt ...
   ahs-tahlt ... se-mehy-re   személyre.
Can I see the menu please?
   megh-nehz-he-tem ahz   Megnézhetem az étlapot?
   eht-lah-pot?
I would like the set lunch.
   me-nüt keh-rek   Menüt kérek.
What does it include?
   mi vahn ben-ne?   Mi van benne?
Is service included in the bill?
   ahz aar tahr-tahl-   Az ár tartalmazza
   mahz-zah ah   a felszolgálást?
   fel-sol-ghaa-laasht?
Not too spicy please.
   nem tool füü-se-re-shen, Nem túl fűszeresen, kérem.
   keh-rem

| ashtray | hah-mu-tahr-toh | hamutartó |
| the bill | ah saam-lah | a számla |

a cup	edj cheh-se	egy csésze
dessert	eh-desh-shehgh	édesség
a drink	edj i-tahl	egy ital
a fork	edj vil-lah	egy villa
fresh	frish	friss
a glass	edj po-haar	egy pohár
a knife	edj kehsh	egy kés
a plate	edj taa-nyehr	egy tányér
spicy	füü-se-resh	fűszeres
a spoon	edj kah-naal	egy kanál
stale	nem frish	nem friss
sweet	eh-desh	édes
teaspoon	teaash-kah-naal	teáskanál
toothpick	fogh-pis-kaa-loh	fogpiszkáló

HUNGARIAN

Vegetarian Meals

I am a vegetarian.
ve-ghe-taa-ri-aa-nush vah-djok Vegetáriánus vagyok.

I don't eat meat.
nem e-sem hoosht Nem eszem húst.

I don't eat chicken fish or ham.
nem e-sem chir-keht, hah-laht, shon-kaat Nem eszem csirkét, halat, sonkát.

Starters   Előételek

Hortobágyi húsos palacsinta
    Pancake stuffed with stewed and minced meat and herbs, and covered with a sauce of gravy and sour cream.

Libamáj
Goose liver; a particular delicacy in Hungary. May be cooked in several ways, either in a light meat stock, with onion and water, in milk, or fried. Often served cold with bread as a starter.

Rántott gomba
Fried mushrooms in breadcrumbs, generally served with rice and tartar sauce or mayonnaise.

Rántott sajt
Fried cheese in breadcrumbs, served like *rántott gomba*.

Soups   Levesek

Bableves
Bean soup with turnip, carrot and sour cream.

Gombaleves
A delicious mushroom soup with seasoning, onion, sour cream and parsley.

Gulyásleves
Goulash soup, chopped meat fried in onions and paprika, and added to water or stock, with potatoes and a dash of white wine.

Halászlé
A strong and rich broth of usually several kinds of fish (but always containing carp) in large pieces, with tomatoes, green paprika and paprika. Beware, this soup can have a bite to it! Usually brought to the table in a small cauldron, 'bogrács', on a tripod.

Hideg gyümölcsleves
Cold fruit soup, often cherry 'meggy', prepared with cream, lemon peel, cinnamon and red wine.

Káposzta leves
Cabbage soup; comes in several variations. A popular one is 'Hangover' soup: korhelyleves with sauerkraut, smoked sausage, onion, paprika and sour cream.

Újházy Tyúkhúsleves
Chicken and meat stock soup with root vegetables and vermicelli.

Dishes of the Day   Készételek

Lecsó
A delicious thick stew of onions, tomatoes, green peppers and lard. Can be served either as a vegetarian dish with rice, or with smoked sausage.

Pörkölt
Beef 'marha', pork 'sertés', veal 'borjú', game 'vad' stew cooked in lard with onions, bacon and paprika, plus the obligatory sour cream.

Töltött káposzta
Similar to töltött paprika, but the meat filling is stuffed in cabbage leaves or cooked as meat balls in the sauce.

Töltött paprika
Green peppers stuffed with a mixture of minced meat, bacon, egg, onion, rice, and baked in a sauce of sour cream.

Meat   Hús

Aprópecsenye
Braised cutlets of pork with paprika, onion and sour cream. Served with vinegar or lemon juice.

Bécsi szelet
Wiener schnitzel veal cutlet deep fried in a coating of flour, beaten eggs and breadcrumbs.

Köménymagos sertéshús
Pork stew with rice, onion, lard, tomato purée and caraway seeds.

Natúrszelet
Leg of veal dipped into flour and fried.

Párizsi szelet
As above, except that the final coating of breadcrumbs is substituted by another layer of flour.

Rántott szelet sertéshús
Pork chops in breadcrumbs, fried in a coating of flour, beaten eggs and breadcrumbs.

Sült csülök
Knuckle of pork boiled, then coated in flour and fried. Served with horseradish.

Fish   Hal

Gombás fogas
Pike-perch, sometimes known as 'süllő', braised with mushrooms and a sauce of white wine, butter, lemon juice, eggs and bone stock.

Rántott hal
Fish in breadcrumbs. May be carp 'ponty' or catfish 'harcsa', or one of several other freshwater types, rolled in flour, egg and breadcrumbs, and fried.

Poultry   Baromfi

Becsinált csirke
Chicken fricassee fried with cauliflower, kohlrabi, celery root, carrot, turnip and mushrooms then braised in stock with lemon juice. Flavoured with egg yolks.

Pirított liba máj
Fried goose liver, first boiled in milk and then fried without seasoning.

Rántott csirke
Deep-fried chicken in breadcrumbs.

Tejfölös csirke
Chicken braised in a sour cream, lemon and butter sauce.

Game   Vad

Fácán narancsos mártással
Pheasant in orange sauce, cooked with carrots, onions, mushrooms, lemon peel and smoked meat. Before serving it is boiled in stock and sugar and orange peel added.

Nyúl vörös borban
Hare braised in red wine, with butter, pork cubes and an onion.

Őzgerinc 'remek' módon
Saddle of venison roast in a rich sauce of sour cream, lemon juice and butter with smoked bacon, carrots, turnips and mustard.

Vaddisznókotlett
Wild-boar cutlets fried in a coating of egg, spices and crispy breadcrumbs with a dressing of mustard sauce.

Salads **Saláták**

Salads are very frequently mixed with a vinegar dressing or pickled, and include:

cabbage	*káposzta*
gherkin	*uborka*
lettuce	*fejes saláta*
tomato	*paradicsom*

Vegetables & Garnishes **Köretek & Főzelékek**

cabbage	*káposzta*
green beans	*zöld bab*
onion	*hagyma*
potato	*burgonya/krumpli*
boiled potatoes	*főtt krumpli*
roast potatoes	*sült krumpli*
chips	*hasábburgonya*

Pasta **Tészták**

Káposztás kocka
   Cabbage, fried and mixed with sour cream, then added to rolled and chopped pasta.

Lángos
   An institution in Hungary, light dough mixed with puréed potato, quick-fried in deep fat and served sweet (with jams or sugar) or salty (with cheese or sour cream).

Túrós csusza
   Fine white noodles mixed with cottage cheese or curds, and lashings of sour cream. Comes in two general variations: with bacon pieces, or sweet with powdered sugar.

Desserts   Édességek
Dobostorta
  A sponge cake with layers of buttered cocoa and topped with a hard brown caramel coating.
Gesztenyepüré
  Mashed and sieved sweet chestnuts cooked in milk with vanilla and served with cream and/or rum.
Rétes
  Strudel pastry filled with a variety of fruits such as sourcherry 'meggy', apple 'alma', walnut 'dió', poppy seed 'mák', or a particular Hungarian favourite, cottage cheese 'túró'.

Nonalcoholic Drinks
drinks	*italok*
ice	*jég*
mineral water	*ásványvíz*
sparkling mineral water	*kristályvíz*
soft drinks	*üdítők*
orange	*narancs*
lemon	*citrom*
apple	*alma*

Alcoholic Drinks   Italok
beer	*sör*
bottled	*üveges*
draught	*csapolt*
champagne	*pezsgő*
wine	*bor*
white	*fehér*

red	*vörös*
dry	*száraz*
sweet	*édes*

Shopping

How much is it?

meny-nyi-be ke-rül?	Mennyibe kerül?

bookshop	*kerny-vesh-bolt*	könyvesbolt
camera shop	*fo-toh-üz-let*	fotóüzlet
clothing store	*ru-haa-zah-ti bolt*	ruházati bolt
delicatessen	*de-li-kaat-üz-let*	delikátüzlet
general store, shop	*aa-ru-haaz*	áruház
laundry	*pah-tyo-laht*	patyolat
market	*pi-ats*	piac
newsagency	*ooy-shaa-ghosh*	újságos
stationer's	*pah-peer-üz-let*	papírüzlet
pharmacy	*djohdj-ser-taar*	gyógyszertár
shoeshop	*tsi-poer-üz-let*	cipőüzlet
souvenir shop	*ah-yaan-dehk-bolt*	ajándékbolt
supermarket	*eh-lel-mi-ser-aa-ru-haaz*	élelmiszeráruház
vegetable shop	*zerld-sheh-ghesh*	zöldséges

I would like to buy ...

se-ret-nehk ... t ven-ni	Szeretnék ...t venni

Do you have others?

vahn vah-lah-mi maash?	Van valami más?

I don't like it.
ez nem tet-sik
Ez nem tetszik.

Can I look at it?
megh-nehz-he-tem ezt?
Megnézhetem ezt?

I'm just looking.
chahk neh-ze-loer-derm
Csak nézelődöm.

Can you write down the price?
le-eer-naa ahz aa-raat?
Leírná az árát?

Do you accept credit cards?
el-fo-ghahd-nahk hi-tel-kaar-tyaat?
Elfogadnak hitelkártyát?

Could you lower the price?
tud-naa cherk-ken-te-ni ahz aa-raht?
Tudná csökkenteni az árat?

I don't have much money.
ninch shok pehn-zem
Nincs sok pénzem.

Can I help you?
she-gheet-he-tek?
Segíthetek?

Will that be all?
ez min-den?
Ez minden?

Would you like it wrapped?
be-cho-mah-ghol-yuk?
Becsomagoljuk?

Sorry, this is the only one.
shay-nosh chahk ez ahz edj vahn
Sajnos csak ez az egy van.

How much/many do you want?
meny-nyit/haany dah-rah-bot se-ret-ne?
Mennyit/hány darabot szeretne?

Souvenirs

earrings	*fül-be-vah-loh*	fülbevaló
handicraft	*keh-zi-mun-kah*	kézimunka
necklace	*nyahk-laants*	nyaklánc
pottery	*ah-djagh-aa-ru*	agyagáru
ring	*djüü-rüü*	gyűrű
rug	*ki-shebb soer-nyegh*	kisebb szőnyeg

Clothing

clothing	*ru-haa-zaht*	ruházat
coat	*kah-baat*	kabát
dress	*ru-hah*	ruha
jacket	*zah-koh*	zakó
jumper (sweater)	*pu-loh-ver*	pulóver
shirt	*ingh*	ing
shoes	*tsi-poer*	cipő
skirt	*sok-nyah*	szoknya
trousers	*nahd-raagh*	nadrág

It doesn't fit.
    nem yoh meh-ret   Nem jó méret.

It is too ...
    ez tool ...   Ez túl ...

big	*nadj*	nagy
small	*kichi*	kicsi
short	*rer-vid*	rövid
long	*hos-soo*	hosszú
tight	*so-rosh*	szoros
loose	*boer*	bő

Materials

cotton	*pah-mut*	pamut
handmade	*keh-zi-mun-kah*	kézimunka
leather	*boer*	bőr
brass	*rehz*	réz
gold	*ah-rahny*	arany
silver	*e-züsht*	ezüst
pure alpaca	*tis-tah ahl-pah-kah*	tiszta alpaka
silk	*she-yem*	selyem
wool	*djahp-yoo*	gyapjú

Colours

black	*fe-ke-te*	fekete
blue	*kehk*	kék
brown	*bahr-nah*	barna
green	*zerld*	zöld
orange	*nah-rahnch-shaar-ghah*	narancssárga
pink	*roh-zhah-seen*	rózsaszín
red	*pi-rosh*	piros
white	*fe-hehr*	fehér
yellow	*shaar-ghah*	sárga

Toiletries

comb	*feh-shüü*	fésű
condoms	*ko-ton*	koton
deodorant	*de-zo-dor*	dezodor
hairbrush	*hahy-ke-fe*	hajkefe
moisturising cream	*krehm saa-rahz boer-re*	krém száraz bőrre

HUNGARIAN

razor	*bo-rot-vah*	borotva
sanitary napkins	*e-ghehs-shehgh-üdji be-teht*	egészségügyi betét
shampoo	*shahm-pon*	sampon
shaving cream	*bo-rot-vaal-ko-zoh krehm*	borotválkozókrém
soap	*sahp-pahn*	szappan
sunblock cream	*nahp-o-lahy*	napolaj
tampons	*tahm-pon*	tampon
tissues	*pah-peer-zheb-ken-doer*	papírzsebkendő
toilet paper	*veh tseh pah-peer*	WC papír
toothbrush	*fogh-ke-fe*	fogkefe
toothpaste	*fogh-krehm*	fogkrém

Stationery & Publications

map	*tehr-kehp*	térkép
newspaper	*ooy-shaagh*	újság
newspaper in English	*ahn-ghol nyel-vüü ooy-shaagh*	angol nyelvű újság
novels in English	*ahn-ghol nyel-vüü re-gheh-nyek*	angol nyelvű regények
paper	*pah-peer*	papír
pen (ballpoint)	*go-yohsh-toll*	golyóstoll
scissors	*ol-loh*	olló

Photography

How much is it to process this film?

meny-nyi-be ke-rül eloer-heev-ni ezt ah fil-met?	Mennyibe kerül előhívni ezt a filmet?

When will it be ready?

mi-kor les kehs?	Mikor lesz kész?

I'd like a film for this camera.

edj fil-met se-ret-nehk eb-be ah fehny-keh-pe-zoer-ghehp-be	Egy filmet szeretnék ebbe a fényképezőgépbe.

HUNGARIAN

B&W (film)	*fe-ke-te fe-hehr-film*	fekete-fehér film
camera	*fehny-keh-pe-zoer-ghehp*	fényképezőgép
colour (film)	*see-nesh-film*	színesfilm
film	*film*	film
lash	*vah-ku*	vaku
lens	*len-che*	lencse
light meter	*fehny-meh-roer*	fénymérő

Smoking

A packet of cigarettes, please.

edj cho-mahgh tsi-ghah-ret-taat keh-rek	Egy csomag cigarettát kérek.

Are these cigarettes strong/mild?

ez ah tsi-ghah-ret-tah e-roersh/djen-ghe?	Ez a cigaretta erős/gyenge?

Do you have a light?
vahn tü-ze?   Van tüze?

cigarette papers	*tsi-ghah-ret-tah pah-peer*	cigaretta papír
cigarettes	*tsi-ghah-ret-tah*	cigaretta
filtered	*füsht-süü-roersh*	füstszűrős
lighter	*ern-djooy-toh*	öngyújtó
matches	*dju-fah*	gyufa
menthol	*men-to-losh*	mentolos
pipe	*pi-pah*	pipa
tobacco (pipe)	*pi-pah-do-haany*	pipadohány

Sizes & Comparisons

small	*ki-chi*	kicsi
big	*nahdj*	nagy
heavy	*ne-hehz*	nehéz
light	*kerny-nyüü*	könnyű
more	*terbb*	több
less	*ke-ve-shebb*	kevesebb
too much/many	*tool shok*	túl sok
many	*shok*	sok
enough	*e-lehgh*	elég
also	*sin-tehn*	szintén
a little bit	*edj ki-chi*	egy kicsi

Health

Where is ...?
> *hol vahn ...?* Hol van ...?

the doctor	*ahz or-vosh*	az orvos
the hospital	*ah kohr-haaz*	a kórház
the chemist	*ah djohdj-ser-taar*	a gyógyszertár
the dentist	*ah fogh-or-vosh*	a fogorvos

I am sick.
> *ros-sul vah-djok* Rosszul vagyok.

My friend is sick.
> *ah bah-raa-tom ros-sul vahn* A barátom rosszul van.

Could I see a female doctor?
> *edj dok-tor-noert ke-re-shek?* Egy doktornőt keresek?

What's the matter?
> *mi ah prob-leh-mah?* Mi a probléma?

Where does it hurt?
> *hol faay?* Hol fáj?

It hurts here.
> *itt faay* Itt fáj.

My ... hurts.
> *ah/ahz ... faay* A/az ... fáj.

Parts of the Body

ankle	*bo-kaam*	bokám
arm	*kah-rom*	karom
back	*haa-tahm*	hátam

chest	*mell-kah-shom*	mellkasom
ear	*fü-lem*	fülem
eye	*se-mem*	szemem
finger	*uy-yahm*	ujjam
foot	*laab-fe-yem*	lábfejem
hand	*ke-zem*	kezem
head	*fe-yem*	fejem
heart	*see-vem*	szívem
leg	*laa-bahm*	lábam
mouth	*saam*	szám
nose	*or-rom*	orrom
ribs	*bor-daam*	bordám
skin	*boer-rerm*	bőröm
spine	*ghe-rin-tsem*	gerincem
stomach	*djom-rom*	gyomrom
teeth	*fo-ghahm*	fogam
throat	*tor-kom*	torkom

Ailments

(I have ...)

an allergy	*ahl-ler-ghi-aash vah-djok*	Allergiás vagyok.
a blister	*hoh-yahgh vahn rahy-tahm*	Hólyag van rajtam.
a burn	*megh-eh-ghet-tem mah-ghahm*	Megégettem magam.
a cold	*megh-faaz-tahm*	Megfáztam.
constipation	*sehk-re-ke-deh-shem vahn*	Székrekedésem van.
cough	*ker-her-gherk*	köhögök

diarrhoea	*hahsh-me-neh-shem vahn*	Hasmenésem van.
fever	*laa-zahm vahn*	Lázam van.
a headache	*faay ah fe-yem*	Fáj a fejem.
hepatitis	*maay-djul-lah-daa-shom vahn*	Májgyulladásom van.
influenza	*in-flu-en-zaash va-djok*	Influenzás vagyok.
low/high blood pressure	*ah-lah-chony/ mah-ghahsh ah vehr-nyo-maa-shom*	Alacsony/ Magas a vérnyomásom.
a pain	*faay-dahl-mahm vahn*	Fájdalmam van.
sore throat	*faay ah tor-kom*	Fáj a torkom.
sprain	*fi-tsah-mom vahn*	Ficamom van.
a stomachache	*faay ah djom-rom*	Fáj a gyomrom.
sunburn	*le-ehgh-tem*	Leégtem.
a venereal disease	*ne-mi be-tegh-sheh-ghem vahn*	Nemi betegségem van.
worms	*ghi-lis-taam vahn*	Gilisztám van.

HUNGARIAN

Some Useful Words & Phrases

(I'm ...)

diabetic	*tsu-kor-be-tegh vah-djok*	Cukorbeteg vagyok.
epileptic	*e-pi-lep-si-aash vah-djok*	Epilepsziás vagyok.
asthmatic	*ahst-maash vah-djok*	Asztmás vagyok.

I'm allergic to antibiotics/
penicillin.
> *ahl-ler-ghi-aash vah-djok* Allergiás vagyok
> *ahz ahn-ti-bi-o-ti-kum-rah/* az antibiotikumra/
> *ah pe-ni-tsi-lin-re* a penicillinre.

I'm pregnant.
> *ter-hesh vah-djok* Terhes vagyok.

I'm on the pill.
> *fo-ghahm-zaash-ghaat-loh* Fogamzásgátlótablettát
> *tab-let-taat se-dek* szedek.

I haven't had my period
for ... months.
> *nem yertt meg ah mensh-* Nem jött meg a menstruációm
> *truaa-tsiohm ...* ... hónapja.
> *hoh-nahp-yah*

I have been vaccinated.
> *be vah-djok olt-vah* Be vagyok oltva.

I have my own syringe.
> *vahn shah-yaat tüüm* Van saját tűm.

I feel better/worse.
> *yob-bahn/ros-sahb-bul* Jobban/rosszabbul vagyok.
> *vah-djok*

accident	*bah-le-shet*	baleset
addiction	*kaa-rosh sen-ve-dehy*	káros szenvedély
antibiotics	*ahn-ti-bi-o-ti-kum*	antibiotikum
antiseptic	*fer-toer-zehsh-ghaat-loh*	fertőzésgátló
aspirin	*as-pi-rin*	aszpirin
bandage	*ker-tehsh*	kötés

bite	*hah-rah-paash*	harapás
blood test	*vehr-vizh-ghaa-laht*	vérvizsgálat
contraceptive	*fo-ghahm-zaash-ghaat-loh*	fogamzásgátló
injection	*in-yek-tsi-oh*	injekció
injury	*sheh-rü-lehsh*	sérülés
medicine	*or-vosh-shaagh*	orvosság
menstruation	*mensht-ru-aa-tsioh*	menstruáció
vitamins	*vi-tah-mi-nok*	vitaminok
wound	*sheb*	seb

HUNGARIAN

At the Chemist

I need medication for ...
   djohdj-ser-re vahn sük-sheh-ghem ...   Gyógyszerre van szükségem ...
I have a prescription.
   vahn edj re-tsep-tem   Van egy receptem.

At the Dentist

I have a toothache.
   faay ah fo-ghahm   Fáj a fogam.
I've lost a filling.
   ki-e-shett ah ter-mehsh   Kiesett a tömés.
I've broken a tooth.
   el-tert edj fo-ghahm   Eltört egy fogam.
My gums hurt.
   faay ahz ee-nyem   Fáj az ínyem.
I don't want it extracted.
   nem ah-kah-rom ki-hoo-zaht-ni   Nem akarom kihúzatni.

Please give me an anaesthetic.

keh-rem ahd-yon	Kérem adjon
ehr-zehsh-te-le-nee-toert	érzéstelenítőt.

Time & Dates

What time is it?

haany oh-rah?	Hány óra?

What date is it today?

haa-nyah-di-kah vahn mah?	Hányadika van ma?

It is ... o'clock.

... oh-rah vahn	... óra van.

in the morning	*regh-ghel*	reggel
in the afternoon	*deh-lu-taan*	délután
in the evening	*esh-te*	este

Days of the Week

Monday	*heht-foer*	hétfő
Tuesday	*kedd*	kedd
Wednesday	*ser-dah*	szerda
Thursday	*chü-ter-terk*	csütörtök
Friday	*pehn-tek*	péntek
Saturday	*som-baht*	szombat
Sunday	*vah-shaar-nahp*	vasárnap

Months

January	*yah-nu-aar*	január
February	*feb-ru-aar*	február
March	*maar-tsi-ush*	március
April	*aap-ri-lish*	április
May	*maa-yush*	május
June	*yoo-ni-ush*	június
July	*yoo-li-ush*	július
August	*ah-u-ghus-tush*	augusztus
September	*sep-tem-ber*	szeptember
October	*ok-toh-ber*	október
November	*no-vem-ber*	november
December	*de-tsem-ber*	december

Seasons

summer	*nyaar*	nyár
autumn	*oers*	ősz
winter	*tehl*	tél
spring	*tah-vahs*	tavasz

Present

today	*mah*	ma
this morning	*mah regh-ghel*	ma reggel
tonight	*mah esh-te*	ma este
this week	*e-zen ah heh-ten*	ezen a héten
year	*eb-ben ahz ehv-ben*	ebben az évben
now	*mosht*	most

HUNGARIAN

HUNGARIAN

Past

yesterday	*tegh-nahp*	tegnap
day before yesterday	*tegh-nahp-e-loertt*	tegnapelőtt
last night	*tegh-nahp esh-te*	tegnap este
last week/year	*moolt heh-ten/* *moolt ehv-ben*	múlt héten/ vbenmúlt évben

Future

tomorrow	*hol-nahp*	holnap
day after tomorrow	*hol-nahp-u-taan*	holnapután
tomorrow evening	*hol-nahp esh-te*	holnap este
next week	*yer-voer heh-ten*	jövő héten
next year	*yer-voer-re*	jövőre

During the Day

afternoon	*deh-lu-taan*	délután
dawn, very early morning	*hahy-nahl*	hajnal
day	*nahp*	nap
early	*ko-raan*	korán
midnight	*ehy-fehl*	éjfél
morning	*regh-ghel*	reggel
night	*ehy-yel*	éjjel
noon	*dehl*	dél
sundown	*nahp-le-men-te*	naplemente
sunrise	*nahp-fel-kel-te*	napfelkelte

Numbers & Amounts

0	*nul-lah*	nulla
1	*edj*	egy
2	*ket-toer*	kettő
3	*haa-rom*	három
4	*nehdj*	négy
5	*ert*	öt
6	*haht*	hat
7	*heht*	hét
8	*nyolts*	nyolc
9	*ki-lents*	kilenc
10	*teez*	tíz
20	*hoos*	húsz
30	*hahr-mints*	harminc
40	*nedj-ven*	negyven
50	*ert-ven*	ötven
60	*haht-vahn*	hatvan
70	*het-ven*	hetven
80	*nyolts-vahn*	nyolcvan
90	*ki-lents-ven*	kilencven
100	*saaz*	száz
1000	*e-zer*	ezer
one million	*edj mil-li-oh*	egy millió
1st	*el-shoer*	első (1.)
2nd	*maa-sho-dik*	második (2.)
3rd	*hahr-mah-dik*	harmadik (3.)

1/4	*edj-ne-djed*	egynegyed
1/3	*edj-hahr-mahd*	egyharmad
1/2	*fehl*	feål
3/4	*haa-rom-ne-djed*	haåromnegyed

Some Useful Words

a little (amount)	*edj ke-vehsh*	egy kevés
double	*dup-lah*	dupla
a dozen	*edj tu-tsaht*	egy tucat
Enough!	*e-lehgh!*	Elég!
few	*neh-haany*	néhány
less	*ke-ve-shebb*	kevesebb
many	*shok*	sok
more	*terbb*	több
once	*edj-ser*	egyszer
a pair	*edj paar*	egy pár
percent	*saa-zah-lehk*	százalék
some	*vah-lah-meny-nyi*	valamennyi
too much	*tool shok*	túl sok
twice	*keht-ser*	kétszer

Abbreviations

db	piece
de./du.	am/pm
É/D	Nth/Sth
EK	UK
EU	EU
ENSZ	UN
gr/kg	gm/kg
id.	snr
ifj.	jnr
i.sz./i.e.	AD/BC
kb.	approx.
Oszt./Közp.	Dept/HQ
stb.	etc
u.i./ford.	ps/pto
u/ú/krt/k	St/Rd/Blvd/Lane
l.Vh/2.Vh	WWI/WWII

HUNGARIAN

Polish

Polish

Introduction

A member of the Slavonic linguistic family, the Polish language has been developing for over a millennium. It belongs to the group of West Slavonic languages, together with Czech, Slovak and Lusatian, and is now the official language of Poland, spoken by some 99% of the country's 38 million people. It is also spoken among Polish communities scattered all over the globe, of which the largest live in the USA, the major nucleus being Chicago.

In the Middle Ages Polish adapted the Roman alphabet and gradually started to replace Latin, by then the lingua franca and language used by the Crown's state offices, administration and the Church. However, in order to write down the complex sounds of the Polish tongue, a number of consonant clusters and diacritical marks had to be devised. In effect, the visual appearance of Polish is pretty fearsome for people outside the Slavonic circle, and it's no doubt a difficult language to master. It has a complicated grammar, with the word endings changing depending on case, number and gender, and the rules abounding in exceptions. There is some good news, however. Polish is a phonetic language, which means that there's a consistent relationship between pronunciation and spelling. The stress almost always goes on the second-to-last syllable of a word.

As in Spanish, French or German, the Polish language uses two forms when addressing people: the familiar informal 'ty' (you), and the formal and more polite 'Pan' (literally Sir) or 'Pani' (Madam). Throughout this chapter, formal usage is given unless otherwise indicated.

Pronunciation

As was mentioned earlier, a letter or a cluster of letters in Polish is always pronounced the same way. Consequently, if you learn the basic rules and do a bit of practice, you'll be able to pronounce Polish words and phrases fairly correctly, and have no problems being understood.

Vowels

Polish vowels are pure, of roughly even length and consisting of one sound only. Their approximate pronunciation is as follows:

a	as the 'u' in 'cut'
e	as the 'e' in 'ten'
i	similar to the 'ee' in 'feet' but shorter
o	as the 'o' in 'not'
u	a bit shorter than 'oo' in 'book'
y	similar to 'i' in 'bit'

There are three specifically Polish vowels:

ą	a nasal vowel sounding like the French 'an', similar to 'own' in 'sown'
ę	also nasalised, like the French 'un'; pronounced as **e** when it's the final letter
ó	sounds the same as the Polish **u**

Consonants

A number of consonants have roughly similar sounds in English and Polish. These are **b**, **d**, **f**, **k**, **l**, **m**, **n**, **p**, **t**, **v** and **z**. Here is the approximate pronunciation of those Polish consonants and clusters of consonants which sound distinctly different:

POLISH

c	as the 'ts' in 'cats'
ch	similar to the 'ch' in the Scottish 'loch'
cz	as the 'ch' in 'church'
ć	a much softer 'ts' sound than Polish **c**; it is replaced by 'ci' before a vowel but sounds the same
dz	similar to 'ds' in 'beds' but shorter
dż	as the 'j' in 'jam'
dź	like **dz** but softer; it is written as 'dzi' before a vowel
g	as the 'g' in 'get'
h	the same as **ch**
j	as the 'y' in 'yet'
ł	as the 'w' in 'wine'
ń	as the 'ny' in 'canyon'; sounds the same as the Spanish 'ñ' (as in *mañana*); it's written as 'ni' before vowels
r	always trilled
rz	as the 's' in 'pleasure'
s	as the 's' in 'set'
sz	as the 'sh' in 'show'
ś	like **s** but much softer; is written as 'si' before vowels, with the same sound
w	as the 'v' in 'van'
ż	the same as **rz**
ź	a softer version of **z**; is replaced by 'zi' before a vowel
szcz	the most awful-looking combination, appearing in a number of words; pronounced as 'shch' in 'fresh cheese'.

The following voiced consonants (or their clusters) become voiceless when they are at the end of a word: **b** sounds like **p**; **d** like **t**; **g** like **k**; **w** like **f**; **z** like **s**, and **rz** like **sz**.

Finally, if you need some practice, here is the favourite Polish tongue-twister: 'Chrząszcz brzmi w trzcinie'.

Greetings & Civilities
Top 10 Useful Phrases

Hello.
chehsts Cześć. (inf)

Goodbye.
do vee-dzeh-nyah Do widzenia.

Yes.
tahk Tak.

No.
nyeh Nie.

Excuse me.
psheh-prah-shahm Przepraszam.

Please.
pro-sheh Proszę.

Thank you (very much).
dzhehn-koo-yeh (bahr-dzo) Dziękuję (bardzo).

You're welcome.
pro-sheh Proszę.

That's all right.
fpo-zhont-koo W porządku.

May I? Do you mind?
chi mo-geh? Czy mogę?
chi mah pahn/pah-nee tsos Czy ma Pan/Pani coś
psheh-tseev-koh? przeciwko?

POLISH

Greetings

Good morning.
dzhehn do-bri   Dzień dobry.

Good evening.
do-bri vyeh-choor   Dobry wieczór.

Good night. (when leaving)
do-brah-nots   Dobranoc.

How are you?
yahk syeh mahsh?   Jak się masz? (inf)
yahk syeh pahn/pah-nee   Jak się Pan/Pani miewa?
myeh-vah?

Very well, thank you.
dzhehn-koo-yeh, bahr-dzo   Dziękuję, bardzo dobrze.
dob-zheh

Forms of Address

Madam/Mrs	*pah-nee*	Pani
Mister/Sir	*pahn*	Pan
Miss	*pahn-nah*	Panna
companion	*ko-leh-gah*	kolega
friend	*pshi-yah-tsyehl*	przyjaciel

When addressing women, the term Pani is almost always used.

Small Talk

Meeting People

What is your name?
yahk tsi nah ee-myeh?   Jak Ci na imię? (inf)
yahk pah-nah/pah-nee   Jak Pana/Pani godność?
god-nostsh?

My name is ...
   mahm nah ee-myeh ...   Mam na imię ... (given name)
   nah-zi-vahm syeh ...   Nazywam się ... (full name)
This is Mr/Mrs/Miss ...
   to yehst pahn/pah-nee/   To jest Pan/Pani/Pani ...
   pah-nee ...
Pleased to meet you.
   mee-wo mee pah-nah/   Miło mi Pana/Panią poznać.
   pah-nyom poz-nahtsh
I (don't) like ...
   (nyeh) loo-byeh ...   (Nie) Lubię ...

Nationalities

Where are you from?
   syah-kyeh-go krah-yoo   Z jakiego kraju
   po-ho-dzhish?   pochodzisz? (inf)
   syah-kyeh-go krah-yoo   Z jakiego kraju Pan/Pani
   pahn/pah-nee po-ho-dzhi?   pochodzi?
I am from England.
   yehs-tehm sahn-glee   Jestem z Anglii.

POLISH

Australia	*ahw-strah-lyah*	Australia
Canada	*kah-nah-dah*	Kanada
England	*ahn-glyah*	Anglia
Ireland	*eer-lahn-dyah*	Irlandia
New Zealand	*no-vah zeh-lahn-dyah*	Nowa Zelandia
Scotland	*shkots-yah*	Szkocja
USA	*stah-ni zyehd-no-cho-neh*	Stany Zjednoczone
Wales	*vahl-yah*	Walia

Occupations

What is your profession?

| *yah-kee yehst pah-nah/* | Jaki jest Pana/Pani zawód? |
| *pah-nee zah-voot?* | |

I am an actor.

| *yehs-tehm ahk-to-rehm* (m) | Jestem aktorem. |

actor	*ahk-tor* (m)	aktor
	ahk-tor-kah (f)	aktorka
artist	*ahr-tis-tah* (m)	artysta
	ahr-tist-kah (f)	artystka
business person	*bees-nehs-mehn*	biznesmen
doctor	*leh-kahsh* (m)	lekarz
	leh-kahr-kah (f)	lekarka
engineer	*een-zhi-nyehr*	inżynier
factory worker	*ro-bot-neek* (m)	robotnik
	ro-bot-nee-tsah (f)	robotnica
farmer	*rol-neek*	rolnik
journalist	*dzhehn-nee-kahzh* (m)	dziennikarz
	dzhehn-nee-kahr-kah (f)	dziennikarka
lawyer	*prahv-neek* (m)	prawnik
	prahv-neech-kah (f)	prawniczka
manual worker	*prah-tsov-neek fee-zich-ni*	pracownik fizyczny
mechanic	*meh-hah-neek* (m)	mechanik
nurse	*pyeh-lehn-gnyahzh* (m)	pielęgniarz
	pyeh-lehn-gnyahr-kah (f)	pielęgniarka

office worker	*oo-zhehnd-neek* (m)	urzędnik
	oo-zhehnd-neech-kah (f)	urzędniczka
scientist	*nah-oo-ko-vyehts*	naukowiec
student	*stoo-dehnt* (m)	student
	stoo-dehn-tkah(f)	studentka
teacher	*nah-oo-chi-tsyehl* (m)	nauczyciel
	nah-oo-chi-tsyehl-kah (f)	nauczycielka
waiter	*kehl-nehr* (m)	kelner
	kehl-nehr-kah (f)	kelnerka
writer	*pee-sahzh* (m)	pisarz
	pee-sahr-kah (f)	pisarka

Religion

What is your religion?
  yah-kyeh-go yehs-tehs viz-nah-nyah? Jakiego jesteś wyznania? (inf)
  yah-kyeh-go yehst pahn/ pah-nee viz-nah-nyah? Jakiego jest Pan/Pani wyznania?

I am not religious.
  yehs-tehm nyeh-vyeh-zhon-tsi/nyeh-vyeh-zhon-tsah Jestem niewierzący/ niewierząca.

I am Catholic.
  yehs-tehm kah-to-lee-kyehm (m) Jestem katolikiem.

| Buddhist | *bood-dis-tah* (m) | buddysta |
| | *bood-dist-kah* (f) | buddystka |

Catholic	*kah-to-leek* (m)	katolik
	kah-to-leech-kah (f)	katoliczka
Christian	*hsheh-stsi-yah-neen* (m)	chrześcijanin
	hsheh-stsi-yahn-kah (f)	chrześcijanka
Hindu	*heen-doo-ees-tah* (m)	hinduista
	heen-doo-eest-kah (f)	hinduistka
Jewish	*yoo-dah-ees-tah* (m)	judaista
	yoo-dah-eest-kah (f)	judaistka
Muslim	*moo-zoow-mah-neen* (m)	muzułmanin
	moo-zoow-mahn-kah (f)	muzułmanka

Family

Are you married?

| *chi yehst pahn zho-nah-ti?* (m) | Czy jest Pan żonaty? |
| *chi pah-nee yehst mehn-zhaht-kom?* (f) | Czy Pani jest mężatką? |

I am single.

| *yehs-tehm kah-vah-leh-rehm* (m)/*nyeh-zah-mehnzh-nah* (f) | Jestem kawalerem/niezamężna. |

I am married.

| *yehs-tehm zho-nah-ti* (m)/*zah-mehnzh-nah* (f) | Jestem żonaty/zamężna. |

How many children do you have?
ee-leh mah pahn/pah-nee dzhe-tsi?

Ile ma Pan/Pani dzieci?

I don't have any children.
nyeh mahm dzhe-tsi

Nie mam dzieci.

I have a daughter/a son.
mahm tsoor-keh/si-nah

Mam córkę/syna.

How many brothers/sisters do you have?
ee-loo mah pahn/pah-nee brah-tsi?

Ilu ma Pan/Pani braci?

ee-leh mah pahn/pah-nee syoostr?

Ile ma Pan/Pani sióstr?

Do you have a girlfriend/boyfriend?
chi mahsh dzhev-chi-neh/ hwo-pah-kah?

Czy masz dziewczynę/ chłopaka? (inf)

brother	*braht*	brat
children	*dzhe-tsi*	dzieci
daughter	*tsoor-kah*	córka
family	*ro-dzi-nah*	rodzina
father	*oy-tsyehts*	ojciec
grandfather	*dzyah-dehk*	dziadek
grandmother	*bahb-tsyah*	babcia
husband	*monzh*	mąż
mother	*maht-kah*	matka
sister	*syos-trah*	siostra
son	*sin*	sy
wife	*zho-nah*	żona

Feelings

I am ...

yehs-tehm ...	Jestem ...
happy	*shchehn-sli-vi*	szczęśliwy
angry	*zwi*	zły
hungry	*gwod-ni*	głodny
thirsty	*sprahg-nyo-ni*	spragniony
grateful	*vdzhen-chni*	wdzięczny

I am cold/hot.
    yehst mi zyee-mno/   Jest mi zimno/gorąco.
    go-ron-tso
I am in a hurry.
    spyeh-sheh syeh   Spieszę się.
I am right.
    mahm rah-tsyeh   Mam rację.

Language Problems

Do you speak English?
    chi pahn/pah-nee   Czy Pan/Pani mówi po
    moo-vi po ahn-gyehl-skoo? angielsku?
Does anyone here speak
English?
    chi ktos too moo-vi po   Czy ktoś tu mówi po
    ahn-gyehl-skoo?   angielsku?
I speak English.
    moo-vyeh po   Mówię po angielsku.
    ahn-gyehl-skoo
I don't speak Polish.
    nyeh moo-vyeh po   Nie mówię po polsku.
    pol-skoo

Please write that down.
pro-sheh to nah-pee-   Proszę to napisać.
sahtsh

I understand. I see.
ro-zoo-myehm   Rozumiem.

I don't understand.
nyeh ro-zoo-myehm   Nie rozumiem.

Please speak more slowly.
pro-sheh moo-veetsh   Proszę mówić wolniej.
vol-nyehy

Could you repeat that please?
chi mo-zheh pahn/pah-nee   Czy może Pan/Pani
to pov-too-zhitsh?   to powtórzyć?

How do you say ...
yahk po vyeh-dzhetsh ...   Jak powiedzieć ...

What does it mean?
tso to znah-chi?   Co to znaczy?

I speak ...
moo-vyeh ...   Mówię ...

English	*po ahn-gyehl-skoo*	po angielsku
French	*po frahn-tsoos-koo*	po francusku
German	*po nyeh-myehts-koo*	po niemiecku
Italian	*po vwos-koo*	po włosku
Russian	*po ro-siy-skoo*	po rosyjsku
Spanish	*po heesh-pahn-skoo*	po hiszpańsku

POLISH

Some Useful Phrases

It's (not) important.
to (nyeh)-vahzh-neh   To (nie)ważne.

It's (not) possible.
to (nyeh)-mozh-lee-veh   To (nie)możliwe.
Not a problem.
nyeh mah pro-bleh-moo   Nie ma problemu.
Wait!
zah-cheh-kahy!   Zaczekaj! (inf)
pro-sheh zah-cheh-kahtsh!   Proszę zaczekać!
Sure.
o-chi-vees-tsyeh   Oczywiście.
Just a minute.
hvee-lehch-keh   Chwileczkę.

Signs

BAGGAGE COUNTER	ODPRAWA BAGAŻU
CUSTOMS	ODPRAWA CELNA
EMERGENCY EXIT	WYJŚCIE ZAPASOWE
ENTRANCE	WEJŚCIE
EXIT	WYJŚCIE
FREE ADMISSION	WSTĘP WOLNY
HOT/COLD	ZIMNO/CIEPŁO
INFORMATION	INFORMACJA
NO ENTRY	WSTĘP WZBRONIONY
NO SMOKING	PALENIE WZBRONIONE
OPEN/CLOSED	OTWARTE/ZAMKNIĘTE
PROHIBITED	WZBRONIONY
RESERVED	ZAREZERWOWANY
TELEPHONE	TELEFON
TOILETS	TOALETY

Emergencies

POLICE POLICE STATION	POLICJA POSTERUNEK POLICJI

Help!
    po-mo-tsi/rah-toon-koo!   Pomocy!/Ratunku!
Thief!
    zwo-dzhey!   Złodziej!
There's been an accident!
    zdah-zhiw syeh vi-pah-dehk!   Zdarzył się wypadek!
Call a doctor.
    pro-sheh vehz-vahtsh leh-kah-zhah   Proszę wezwać lekarza.
Call an ambulance.
    pro-sheh vehz-vahtsh kah-reht-keh   Proszę wezwać karetkę.

I've been raped.
    zgvahw-tso-no mnyeh   Zgwałcono mnie.
I've been robbed!
    ob-rah-bo-vah-noh mnyeh!   Obrabowano mnie!
Call the police!
    pro-sheh vehz-vahtsh po-leets-yeh!   Proszę wezwać policję!
Where is the police station?
    gdzheh yehst pos-teh-roo-nehk po-lee-tsyee?   Gdzie jest posterunek policji?

POLISH

I am ill.
yehs-tehm ho-ri   Jestem chory.

My friend is ill.
mooy pshi-yah-tsyehl   Mój przyjaciel jest chory.
yehst ho-ri (m)

mo-yah pshi-yah-tsyoow- Moja przyjaciółka jest chora.
kah yehst ho-rah (f)

I am lost.
sgoo-bee-wehm syeh (m)   Zgubiłem się.
sgoo-bee-wahm syeh (f)   Zgubiłam się.

Where are the toilets?
gdzheh som to-ah-leh-ti? Gdzie są toalety?

Help me, please.
pro-sheh mee po-moots   Proszę mi pomóc.

Could you help me please?
chi pahn moogw-bi mee   Czy Pan mógłby mi pomóc?
po-moots? (m)

chi pah-nee mog-wah-   Czy Pani mogłaby mi pomóc?
bi mee po-moots? (f)

Could I please use the
telephone?
chi mo-geh sko-zhis-tahtsh Czy mogę skorzystać z
steh-leh-fo-noo?   telefonu?

I wish to contact my
embassy.
htseh syeh skon-tahk-to- Chcę się skontaktować z
vahtsh smo-yom   moją ambasadą.
ahm-bah-sah-dom

I have medical insurance.
mahm oo-behs-pyeh-   Mam ubezpieczenie
cheh-nyeh sdro-vot-neh   zdrowotne.

My possessions are insured.
mo-yeh zheh-chi som   Moje rzeczy są ubezpieczone.
oo-behs-pyeh-cho-neh

My ... was stolen.
skrah-dzho-no mee ...   Skradziono mi ...
I've lost my ...
skrah-dzho-no mee ...   Skradziono mi ...

luggage	*bah-gahzh*	bagaż
backpack	*pleh-tsahk*	plecak
handbag	*tor-beh*	torbę
money	*pyeh-nyon-dzeh*	pieniądze
passport	*pahsh-port*	paszport
travellers' cheques	*cheh-kee pod-roozh-neh*	czeki podróżne

Forms

name	*ee-myeh ee nahz-vees-ko*	imię i nazwisko
address	*ahd-rehs*	adres
date of birth	*dah-tah oo-ro-dzeh-nyah*	data urodzenia
place of birth	*myehy-stseh oo-ro-dzeh-nyah*	miejsce urodzenia
age	*vyehk*	wiek
sex	*pwehtsh*	płeć
nationality	*nah-ro-do-vostsh*	narodowość
religion	*viz-nah-nyeh*	wyznanie
reason for travel	*mo-tif pod-roo-zhi*	motyw podróży

POLISH

profession	*zah-voot*	zawód
marital status	*stahn tsi-veel-ni*	stan cywilny
passport	*pahsh-port*	paszport
passport number	*noo-mehr pahsh-por-too*	numer paszportu
visa	*vee-zah*	wiza
identity card	*do-voot tosh-sah-mosh-tsee*	dowód tożsamości
birth certificate	*sfyah-dehts-tvo oo-ro-dzeh-nyah*	świadectwo urodzenia
driver's licence	*prah-vo yahz-di*	prawo jazdy
car registration	*reh-yehs-trah-tsyah sah-mo-ho-doo*	rejestracja samochodu

POLISH

Getting Around

ARRIVALS	PRZYJAZDY
BUS STATION	DWORZEC AUTO-BUSOWY
BUS STOP	PRZYSTANEK AUTO-BUSOWY
DEPARTURES	ODJAZDY
STATION	STACJA/DWORZEC
SUBWAY	METRO
TICKET OFFICE	KASA BILETOWA
TIMETABLE	ROZKŁAD JAZDY
TRAIN STATION	STACJA KOLEJOWA/DWORZEC KOLEJOWY

What time does the ...
arrive/leave?

o ktoo-rehy go-dzee-nyeh pshi-ho-dzee/ ot-ho-dzee ...?		O której godzinie przychodzi/ odchodzi ...?

(aero)plane	*sah-mo-lot*	samolot
boat	*stah-tehk*	statek
bus	*ahw-to-boos*	autobus
train	*po-tshonk*	pociąg
tram	*trahm-vahy*	tramwaj

Directions

Where is the ...?
   gdzheh yehst ...?   Gdzie jest ...?
How do I get to ... ?
   yahk syeh dos-tahtsh do ...?   Jak się dostać do ...?
Is it far/near from here?
   chi to dah-leh-ko/blees-ko   Czy to daleko/blisko stąd?
   stond?
How can I walk there?
   yahk mozh-nah tahm   Jak można tam dojść?
   doystsh?
Show me (on the map).
   pro-sheh mee po-kah-   Proszę mi pokazać
   zahtsh (nah mah-pyeh)   (na mapie).
Go straight ahead.
   pro-sheh eestsh pros-to   Proszę iść prosto.
It's further down.
   to yehst yesh-cheh   To jest jeszcze dalej.
   dah-lehy

Turn left/right ...
>   *pro-sheh skrehn-tsyeetsh*   Proszę skręcić w lewo/
>   *vleh-vo/fprah-vo ...*   w prawo ...

at the next corner
>   *nah nahy-bleezh-shim*   na najbliższym rogu
>   *ro-goo*

at the traffic lights
>   *nah svyaht-wahh*   na światłach

behind	*zah*	za
in front of	*pshehd*	przed
far	*dah-leh-ko*	daleko
near	*blees-ko*	blisko
opposite	*nah-psheh-tsyeev-ko*	naprzeciwko
over there	*tahm*	tam

Booking Tickets

Excuse me, where is the ticket office?
>   *psheh-prah-shahm,*   Przepraszam, gdzie jest kasa
>   *gdzheh yehst kah-sah*   biletowa?
>   *bee-leh-to-vah?*

Where can I buy a ticket?
>   *gdzheh mo-geh*   Gdzie mogę kupić bilet?
>   *koo-peetsh bee-leht?*

I want to go to ...
>   *htseh syeh dos-tahtsh*   Chcę się dostać do ...
>   *do ...*

Air

Is th

Whe

How

Wha

Wha
chec

Bus

BU

Whe

Whic

Doe

How much is the ticket to ...?
ee-leh kosh-too-yeh
bee-leht do ...?

Ile kosztuje bilet do ...?

Do I need to book?
chi moo-sheh reh-zehr-vo-vahtsh?

Czy muszę rezerwować?

You need to book.
moo-syee pahn/pah-nee reh-zehr-vo-vahtsh

Musi Pan/Pani rezerwować.

I'd like to book a seat to ...
htseh zah-reh-zehr-vo-vahtsh myehy-stseh do ...

Chcę zarezerwować miejsce do ...

It is full.
brahk myehysts

Brak miejsc.

I would like ...		
po-pro-sheh ...		Poproszę ...
a one-way ticket	*bee-leht vyehd-nom stro-neh*	bilet w jedną stronę
a return ticket	*bee-leht pov-rot-ni*	bilet powrotny
two tickets	*dvah bee-leh-ti*	dwa bilety
tickets for all of us	*bee-leh-ti dlah nahs fshist-keeh*	bilety dla nas wszystkich
a student's fare	*bee-leht zeh zneesh-kom stoo-dehn-tskom*	bilet ze zniżką studencką
a child's/ pensioner's fare	*bee-leht dlah dzhets-kah/eh-meh-ri-tah*	bilet dla dziecka/ emeryta

Air

Is there a flight to ...?
chi yehst lot do ...? Czy jest lot do ...?

When is the next flight to ...?
kyeh-di yehst nahs-tehmp-ni lot do ...? Kiedy jest następny lot do ...?

How long is the flight?
yahk dwoo-go trfah lot? Jak długo trwa lot?

What is the flight number?
yah-kee yehst noo-mehr lo-too? Jaki jest numer lotu?

What time do I have to check in?
o ktoo-rehy moo-sheh bitsh nah lot-nees-koo? O której muszę być na lotnisku?

Bus

BUS/TRAM STOP	PRZYSTANEK AUTO-BUSOWY/TRAMWAJOWY

Where is the bus/tram stop?
gdzheh yehst pshis-tah-nehk ahw-to-boo-so-vi/trahm-vah-yo-vi? Gdzie jest przystanek autobusowy/tramwajowy?

Which bus goes to ...?
ktoo-ri ahw-to-boos yeh-dzheh do ...? Który autobus jedzie do ...?

Does this bus go to ...?
chi tehn ahw-to-boos yeh-dzheh do ...? Czy ten autobus jedzie do ...?

How often do buses pass by?
yahk chehn-sto ho-dzom ahw-to-boo-si? Jak często chodzą autobusy?

Could you let me know when
we get to ...?
chi mo-zheh mee pahn/ pah-nee fskah-zahtsh gdi do-yeh-dzheh-mi do ...? Czy może mi Pan/ Pani wskazać gdy dojedziemy do ...?

I want to get off.
htseh vi-syonstsh Chcę wysiąść.

What time is the ... bus?
o ktoo-rehy yehst ... ahw-to-boos? O której jest ... autobus?

next	*nahs-tehmp-ni*	następny
first	*pyehrv-shi*	pierwszy
last	*os-taht-ni*	ostatni

Train

EXIT TO PLATFORMS	WYJŚCIE NA PERONY
LEFT-LUGGAGE OFFICE	PRZECHOWALNIA BAGAŻU
PLATFORM NO	PERON NR
WAITING ROOM	POCZEKALNIA

What platform does the train
for ... leave from?
sktoo-reh-go peh-ro-noo od-ho-dzhee po-tshonk do ...? Z którego peronu odchodzi pociąg do ...?

Is this the right platform for
the train to ...?

   chi steh-go peh-ro-noo   Czy z tego peronu
   od-ho-dzhee po-tshonk   odchodzi pociąg do ...?
   do ...?

The train leaves from
platform ...

   po-tshonk od-ho-dzhee   Pociąg odchodzi z peronu ...
   speh-ro-noo ...

Does this train stop at ...?

   chi tehn po-tshonk zahch-   Czy ten pociąg zatrzymuje
   shi-moo-yeh syeh f ...?   się w ...?

dining car	*vah-gon rehs-tah-oo-rah-tsiy-ni*	wagon restauracyjny
express	*ehks-prehs*	ekspres
local (suburban)	*pod-myehy-skee*	podmiejski
fast (train)	*pos-pyehsh-ni*	pośpieszny
sleeping car	*vah-gon si-pyahl-ni*	wagon sypialny
1st class	*pyehr-fshah klah-sah*	pierwsza klasa
2nd class	*droo-gah klah-sah*	druga klasa

Taxi

Can you take me to ...?

   chi mo-zheh mnyeh pahn   Czy może mnie Pan zawieźć
   zah-vyehstsh do ...?   do ...?

Please take me to ...

   pro-sheh mnyeh   Proszę mnie zawieźć do ...
   zah-vyestsh do ...

POLISH

How much is it to go to ...?
*ee-leh kosh-too-yeh koors
do ...?*   Ile kosztuje kurs do ...?

Instructions

It's here, thank you.
*to too-tahy, dzhen-koo-
yeh*   To tutaj, dziękuję.

The next corner, please.
*nah nahs-tehmp-nim
ro-goo pro-sheh*   Na następnym rogu proszę.

Continue.
*pro-sheh yeh-hahtsh
dah-lehy*   Proszę jechać dalej.

The next street ...
*nahs-tehmp-nah
oo-lee-tsah ...*   Następna ulica ...

(to the) left/right
vleh-vo/fprah-vo   w lewo/w prawo

Stop here!
*pro-sheh syeh too
zah-tshi-mahtsh!*   Proszę się tu zatrzymać!

Please slow down.
pro-sheh zvol-neetsh   Proszę zwolnić.

Please wait here.
*pro-sheh too zah-cheh-
kahtsh*   Proszę tu zaczekać.

Some Useful Phrases

The train is delayed/
cancelled.
*po-tshonk yehst o-pooz-
nyo-ni/od-vo-wah-ni*

Pociąg jest opóźniony/
odwołany.

How long it is delayed?
*ee-leh yehst o-pooz-nyo-
ni?*

Ile jest opóźniony?

There is a delay of ... hours.
*yehst o-pooz-nyo-ni ...
go-dzhee-ni*

Jest opóźniony ... godziny.

Is it a direct train?
*chi to po-tshonk
behs-pos-rehd-ni?*

Czy to pociąg bezpośredni?

Do I need to change?
*chi moo-sheh syeh
psheh-syah-dahtsh?*

Czy muszę się przesiadać?

You must change trains at ...
*moo-syee pahn/pah-nee
syeh psheh-syonstsh f ...*

Musi Pan/Pani się
przesiąść w ...

Is that seat taken?
*chi to myehy-stseh
yehst zah-yehn-teh?*

Czy to miejsce jest zajęte?

I want to get off at ...
htseh vi-syonstsh f ...

Chcę wysiąść w ...

Where can I hire a bicycle?
*gdzhe mo-geh vi-po-zhi-
chitsh ro-vehr?*

Gdzie mogę wypożyczyć
rower?

Car

DETOUR	OBJAZD
FREEWAY	AUTOSTRADA
GARAGE	WARSZTAT SAMOCHO-DOWY
MECHANIC	MECHANIK
NO ENTRY	ZAKAZ WJAZDU
NO PARKING	ZAKAZ POSTOJU
ONE WAY	ULICA JEDNOKIE-RUNKOWA
REPAIRS	NAPRAWY
SELF SERVICE	SAMOOBSŁUGA
STOP	STOP
UNLEADED	BEZOŁOWIOWA

Where can I rent a car?
   gdzheh mo-geh vi-po-zhi-
   chitsh sah-mo-hood?
Gdzie mogę wypożyczyć samochód?

How much is it ...?
   ee-leh to kosh-too-yeh ...?
Ile to kosztuje ...?

daily/weekly
   dzhehn-nyeh/ti-god-nyo-vo
dziennie/tygodniowo

Does that include insurance/ mileage?
   chi to o-behy-moo-yeh
   oo-behs-pyeh-cheh-nyeh/
   psheh-byehk?
Czy to obejmuje ubez-pieczenie/przebieg?

Please fill the tank.
   pro-sheh nah-pehw-neetsh
   bahk
Proszę napełnić bak.

What make is it?

> *yah-kah to mahr-kah?* Jaka to marka?

I want ... litres of petrol.

> *pro-sheh ... leet-roof behn-zi-ni* Proszę ... litrów benzyny.

Please check the oil and water.

> *pro-sheh sprahv-dzheetsh o-lehy ee vo-deh* Proszę sprawdzić olej i wodę.

Where's the next/nearest petrol station?

> *gdzheh yehst nahs-tehmp-nah/nahy-bleezh-shah stah-tsyah behn-zi-no-vah?* Gdzie jest następna/najbliższa stacja benzynowa?

How long can I park here?

> *yahk dwoo-go mo-geh too pahr-ko-vahtsh?* Jak długo mogę tu parkować?

Does this road lead to ...?

> *chi tah dro-gah pro-vah-dzhee do ...?* Czy ta droga prowadzi do ...?

air (for tyres)	*po-vyeh-tsheh*	powietrze
battery	*ah-koo-moo-lah-tor*	akumulator
brakes	*hah-mool-tseh*	hamulce
driver's licence	*prah-vo yahz-di*	prawo jazdy
engine	*syeel-neek*	silnik
lights	*syfyaht-wah*	światła
oil	*o-lehy*	olej
petrol	*behn-zi-nah*	benzyna
puncture	*psheh-bee-tsyeh o-po-ni*	przebicie opony

radiator	*hwod-nee-tsah*	chłodnica
road map	*mah-pah dro-go-vah*	mapa drogowa
tyres	*o-po-ni*	opony
windscreen	*pshehd-nyah shi-bah*	przednia szyba

Car Problems

I need a mechanic.
  po-tsheh-boo-yeh Potrzebuję mechanika.
  meh-hah-nee-kah
The battery is flat.
  ah-koo-moo-lah-tor yehst Akumulator jest rozładowany.
  ros-wah-do-vah-ni
The radiator is leaking.
  hwod-nee-tsah Chłodnica przecieka.
  psheh-tsyeh-kah
I have a flat tyre.
  zwah-pah-wehm goo-meh Złapałem gumę.
It's overheating.
  psheh-gzheh-vah syeh Przegrzewa się.
It's not working.
  nyeh dzhya-wah Nie działa.

Accommodation

CAMPING GROUND	CAMPING
HOTEL	HOTEL
MOTEL	MOTEL
YOUTH HOSTEL	SCHRONISKO
	MŁODZIEŻOWE

POLISH

I am looking for a ... hotel
shoo-kahm ... ho-teh-loo   Szukam ... hotelu

cheap	*tah-nyeh-go*	taniego
clean	*chis-teh-go*	czystego
good	*dob-reh-go*	dobrego

What is the address?
yah-kee yehst ahd-rehs?   Jaki jest adres?

Write down the address,
please.
   pro-sheh nah-pee-sahtsh   Proszę napisać adres.
   ahd-rehs

At the Hotel

Do you have rooms available?
   chi som vol-neh   Czy są wolne pokoje?
   po-ko-yeh?

I would like a ...
   po-pro-sheh o ...   Poproszę o ...

single room	*yeh-din-keh*	jedynkę
double room	*dvooy-keh*	dwójkę
room with a	*po-kooy*	pokój z łazienką
bathroom	*swah-zyehn-kom*	
bed in a dorm	*woozh-ko fsah-lee*	łóżko w sali
	zbyo-ro-vehy	zbiorowej

I want a room ...
  htseh po-kooy ...   Chcę pokój ...

with a bathroom	*swah-zyehn-kom*	z łazienką
with a shower	*sprish-nee-tsehm*	z prysznicem
with a television	*steh-leh-vee-zo-rehm*	z telewizorem
with a window	*sok-nehm*	z oknem

I'm going to stay for ...
  zah-myeh-zhahm   Zamierzam zostać ...
  zos-tahtsh ...

one day	*yeh-dehn dzhen*	jeden dzień
two days	*dvah dnee*	dwa dni
one week	*yeh-dehn ti-dzhehn*	jeden tydzień

Sorry, we're full.
  pshik-ro mee, nyeh mah   Przykro mi, nie ma miejsc.
  myehysts

How long will you be staying?
  yahk dwoo-go zah-myeh-   Jak długo zamie-
  zhah pahn/pah-nee   rza Pan/Pani zostać?
  zos-tahtsh?

How many nights?
  ee-leh no-tsi?   Ile nocy?

It's ... per day/per person.
  kosh-too-yeh ...   Kosztuje ... dziennie/
  dzhehn-nyeh/od o-so-bi   od osoby.

How much is per night/per
person?
  ee-leh kosh-too-yeh   Ile kosztuje za noc/od osoby?
  zah nots/od o-so-bi?

May I see the room?
 chi mo-geh o-behy- Czy mogę obejrzeć pokój?
 zhehtsh po-kooy?

Are there any others?
 chi som een-neh? Czy są inne?

Are there any cheaper rooms?
 chi som tahn-sheh Czy są tańsze pokoje?
 po-ko-yeh?

Could we have another bed
in the room?
 chi mozh-nah Czy można dostawić łóżko?
 dos-tah-veetsh woozh-ko?

Is there a discount for
children?
 chi yehst sneezh-ka dlah Czy jest zniżka dla dzieci?
 dzheh-tsee?

Does it include breakfast?
 chi snyah-dah-nyeh Czy śniadanie jest wliczone?
 yehst vlee-cho-neh?

It's fine, I'll take it.
 fpo-zhond-koo, byo-reh go W porządku, biorę go.

I'm not sure how long I'm
staying.
 nyeh yehs-tehm peh-vyehn Nie jestem pewien jak długo
 yahk dwoo-go zos-tah-neh zostanę.

Is there a lift?
 chi yehst veen-dah? Czy jest winda?

Where is the bathroom?
 gdzheh yehst Gdzie jest łazienka?
 wah-zyehn-kah?

Could you store this
for me?
    chi mo-zheh pahn/pah-nee   Czy może Pan/Pani
    psheh-ho-vahtsh to dlah   przechować to dla mnie?
    mnyeh?
Is there somewhere to wash
clothes?
    chi mozh-nah gdzhesh too   Czy można gdzieś tu uprać
    oop-rahtsh oo-brah-nyeh?   ubranie?
Can I use the kitchen?
    chi mo-geh ko-zhis-tahtsh   Czy mogę korzystać z kuchni?
    skooh-nee?
Can I use the telephone?
    chi mo-geh ko-zhis-   Czy mogę korzystać z
    tahtsh steh-leh-fo-noo?   telefonu?

Requests & Complaints

I have a request.
    mahm prosh-beh   Mam prośbę.
Please change the sheets.
    pro-sheh smyeh-neetsh   Proszę zmienić pościel.
    pos-tsyehl
I can't open/close the window.
    nyeh mo-geh ot-fo-zhitsh/   Nie mogę otworzyć/
    zahmk-nontsh ok-nah   zamknąć okna.
The toilet doesn't flush.
    vo-dah syeh nyeh   Woda się nie spuszcza.
    spoosh-chah
The ... doesn't work.
    ... nyeh dzhya-wah   ... nie działa.

POLISH

I don't like this room.
  nyeh po-do-bah
  mee syeh tehn po-kooy   Nie podoba mi się ten pokój.

It's too ...
  yehst sbit ...   Jest zbyt ...
dark   *tsyehm-ni*   ciemny
expensive   *dro-gee*   drogi
noisy   *gwosh-ni*   głośny
small   *mah-wee*   mały

Some Useful Words & Phrases
I am/We are leaving ...
  vi-yehzh-dzhahm ...   Wyjeżdżam ...
  vi-yehzh-dzhah-mi ...   Wyjeżdżamy ...
now/tomorrow
  zah-rahs/yoot-ro   zaraz/jutro
I'd like to pay now.
  htseh teh-rahs   Chcę teraz zapłacić.
  zah-pwah-tsyeetsh

first name   *ee-myeh*   imię
surname   *nahz-vees-ko*   nazwisko
room number   *noo-mehr po-ko-yoo*   numer pokoju

address   *ahd-rehs*   adres
air-conditioned *klee-mah-ti-zo-*   klimatyzowany
              vah-ni
babysitter   *o-pyeh-koon-kah do*   opiekunka do
              dzhehts-kah   dziecka
balcony   *bahl-kon*   balkon

bathroom	*wah-zyehn-kah*	łazienka
bed	*woozh-ko*	łóżko
bill	*rah-hoo-nehk*	rachunek
blanket	*kots*	koc
chair	*ksheh-swo*	krzesło
clean	*chis-ti*	czysty
cold	*zyeem-ni*	zimny
cupboard	*shahf-kah*	szafka
dark	*chyehm-ni*	ciemny
double bed	*woozh-ko pod-vooy-neh*	łóżko podwójne
electricity	*eh-lehk-trich-nostsh*	elektryczność
excluded	*nyeh vlee-cho-ni*	nie wliczony
fan	*vehn-ti-lah-tor*	wentylator
hot	*go-ron-tsi*	gorący
key	*klooch*	klucz
lift (elevator)	*veen-dah*	winda
lock (n)	*zah-mehk*	zamek
padlock	*kwoot-kah*	kłódka
pillow	*po-doosh-kah*	poduszka
quiet	*chee-hi*	cichy
noisy	*gwosh-ni*	głośny
sheet	*pos-tsyehl*	pościel
shower	*prish-neets*	prysznic
swimming pool	*bah-sehn*	basen
toilet	*to-ah-leh-tah*	toaleta
toilet paper	*pah-pyehr to-ah-leh-to-vi*	papier toaletowy
towel	*rehnch-neek*	ręcznik
window	*ok-no*	okno

POLISH

Around Town

Where is ...?
gdzheh yehst ...?   Gdzie jest ...?

the art gallery	*gah-lehr-yah shtoo-kee*	galeria sztuki
a bank	*bahnk*	bank
a church	*kos-tsyoow*	kościół
the city centre	*tsehn-troom myahs-tah*	centrum miasta
the market	*tahrg/bah-zahr*	targ/bazar
the museum	*moo-zeh-oom*	muzeum
the police station	*pos-teh-roo-nehk po-lee-tsyee*	posterunek policji
the post office	*poch-tah*	poczta
a public toilet	*to-ah-leh-tah poob-leech-nah*	toaleta publiczna
a restaurant	*rehs-tah-oo-rahts-yah*	restauracja
tourist informa-tion	*een-for-mahts-yah too-ris-tich-nah*	informacja turystyczna

What time does it open?
o ktoo-rehy ot-fyeh-rah-yom?   O której otwierają?

What time does it close?
o ktoo-rehy zah-mi-kah-yom?   O której zamykają?

What street is this?
yah-kah to yehst oo-lee-tsa?   Jaka to jest ulica?

For directions, see the Getting Around section, page 253.

At the Post Office

I would like to send ...

	htseh vis-wahtsh ...	Chcę wysłać ...
a letter	*leest*	list
a postcard	*poch-toof-keh*	pocztówkę
a parcel	*pahch-keh*	paczkę
a telegram	*teh-lehg-rahm*	telegram

I would like to buy some stamps.

htseh koo-peetsh pah-reh znahch-koof   Chcę kupić parę znaczków.

How much is the postage?

ee-leh kosh-too-yeh psheh-siw-kah?   Ile kosztuje przesyłka?

How much is it to send this to ...?

ee-leh kosh-too-yeh pshehs-wah-nyeh teh-go do ...?   Ile kosztuje przesłanie tego do ...?

airmail	*poch-tah lot-nee-chah*	poczta lotnicza
envelope	*ko-pehr-tah*	koperta
mail box	*skshin-kah poch-to-vah*	skrzynka pocztowa
registered mail	*psheh-siw-kah po-leh-tso-nah*	przesyłka polecona
stamp	*znah-chehk*	znaczek
surface mail	*psheh-siw-kah zvik-wah*	przesyłka zwykła

Telephone

I want to call ...
htseh zahdz-vo-neetsh ... Chcę zadzwonić ...

The number is ...
to yehst noo-mehr ... To jest numer ...

I want to speak for three
minutes.
htseh ros-mah-vyahtsh Chcę rozmawiać trzy minuty.
chshi mee-noo-ti

How much does a three-
minute call cost?
ee-leh kosh-too-yom chshi Ile kosztują trzy minuty
mee-noo-ti ros-mo-vi? rozmowy?

How much does each extra
minute cost?
ee-leh kosh-too-yeh Ile kosztuje
kahzh-dah do-daht-ko-vah każda dodatkowa
mee-noo-tah? minuta?

I want to make a person-to-
person phone call.
htseh zah-moo-veetsh Chcę zamówić
ros-mo-veh spshi-vo-wah- rozmowę z przywołaniem
nyehm ah-bo-nehn-tah abonenta.

I would like to speak to
Mr/Mrs ...
htseh ros-mah-vyahtsh Chcę rozmawiać z Panem/
spah-nehm/spah-nyom ... z Panią ...

Hello, is ... there?
hah-lo, chi zahs-tah- Halo, czy zastałem ...?
wehm ...?

It's engaged.
  yehst za-yehn-teh   Jest zajęte.
I've been cut off.
  pshehr-vah-no mee   Przerwano mi połączenie.
  po-won-cheh-nyeh

At the Bank

What is the exchange rate?
  yah-kee yehst koors   Jaki jest kurs wymiany?
  vi-myah-ni?
How many zlotys per dollar?
  ee-leh zwo-tih zah   Ile złotych za dolara?
  do-lah-rah?
I want to exchange some
money/travellers' cheques.
  htseh vi-myeh-neetsh   Chcę wymienić pieniądze/
  pyeh-nyon-dzeh/cheh-kee   czeki podróżne.
  pod-roozh-neh
Can I have money transferred
here from my bank?
  chi mozh-nah too-tahy   Czy można tutaj przesłać
  pshehs-wahtsh pyeh-nyon-   pieniądze z mojego banku?
  dzeh smo-yeh-go bahn-koo?
How long will it take to
arrive?
  yahk dwoo-go to potr-fah   Jak długo to potrwa zanim
  zah-neem pshiy-dom?   przyjdą?
I'm expecting some money
from ...
  spo-dzheh-vahm   Spodziewam się
  syeh pyeh-nyehn-dzi s ...   pieniędzy z ...

POLISH

Has my money arrived yet?
chi yoosh pshish-wi   Czy już przyszły moje
mo-yeh pyeh-nyon-dzeh?   pieniądze?

bankdraft	*chehk bahn-ko-vi*	czek bankowy
bank notes	*bahnk-no-ti*	banknoty
black market	*chahr-ni ri-nehk*	czarny rynek
cashier	*kahs-yehr*	kasjer
coins	*mo-neh-ti*	monety
credit card	*kahr-tah*	karta kredytowa
	kreh-di-to-vah	
exchange	*vi-myah-nah*	wymiana
signature	*pot-pees*	podpis

Sightseeing

Do you have a ...?
chi mah pahn/pah-nee ...?   Czy ma Pan/Pani ...?

guidebook	*psheh-vod-neek*	przewodnik
regional map	*mah-peh rehg-yo-noo*	mapę regionu
city map	*plahn myahs-tah*	plan miasta

Where are the main tourist
attractions?
gdzhe som gwoov-neh   Gdzie są główne atrakcje
aht-rahk-tsyeh   turystyczne?
too-ris-tich-neh?
What is that?
tso to yehst?   Co to jest?
How old is it?
ee-leh to mah laht?   Ile to ma lat?

What time does it open/
close?

    o ktoo-rehy ot-fyeh-
    rah-yom/zah-mi-kah-yom?

O której otwierają/zamykają?

What is the admission price?

    ee-leh kosh-too-yeh
    fstehmp?

Ile kosztuje wstęp?

Can I take photographs?

    chi mo-geh ro-beetsh
    zdyehn-chyah?

Czy mogę robić zdjęcia?

ancient	*stah-ri*	stary
archaeological	*ahr-heh-o-lo-geech-ni*	archeologiczny
beach	*plah-zhah*	plaża
botanical gardens	*og-root bo-tah-neech-ni*	ogród botaniczny
building	*boo-di-nehk*	budynek
castle	*zah-mehk*	zamek
cathedral	*kah-tehd-rah*	katedra
city centre	*tsehn-troom*	centrum
church	*kos-tsyoow*	kościół
concert hall	*sah-lah kon-tsehr-to-vah*	sala koncertowa
library	*beeb-lyo-teh-kah*	biblioteka
main square	*gwoov-ni plahts*	główny plac
market	*tahrg/bah-zahr*	targ/bazar
monastery	*klahsh-tor*	klasztor
monument	*pom-neek*	pomnik
mosque	*meh-cheht*	meczet
old town	*stah-reh myahs-to*	stare miasto

old town's square	*ri-nehk*	rynek
palace	*pah-wahts*	pałac
opera house	*o-peh-rah*	opera
ruins	*roo-ee-ni*	ruiny
stadium	*stah-dyon*	stadion
synagogue	*si-nah-go-gah*	synagoga
university	*oo-nee-vehr-si-teht*	uniwersytet

Entertainment

What is there to do in the evenings?
  tso mozh-nah ro-beetsh vyeh-cho-rehm? — Co można robić wieczorem?

Are there places where one can hear folk music?
  chi mozh-nah gdzhesh pos-woo-hahtsh loo-do-vehy moo-zi-ki? — Czy można gdzieś posłuchać ludowej muzyki?

How much is it to get in?
  ee-leh kosh-too-yeh fstehmp? — Ile kosztuje wstęp?

I would like to see/go to ...
  htseh pooystsh ... — Chcę pójść ...

a concert	*nah kon-tsehrt*	na koncert
discotheque	*nah dis-ko-teh-keh*	na dyskotekę
a film	*do kee-nah*	do kina
nightclub	*do kloo-boo nots-neh-go*	do klubu nocnego
theatre	*do teh-aht-roo*	do teatru

In the Country

I'd like to go ...
htseh syeh vib-rahtsh nah ...
Chcę się wybrać na ...

bush walking	*vehn-droov-keh pyeh-shom*	wędrówkę pieszą
mountaineering	*vspee-nahch-keh goor-skom*	wspinaczkę górską
sailing	*zhahg-leh*	żagle
skiing	*nahr-ti*	narty

Where can I stay?
gdzheh mo-geh syeh zah-chshee-mahtsh?
Gdzie mogę się zatrzymać?

Where can I hire equipment/a tent?
gdzheh mo-geh vi-po-zhi-chitsh spshehnt/nah-myot?
Gdzie mogę wypożyczyć sprzęt/namiot?

beach	*plah-zhah*	plaża
bridge	*most*	most
cave	*yahs-kee-nyah*	jaskinia
farm	*gos-po-dahr-stvo*	gospodarstwo
forest	*lahs*	las
harbour	*port*	port
hill	*pah-goo-rehk*	pagórek
lake	*yeh-zyo-ro*	jezioro
mountain	*goo-rah*	góra
mountain range	*mah-siv goor-skee*	masyw górski
national park	*pahrk nah-ro-do-vi*	park narodowy

POLISH

ocean	*o-tseh-ahn*	ocean
river	*zheh-kah*	rzeka
scenery	*krah-yo-brahs*	krajobraz
village	*vyehsh*	wieś
waterfall	*vo-dos-paht*	wodospad

Weather

What's the weather like?
    yah-kah yehst po-go-dah?   Jaka jest pogoda?

The weather is ... today.
    dzhee-syahy yehst...   Dzisiaj jest ...
Will it be ... tomorrow?
    chi yoot-ro behn-dzheh ...?   Czy jutro będzie ...?

bad	*bzhit-ko*	brzydko
cloudy	*poh-moor-nyeh*	pochmurnie
good	*wahd-nyeh*	ładnie
rainy	*dehsh-cho-vo*	deszczowo
sunny	*swo-nehch-nyeh*	słonecznie

cloud	*hmoo-rah*	chmura
dry season	*po-rah soo-hah*	pora sucha
fog	*mgwah*	mgła
frost	*mroos*	mróz
ice	*loot*	lód
mud	*bwo-to*	błoto
rain	*dehshch*	deszcz
the rainy season	*po-rah dehsh-cho-vah*	pora deszczowa
snow	*snyehg*	śnieg

sun	*swon-tseh*	słońce
thunderstorm	*boo-zhah*	burza
weather	*po-go-dah*	pogoda
wind	*vyahtr*	wiatr

Camping

Am I allowed to camp here?
chi mozh-nah too bee-vah-ko-vahtsh? — Czy można tu biwakować?

Is there a campsite nearby?
chi yehst kahm-peeng fpob-lee-zhoo? — Czy jest camping w pobliżu?

backpack	*pleh-tsahk*	plecak
can opener	*ot-fyeh-rahch do kon-sehrf*	otwieracz do konserw
compass	*kom-pahs*	kompas
crampons	*rah-kee*	raki
firewood	*dzeh-vo nah o-pahw*	drzewo na opał
gas cartridge	*po-yehm-neek sgah-zehm*	pojemnik z gazem
hammock	*hah-mahk*	hamak
ice axe	*cheh-kahn*	czekan
mattress	*mah-teh-rahts*	materac
penknife	*stsi-zo-rik*	scyzoryk
rope	*lee-nah*	lina
tent	*nah-myot*	namiot
tent pegs	*shpeel-kee/ sleh-dzheh*	szpilki/śledzie
torch (flashlight)	*lah-tahr-kah*	latarka

POLISH

sleeping bag	*spee-voor*	śpiwór
stove	*ko-hehr*	kocher
water bottle	*bee-don/boo-tehl-kah nah vo-deh*	bidon/butelka na wodę

Food

breakfast	*snyah-dah-nyeh*	śniadanie
lunch/dinner	*o-byaht*	obiad
supper	*ko-lahts-yah*	kolacja

Can I see the menu, please?
  chi mo-ghe pro-syeetsh o meh-noo? — Czy mogę prosić o menu?

What do you recommend?
  tso pahn/pah-nee po-leh-tsah? — Co Pan/Pani poleca?

I prefer ...
  vo-leh ... — Wolę ...

I would like ...
  htsyahw-bim/ htsyah-wah-bim ... — Chciałbym/Chciałabym ...

That's all, thanks.
  to fshist-ko, dzhehn-koo-yeh — To wszystko, dziękuję.

May I have the bill, please?
  po-pro-sheh o rah-hoo-nehk — Poproszę o rachunek.

POLISH

ashtray	*po-pyehl-neech-kah*	popielniczka
the bill	*rah-hoo-nehk*	rachunek
Bon appétit.	*smahch-neh-go*	Smacznego.
Cheers!	*nah zdro-vyeh!*	Na zdrowie!
cup	*fee-lee-zhahn-kah*	filiżanka
fork	*vee-deh-lets*	widelec
fresh	*svyeh-zhi*	świeży
glass	*shklahn-kah*	szklanka
knife	*noosh*	nóż
plate	*tah-lehsh*	talerz
ripe	*doy-zhah-wi*	dojrzały
salad	*sah-waht-kah*	sałatka
spicy	*pee-kahn-tni*	pikantny
spoon	*wizh-kah*	łyżka
sweet	*swot-kee*	słodki
teaspoon	*wi-zhehch-kah*	łyżeczka

POLISH

Methods of Cooking

baked	*pieczone*
boiled	*gotowane*
braised	*duszone*
fried	*smażone*
grilled	*z grilla*
jellied	*w galarecie*
marinated	*marynowane*
roast	*pieczone*
smoked	*wędzone*
steamed	*gotowane na parze*
stewed	*duszone/gotowane*

Breakfast Menu, Staple Foods & Condiments

bread	*chleb*
butter	*masło*
caviar	*kawior*
cheese	*ser*
chips	*frytki*
egg	*jajko*
fried eggs	*jajka sadzone*
soft/hard-boiled egg	*jajko na miękko/twardo*
scrambled eggs	*jajecznica*
eggs on ham/bacon	*jajka na szynce/boczku*
fish	*ryba*
fruit	*owoce*
ham	*szynka*
honey	*miód*
horseradish	*chrzan*
ice	*lód*
jam	*dżem*
ketchup	*ketchup*
lemon	*cytryna*
marmalade	*marmolada*
meat	*mięso*
milk	*mleko*
mustard	*musztarda*
olive oil	*oliwa*
omelette	*omlet*
pasta	*makaron*
pepper	*pieprz*
potatoes	*ziemniaki, kartofle*
rice	*ryż*
a roll	*bułeczka, kajzerka*

salad	*sałatka, surówka*
salt	*sól*
sandwich	*kanapka*
sauce	*sos*
sausage	*kiełbasa*
seasonings	*przyprawy*
sugar	*cukier*
vegetables	*warzywa, jarzyny*
vinegar	*ocet*
water	*woda*

Fruit & Nuts

apples	*jabłka*
apricots	*morele*
blackberries	*jagody*
cherries	*czereśnie*
currants	*porzeczki*
hazelnuts	*orzechy laskowe*
grapes	*winogrona*
oranges	*pomarańcze*
peaches	*brzoskwinie*
pears	*gruszki*
pineapple	*ananas*
plums	*śliwki*
raspberries	*maliny*
strawberries	*truskawki*
walnuts	*orzechy włoskie*
watermelon	*arbuz*
wild strawberries	*poziomki*

POLISH

Vegetarian Meals

I am vegetarian.
   yehs-tehm yah-ro-shehm   Jestem jaroszem.
I don't eat ...
   nyeh yah-dahm ...   Nie jadam ...
meat/ham/fish
   myehn-sah/shin-kee/rib   mięsa/szynki/ryb
dairy products
   nah-byah-woo   nabiału

fasolka po bretońsku
   Baked beans in tomato sauce.
knedle
   Dumplings stuffed with plums or apples.
kopytka
   Dumplings made from potato flour and boiled.
leniwe pierogi
   Boiled dumplings with cottage cheese.
naleśniki
   Fried pancakes; can be with cottage cheese, *z serem*, or with
   jam, *z dżemem*; served with sour cream and sugar.
pierogi
   Dumplings made from noodle dough, stuffed and boiled; the
   most popular are those with cottage cheese, *z serem*; with
   blueberries, *z jagodami*; with cabbage and wild mushrooms,
   z kapustą i grzybami, and with minced meat, *z mięsem.*
placki ziemniaczane
   Fried pancakes made from grated raw potatoes with egg and
   flour, served with sour cream, *ze śmietaną,* or sugar, *z cukrem.*
pyzy
   Ball-shaped steamed dumplings.

POLISH

Starters & Buffet Meals

befsztyk tatarski (or *tatar*)
Raw minced beef with onion, raw egg yolk and often with chopped dill cucumber; eat it only in reputable restaurants.

łosoś wędzony
Smoked salmon.

karp w galarecie
Jellied carp.

nóżki w galarecie
Jellied pig's knuckles.

sałatka jarzynowa
Vegetable salad commonly known as Russian salad.

śledź w oleju
Herring in oil with chopped onion; a staple of virtually every menu.

śledź w śmietanie
Herring in sour cream.

węgorz wędzony
Smoked eel.

Soups

barszcz czerwony
Beetroot broth; the most typical Polish soup; can be served clear, *barszcz czysty*; with tiny ravioli-type dumplings stuffed with meat, *barszcz z uszkami*; or served with a hot pastry filled with meat, *barszcz z pasztecikiem*.

botwinka
Another summertime soup but this is hot; made from the stems and leaves of baby beetroots; often includes a hard boiled egg inside.

chłodnik
  Cold beetroot soup with sour cream and fresh vegetables;
  originally Lithuanian but widespread in Poland; served in
  summer only.

flaki
  Seasoned tripe cooked in bouillon with vegetables; increas-
  ingly popular on menus.

grochówka
  Pea soup, sometimes served with croutons, *z grzankami*.

kapuśniak
  A sauerkraut soup with potatoes.

kartoflanka/zupa ziemniaczana
  Potato soup.

krupnik
  A thick barley soup containing a variety of vegetables and
  occasionally small chunks of meat.

rosół
  Beef or chicken bouillon usually served with pasta, *z maka-
  ronem*.

(zupa) grzybowa
  Mushroom soup.

(zupa) jarzynowa
  Vegetable soup.

(zupa) ogórkowa
  Cucumber soup, more often than not with potatoes and other
  vegetables.

(zupa) szczawiowa
  Sorrel soup, most likely to appear with hard-boiled egg.

żurek
  Another Polish speciality; rye-flour soup thickened with sour
  cream; most likely to be served with hard-boiled egg, *z*

jajkiem, with sausage, *z kiełbasą*, or both; often served with mashed potatoes.

Meat

befsztyk

Beef steak; if you find an addition saying *po angielsku* (literally 'in English style'), it means it will be rare; if you want medium, ask for *średnio wysmażony*, and for well-done, ask for *dobrze wysmażony*.

bigos

Polish national dish made with sauerkraut, fresh chopped cabbage and a variety of meats including pork, beef, game, sausage and bacon, cooked together on very low fire for several hours; in cheap eateries it ranges from poor to very poor – try it in a top-class restaurant or, better still, in a private home.

bryzol

Grilled beef steak.

golonka

Boiled pig's knuckle served with horseradish; a favourite dish for many Poles.

gołąbki

Cabbage leaves stuffed with minced beef and rice, and occasionally with mushrooms.

gulasz

Goulash; can be served either as a main course or a soup; originally Hungarian.

kotlet mielony

A minced-meat cutlet fried in a similar coat as the *kotlet schabowy*, though the contents are doubtful in seedy restaurants; Poles nickname it 'a review of the week' – avoid it.

kotlet schabowy
  Fried pork cutlet coated in breadcrumbs, flour and egg; ubiquitous on every menu; the name sometimes bears an additional *panierowany* to distinguish it from the less common sautéed version.

pieczeń wołowa/wieprzowa
  Roast beef/pork.

placek po węgiersku
  A more sophisticated version of a fried pancake, 'in Hungarian style' is made of potato and served with goulash.

polędwica pieczona
  Roast fillet of beef.

rumsztyk
  Rump steak.

schab pieczony
  Roast loin of pork seasoned with prunes and a variety of herbs.

stek
  Steak; in obscure restaurants you may find it made of minced meat.

sztuka mięsa
  Boiled beef served with horseradish.

zraz zawijany
  Stewed beef rolls stuffed with mushrooms or/and bacon and served in sour cream sauce.

Fish

Fish dishes don't abound on the menus of average restaurants but there are some places in big cities which specialise in fish. The most common sea fish is cod, *dorsz*. Of the freshwater types you're most likely to encounter carp, *karp*, and trout, *pstrąg*.

The usual method of preparation is frying, in flour, egg and breadcrumbs. Other seafood is rare and is found only in top-end establishments.

Poultry

kurczak pieczony
Roast chicken, the most common of the poultry dishes.
kotlet de Volaille
Chicken fried in breadcrumbs with egg.
kaczka z jabłkami
Roast duck stuffed with apples.

Game

pieczeń z dzika
Roast wild boar.
zając w śmietanie
Roast hare in a sour cream sauce.
comber sarni
Saddle of venison roast in sauce.
pieczeń z żubra
Roast European bison; this is a dish which seld
restaurant menus, and is worth trying more f
for taste.

Salads & Accompaniments

bukiet surówek
Mixed vegetable salad, its ingr
the season, and imagination of th

ćwikła z chrzanem
  Boiled and grated beetroot with horseradish.
fasolka szparagowa
  Green beans, boiled and served with fried breadcrumbs.
grzyby marynowane
  Pickled wild mushrooms.
marchewka z groszkiem
  Boiled carrot with green peas.
mizeria ze śmietaną
  Sliced fresh cucumbers in sour cream.
kasza gryczana
  Steamed buckwheat groats.
ogórek kiszony
  Dill cucumber.
pieczarki z patelni
  Fried mushrooms.
sałatka z pomidorów
  Tomato salad, most likely to be with onion.
surówka z kiszonej kapusty
  Sauerkraut, sometimes with apple and onion.
ziemniaki
  Potatoes – by far the most common supplement to main
  courses; boiled and often served mashed.

Desserts

d fruit compote	*kompot*
eam	*lody*
colate	*czekoladowe*
e	*kawowe*
	owocowe
	waniliowe

ice cream with whipped cream and fruit	*melba*
jelly	*galaretka*
milk pudding	*budyń*
pastry, cake	*ciastko*
apple cake	*szarlotka*
cheese cake	*sernik*
chocolate cake	*tort czekoladowy*
doughnut	*pączek*
honey cake	*piernik*
poppy seed roll	*makowiec*
whipped cream	*bita śmietana*

Nonalcoholic Drinks

coffee	*kawa*
expresso	*z ekspresu*
with cream	*ze śmietanką*
fruit juice	*sok owocowy*
mineral water	*woda mineralna*
soda water	*woda sodowa*
tea	*herbata*
with lemon	*z cytryną*

Alcoholic Drinks

beer	*piwo*
bottled	*butelkowe*
canned	*puszkowe*
draught	*kuflowe*
champagne	*szampan*
cognac	*koniak*

POLISH

vodka	*wódka*	
wine	*wino*	
dry		*wytrawne*
red/white		*czerwone/białe*
sparkling		*musujące*
sweet		*słodkie*

Shopping

How much is it?
ee-leh to kosh-too-yeh?   Ile to kosztuje?

bookshop	*ksyen-gahr-nyah*	księgarnia
camera shop	*sklehp fo-to-grah-feech-ni*	sklep fotograficzny
delicatessen	*deh-lee-kah-teh-si*	delikatesy
general/ department store	*dom to-vah-ro-vi*	dom towarowy
jewellery shop	*yoo-bee-lehr*	jubiler
laundry	*prahl-nyah*	pralnia
market	*tahrg/bah-zahr*	targ/bazar
newsagency	*kyosk roo-hoo*	kiosk Ruchu
pharmacy	*ahp-teh-kah*	apteka
shoe shop	*sklehp o-boov-ni-chi*	sklep obuwniczy
souvenir shop	*sklehp spah-myont-kah-mee*	sklep z pamiątkami
stationers	*sklehp pah-pyehr-nee-chi*	sklep papierniczy
supermarket	*sahm spo-zhiv-chi*	sam spożywczy
vegetable shop	*sklehp vah-zhiv-nee-chi*	sklep warzywniczy

POLISH

Please give me ...
po-pro-sheh o ... Poproszę o ...

Do you have others?
chi som een-neh? Czy są inne?

I don't like it.
nyeh po-do-bah mee syeh Nie podoba mi się.

Can I look at it?
chi mo-geh to o-behy-zhehtsh? Czy mogę to obejrzeć?

I'm just looking.
vwahs-nyeh o-glon-dahm Właśnie oglądam.

Can you write down the price?
chi mo-zheh pahn/pah-nee nah-pee-sahtsh tseh-neh? Czy może Pan/Pani napisać cenę?

Do you accept credit cards?
chi ahk-tsehp-too-yeh-tsyeh kahr-ti kreh-di-to-veh? Czy akceptujecie karty kredytowe?

Can I help you?
chim mo-geh swoo-zhitsh? Czym mogę służyć?

Will that be all?
chi to vshist-ko? Czy to wszystko?

How much/many do you want?
ee-leh pahn/pah-nee so-byeh zhi-chi? Ile Pan/Pani sobie życzy?

Souvenirs

amber	*boor-shtin*	bursztyn
books	*ksyonzh-kee*	książki
cut glass	*krish-tah-wi*	kryształy
handicraft	*shtoo-kah loo-do-vah*	sztuka ludowa
jewellery	*bee-zhoo-teh-ryah*	biżuteria
paper cut-outs	*vi-tsyee-nahn-kee*	wycinanki
records (LPs)	*pwi-ti*	płyty

Clothing

coat	*pwahshch*	płaszcz
dress	*soo-kyehn-kah*	sukienka
jacket	*koort-kah*	kurtka
jumper (sweater)	*sveh-tehr*	sweter
shirt	*ko-shoo-lah*	koszula
shoes	*boo-ti*	buty
skirt	*spood-nee-tsah*	spódnica
trousers	*spod-nyeh*	spodnie

It doesn't fit.
    to nyeh pah-soo-yeh   To nie pasuje.
It is too ...
    yehst zah ...   Jest za ...

big	*doo-zhi*	duży
small	*mah-wi*	mały
short	*kroot-kee*	krótki
long	*dwoo-gee*	długi
tight	*op-tsyees-wi*	obcisły
loose	*loozh-ni*	luźny

POLISH

General

bag	*tor-bah*	torba
battery (radio)	*bah-tehr-yah*	bateria
bottle	*boo-tehl-kah*	butelka
bottle opener	*ot-fyeh-rahch do boo-teh-lehk*	otwieracz do butelek
box	*poo-dehw-ko*	pudełko
button	*goo-zeek*	guzik
can opener	*ot-fyeh-rahch do kon-sehrf*	otwieracz do konserw
candles	*svyeh-tseh*	świece
discount	*ob-neesh-kah*	obniżka
gold	*zwo-to*	złoto
needle (sewing)	*eeg-wah*	igła
packet	*pahch-kah*	paczka
receipt	*pah-rah-gon*	paragon
silver	*srehb-ro*	srebro
thread	*nee-tsyee*	nici

Materials

cotton	*bah-vehw-nah*	bawełna
denim	*dreh-leeh*	drelich
handmade	*rehnch-nyeh ro-byo-neh*	ręcznie robione
leather	*skoo-rah*	skóra
linen	*lehn*	len
nylon	*ni-lon*	nylon
plactic	*plahs-tik*	plastyk
polyester	*po-lee-ehs-tehr*	polyester
silk	*yehd-vahb*	jedwab

suede	*zahmsh*	zamsz
velvet	*ahk-sah-meet*	aksamit
wool	*vehw-nah*	wełna

Colours

black	*chahr-ni*	czarny
blue	*nyeh-byehs-kee*	niebieski
brown	*bron-zo-vi*	brązowy
dark	*tsyem-ni*	ciemny
green	*zyeh-lo-ni*	zielony
light	*yahs-ni*	jasny
orange	*po-mah-rahn-cho-vi*	pomarańczowy
pink	*roo-zho-vi*	różowy
purple	*poor-poo-ro-vi*	purpurowy
red	*chehr-vo-ni*	czerwony
white	*byah-wi*	biały
yellow	*zhoow-ti*	żółty

Toiletries

comb	*gzheh-byehn*	grzebień
condoms	*preh-zehr-vah-ti-vi*	prezerwatywy
hairbrush	*shchot-kah do vwo-soof*	szczotka do włosów
moisturising cream	*krehm nah-veel-zhah-yon-tsi*	krem nawilżający
razorblades	*mah-shin-kah do go-leh-nyah*	maszynka do golenia
sanitary napkins	*pod-pahs-kee*	podpaski
shampoo	*shahm-pon*	szampon

shaving cream	*krehm do go-leh-nyah*	krem do golenia
soap	*mid-wo*	mydło
sunblock cream	*krehm psheh-tsyeev-swo-nehch-ni*	krem przeciwsłoneczny
tampons	*tahm-po-ni*	tampony
tissues	*sehr-veht-kee*	serwetki
toilet paper	*pah-pyehr to-ah-leh-to-vi*	papier toaletowy
toothbrush	*shchot-kah do zehm-boof*	szczotka do zębów
toothpaste	*pahs-tah do zehm-boof*	pasta do zębów

Stationery & Publications

map	*mah-pah*	mapa
newspaper	*gah-zeh-tah*	gazeta
newspaper in English	*gah-zeh-tah vyehn-zi-koo ahn-gyehls-keem*	gazeta w języku angielskim
novels in English	*po-vyehs-tsyee vyehn-zi-koo ahn-gyehls-keem*	powieści w języku angielskim
paper	*pah-pyehr*	papier
pen (ballpoint)	*dwoo-go-pees*	długopis

Photography

Can you process this film?

chi mozh-nah too vi-vo-wahtsh tehn feelm?	Czy można tu wywołać ten film?

POLISH

When will it be ready?
*kyeh-di behn-dzheh
go-to-vi?*   Kiedy będzie gotowy?
I want a film for this
camera.
*htseh feelm do teh-go
ah-pah-rah-too*   Chcę film do tego aparatu.

B&W (film)	*chahr-no-byah-wi*	czarnobiały
camera	*ah-pah-raht*	aparat
colour (film)	*ko-lo-ro-vi*	kolorowy
film	*feelm*	film
flash	*lahm-pah bwis-ko-vah*	lampa błyskowa
lens	*o-byehk-tiv*	obiektyw
light metre	*svyaht-wo-myehzh*	światłomierz

Smoking

A packet of cigarettes,
please.
*po-pro-sheh pahch-keh
pah-pyeh-ro-soof*   Poproszę paczkę papierosów.
Are these cigarettes strong/
mild?
*chi teh pah-pyeh-ro-si
som mots-neh/
wah-god-neh?*   Czy te papierosy są
                                  mocne/łagodne?
Do you have a light?
*chi mo-geh pro-syeetsh
o o-gyen?*   Czy mogę prosić o ogień?

cigarettes	*pah-pyeh-ro-si*	papierosy
cigarette papers	*bee-boow-kee do ti-to-nyoo*	bibułki do tytoniu
filtered	*sfeel-trehm*	z filtrem
lighter	*zah-pahl-neech-kah*	zapalniczka
matches	*zah-pahw-kee*	zapałki
menthol	*mehn-to-lo-veh*	mentolowe
pipe	*fahy-kah*	fajka
tobacco	*ti-ton*	tytoń
unfiltered	*behs feel-trah*	bez filtra

Sizes & Comparisons

small	*mah-wi*	mały
big	*doo-zhi*	duży
heavy	*tsyehn-shkee*	ciężki
light	*lehk-kee*	lekki
more	*vyehn-tsehy*	więcej
less	*mnyehy*	mniej
too much/many	*zah doo-zho*	za dużo
many	*doo-zho*	dużo
enough	*vis-tahr-chi*	wystarczy
also	*tahk-zheh*	także
a little bit	*tro-heh*	trochę

Health

chemist	*ahp-teh-kahsh*	aptekarz
dentist	*dehn-tis-tah*	dentysta
doctor	*leh-kahsh*	lekarz
hospital	*shpee-tahl*	szpital

I am sick.
   yehs-tehm ho-ri — Jestem chory.

My friend is sick.
   mooy pshi-yah-tsyehl — Mój przyjaciel jest chory.
   yehst ho-ri (m)
   mo-yah pshi-yah-tsyoow- — Moja przyjaciółka jest chora.
   kah yehst ho-rah (f)

I need a female doctor,
please.
   po-chsheh-boo-yeh — Potrzebuję ginekologa.
   gee-neh-ko-lo-gah

Could you please call a
doctor?
   pro-sheh vehs-vatsh — Proszę wezwać lekarza.
   leh-kah-zhah

What's the matter?
   tso pah-noo/pah-nee — Co Panu/Pani dolega?
   do-leh-gah?

Where does it hurt?
   gdzheh pah-nah/pah-nyom — Gdzie Pana/Panią boli?
   bo-lee?

It hurts here.
   too mnyeh bo-lee — Tu mnie boli.

I feel dizzy.
   mahm zahv-ro-ti gwo-vi — Mam zawroty głowy.

I'm having trouble breathing.
   mahm prob-leh-mi — Mam problemy
   zot-di-hah-nyehm — z oddychaniem.

POLISH

I've been vomiting.
vi-myo-to-vah-wehm (m) Wymiotowałem.
vi-myo-to-vah-wahm (f) Wymiotowałam.
I can't sleep.
nyeh mo-geh spahtsh Nie mogę spać.
My ... hurts.
bo-lee mnyeh ... Boli mnie ...

Parts of the Body

arm	*rah-myeh*	ramię
back	*pleh-tsi*	plecy
blood	*krehf*	krew
bone	*koshch*	kość
ear	*oo-ho*	ucho
eye	*o-ko*	oko
face	*tfahsh*	twarz
finger	*pah-lehts*	palec
hand	*rehn-kah*	ręka
head	*gwo-vah*	głowa
leg	*no-gah*	noga
neck	*shi-yah*	szyja
skin	*skoo-rah*	skóra
throat	*gahr-dwo*	gardło

Ailments

I have ...
mahm ... Mam ...

blood pressure	*tsyees-nyeh-nyeh krfee*	ciśnienie krwi
low/high	*nees-kyeh/vi-so-kyeh*	niskie/wysokie

a cold	*psheh-zyehm-byeh-nyeh*	przeziębienie
constipation	*zaht-fahr-dzeh-nyeh*	zatwardzenie
a cough	*kah-shehl*	kaszel
food poisoning	*zaht-roo-tsyeh po-kahr-mo-veh*	zatrucie pokarmowe
frostbite	*od-mro-zheh-nyeh*	odmrożenie
a headache	*bool gwo-vi*	ból głowy
indigestion	*nyeh-strahv-nostsh*	niestrawność
an infection	*een-fehk-tsyeh*	infekcję
influenza	*gri-peh*	grypę
a migraine	*mee-greh-neh*	migrenę
a pain	*bool*	ból
sprain	*zveeh-nyehn-tsyeh*	zwichnięcie
a sore throat	*vzhoot gahrd-wah*	wrzód gardła
venereal disease	*ho-ro-beh veh-neh-rich-nom*	chorobę weneryczną
worms	*ro-bah-kee*	robaki

Some Useful Words & Phrases

I'm ...

   yehs-tehm ...   Jestem ...

asthmatic	*ahst-mah-ti-kyehm*	astmatykiem
diabetic	*dyah-beh-ti-kyehm*	diabetykiem
epileptic	*eh-pee-lehp-ti-kyehm*	epileptykiem

I'm allergic to antibiotics/
penicillin.

   yehs-tehm oo-choo-lo-   Jestem uczulony na
   ni nah ahn-ti-byo-ti-kee/   antybiotyki/
   pehn-tsi-lee-neh   penicylinę.

I'm pregnant.
   yehs-tehm ftsyon-zhi   Jestem w ciąży.
I'm on the pill.
   byo-reh pee-goow-kee   Biorę pigułki
   ahn-ti-kon-tsehp-tsiy-neh   antykoncepcyjne.
I haven't had my period for
... months.
   nyeh myah-wahm ok-reh-   Nie miałam okresu od ...
   soo ot ... myeh-syehn-tsi   miesięcy.
I've been vaccinated.
   yehs-tehm zahsh-cheh-   Jestem zaszczepiony.
   pyo-ni
I feel better/worse.
   choo-yeh syeh leh-pyehy/   Czuję się lepiej/gorzej.
   go-zhehy

accident	*vi-pah-dehk*	wypadek
acupuncture	*ah-koo-poonk-too-rah*	akupunktura
addiction	*nah-wook*	nałóg
antibiotics	*ahn-ti-byo-ti-kee*	antybiotyki
antiseptic	*ahn-ti-sehp-tich-ni*	antyseptyczny
bandage	*bahn-dahzh*	bandaż
bite	*oo-kon-sheh-nyeh*	ukąszenie
contraceptives	*syrot-kee ahn-ti-kon-tsehp-tsiy-neh*	środki antykoncepcyjne
injection	*zahst-shik*	zastrzyk
injury	*rah-nah*	rana
medicine	*lehk/leh-kahrs-tfo*	lek/lekarstwo
menstruation	*myeh-syonch-kah*	miesiączka
oxygen	*tlehn*	tlen

| urine | *moch* | mocz |
| vitamins | *vee-tah-mee-ni* | witaminy |

At the Chemist

I need medication for ...
  pot-sheh-boo-yeh lehk   Potrzebuję lek na ...
  nah ...
I have a prescription.
  mahm reh-tsehp-teh   Mam receptę.

At the Dentist

I have a toothache.
  bo-lee mnyeh zomp   Boli mnie ząb.
I've broken a tooth.
  zwah-mahw mee syeh   Złamał mi się ząb.
  zomp
My gums hurt.
  bo-lom mnyeh dzyon-swah   Bolą mnie dziąsła.
Please give me anaesthetic.
  pro-sheh o   Proszę o
  znyeh-choo-leh-nyeh   znieczulenie
I don't want it extracted.
  nyeh htseh go oo-soo-   Nie chcę go usunąć.
  nontsh

Times & Dates

What time is it?
  ktoo-rah yehst   Która jest godzina?
  go-dzee-nah?

POLISH

Could you write it down?
chi mo-zheh pahn/pah-nee Czy może Pan/Pani to
to nah-pee-sahtsh? napisać?

What is the date today?
ktoo-ri yehst dzhee-syay? Który jest dzisiaj?

It's 2 June.
yehst droo-gee chehrf-tsah Jest 2-gi czerwca.

in the morning	*rah-no*	rano
in the afternoon	*po po-wood-nyoo*	po południu
in the evening	*vyeh-cho-rehm*	wieczorem

Days of the Week

Monday	*po-nyeh-dzhah-wehk*	poniedziałek
Tuesday	*fto-rehk*	wtorek
Wednesday	*sro-dah*	środa
Thursday	*chfahr-tehk*	czwartek
Friday	*pyon-tehk*	piątek
Saturday	*so-bo-tah*	sobota
Sunday	*nyeh-dzheh-lah*	niedziela

Months

January	*sti-chehn*	styczeń
February	*loo-ti*	luty
March	*mah-zhehts*	marzec
April	*kfyeh-tsehn*	kwiecień
May	*mahy*	maj
June	*chehr-vyehts*	czerwiec
July	*lee-pyehts*	lipiec
August	*syehr-pyehn*	sierpień

September	*vzheh-syehn*	wrzesień
October	*pahz-dzhehr-neek*	październik
November	*lees-to-paht*	listopad
December	*groo-dzhehn*	grudzień

Seasons

summer	*lah-toh*	lato
autumn	*yeh-syehn*	jesień
winter	*zee-mah*	zima
spring	*vyos-nah*	wiosna

Present

today	*dzhee-syahy/dzhees*	dzisiaj/dziś
this morning	*dzhees rah-no*	dziś rano
this afternoon	*dzhees po po-wood-nyoo*	dziś po południu
tonight	*dzhees vyeh-cho-rehm*	dziś wieczorem
this week/year	*ftim ti-god-nyoo/ ro-koo*	w tym tygodniu/ roku
immediately	*nah-tih-myahst*	natychmiast
now	*teh-rahs*	teraz

Past

yesterday	*fcho-rahy*	wczoraj
day before yesterday	*psheht-fcho-rahy*	przedwczoraj
last night	*fcho-rahy vno-tsi*	wczoraj w nocy
last week/year	*vzhehs-wim ti-god-nyoo/ro-koo*	w zeszłym tygodniu/roku

Future

tomorrow	*yoot-ro*	jutro
day after tomorrow	*po-yoot-sheh*	pojutrze
next week/year	*fpshish-wim ti-god-nyoo/ro-koo*	w przyszłym tygodniu/roku

During the Day

sunrise	*fs-hoot*	wschód
morning	*rah-no*	rano
noon	*po-wood-nyeh*	południe
afternoon	*po-po-wood-nyeh*	popołudnie
sunset	*zah-hoot*	zachód
evening	*vyeh-choor*	wieczór
midnight	*poow-nots*	północ

Numbers & Amounts

0	*zeh-ro*	zero
1	*yeh-dehn*	jeden
2	*dvah*	dwa
3	*chshi*	trzy
4	*chteh-ri*	cztery
5	*pyehntsh*	pięć
6	*shehstsh*	sześć
7	*syeh-dehm*	siedem
8	*o-syehm*	osiem
9	*dzheh-vyehntsh*	dziewięć
10	*dzheh-syehntsh*	dziesięć
11	*yeh-deh-nahs-tsheh*	jedenaście

POLISH

POLISH

12	*dvah-nahs-tsheh*	dwanaście
13	*chshi-nahs-tsheh*	trzynaście
14	*chtehr-nahs-tsheh*	czternaście
15	*pyeht-nahs-tsheh*	piętnaście
16	*shehs-nahs-tsheh*	szesnaście
17	*syeh-dehm-nahs-tsheh*	siedemnaście
18	*o-syehm-nahs-tsheh*	osiemnaście
19	*dzheh-vyeht-nahs-tsheh*	dziewiętnaście
20	*dvah-dzhehs-tshah*	dwadzieścia
21	*dvah-dzhehs-tshah yeh-dehn*	dwadzieścia jeden
22	*dvah-dzhehs-tshah dvah*	dwadzieścia dwa
30	*chshi-dzhehs-tshee*	trzydzieści
40	*chtehr-dzhehs-tshee*	czterdzieści
50	*pyehn-dzheh-syont*	pięćdziesiąt
60	*shehsy-dzheh-syont*	sześćdziesiąt
70	*syeh-dehm-dzheh-syont*	siedemdziesiąt
80	*o-syehm-dzheh-syont*	osiemdziesiąt
90	*dzheh-vyehn-dzheh-syont*	dziewięćdziesiąt
100	*sto*	sto
1000	*ti-syonts*	tysiąc
one million	*mee-lyon*	milion
1/4	*yehd-nah chfahr-tah*	jedna czwarta
1/3	*yehd-nah chsheh-tsyah*	jedna trzecia

1/2	*yehd-nah droo-gah*	jedna druga
3/4	*chshi chfahr-teh*	trzy czwarte
1st	*pyehr-fshi*	pierwszy
2nd	*droo-gee*	drugi
3rd	*chsheh-tshee*	trzeci

Some Useful Words

a little (amount)	*tro-heh*	trochę
double	*pod-vooy-nyeh*	podwójnie
a dozen	*too-zyeen*	tuzin
enough	*do-sitsh*	dosyć
few	*keel-kah*	kilka
less	*mnyehy*	mniej
a lot	*doo-zho*	dużo
many	*doo-zho*	dużo
more	*vyehn-tsehy*	więcej
once	*yeh-dehn rahs*	jeden raz
a pair	*pah-rah*	para
percent	*pro-tsehnt*	procent
some	*tro-heh*	trochę
too much	*zah doo-zho*	za dużo
twice	*dvah rah-zi*	dwa razy

POLISH

Abbreviations

Al.	avenue
CEPELIA	a network of folk art shops
doc.	associate professor
dr	doctor (university title)
EWG	EC
godz.	hour
IT	tourist information
inż.	engineer
itd.	etc.
LOT	Polish Airlines
m.	flat, apartment (used in addresses)
mgr	Master of Arts, Master of Science
min.	minute
Ob.	citizen (placed before names in official correspondence)
PKO	Polish Savings Bank
PKP	Polish State Railways
PKS	Polish State Coachlines
prof.	professor
PTTK	Polish Tourists & Country-Lovers' Association
PZMot	Polish Automobile Federation
ul.	street (used in addresses)
W.P.	Sir/Madam (an elegant form of address in correspondence, placed before the name)
w/w	above mentioned

POLISH

Romanian

Romanian

Introduction

Romanian belongs to the group of Romance languages which are the modern descendants of Latin and include French, Italian, Portuguese and Spanish. The Romanian language represents the present stage of evolution of the Latin that has been spoken in the Danubian provinces, in the north-eastern part of the Roman Empire, since early Roman occupation. The transformation process of Latin into Romanian, between the 5th and 8th centuries AD, saw the development of the main characteristics of Romanian which distinguish it today.

The sounds of the Romanian language (the phonological system) and its grammatical structure (morphology and syntax) are mostly of Latin origin; the declension and conjugation of nouns, pronouns, adjectives and verbs display many similarities, such as the retention of three genders (masculine, feminine, neuter) and of four verb conjugations. Words of Latin origin are in widespread use to describe everyday concepts such as parts of the human body, various kinds of animals, food, natural phenomena, and notions concerning time.

As a result of historical contact with other peoples, some words of Hungarian, Turkish, Greek and Bulgarian origin have penetrated the Romanian vocabulary. However, Romanian's close connection to Latin has caused Romania to be considered a Latin island in a Slav sea.

Romania has 22 million inhabitants, all of whom speak Romanian. It is also spoken in areas of the former USSR, and there are half a million Romanian speakers in Hungary, and around 200,000 Romanians in Bulgaria. There is little dialectal variation, although in the north-east of Romania, people frequently use 'se' and 'si' (pronounced 'she' and 'shi') instead of 'ce' and 'ci ' ('che' and 'chi').

Romanian uses different forms of words depending on whether a man or a woman is being referred to. As a rule, feminine forms of words are distinguished from masculine by the suffix 'a'or 'ă'. In this chapter, the two forms are generally separated by a slash: for example, 'farmer' is given as 'fermier/ ă', meaning that a male farmer is a 'fermier' and a female farmer is a 'fermieră'.

Pronunciation

The Romanian language is written more or less as it is spoken, although a few letters are unfamiliar to English speakers. Pronunciation is particularly straightforward as each letter is always pronounced in the same way, and there is no distinction between short and long vowels.

Vowels

a	an 'ah' sound, as the 'a' in 'father'
e	as the 'e' in 'soufflé'
i	as the 'i' in 'in'
o	as the 'o' from 'pot'
u	as the 'u' from 'pull'

The Romanian language has two special vowels:

ă	as the 'er' in 'brother'
î	prepare your lips to say 'i' but say 'u'. There is no equivalent in English.

In the simplified phonetic translation here we use the same letters, 'ă' and 'î'.

Consonants

In the Romanian language all the consonants are read as in English except for the following:

c	as the 'k' in 'king', except before 'e' and 'i', when it is pronounced as the 'ch' as in 'church'
ch	always as the 'k' in 'king'
g	as the 'g' in 'get', except befor e 'e' and 'i', when it is pronounced as the 'j' in 'jeans'
gh	always as the 'g' in 'get'
r	always rolled

The Romanian language has two different consonants:

ş	as the 'sh' as in 'ship'
ţ	a 'ts' sound like the 'z' in the German 'zwei', 'zehn'

Double vowels, such as 'ii' or 'ee', or double consonants such as 'nn', are pronounced as two distinct sounds.

These are the rules of the Romanian pronunciation and you'll discover that it's a very easy language to read. Romanians will be very appreciative if you make an effort to speak the language.

ROMANIAN

Greetings & Civilities
Top 10 Useful Phrases

Hello.
bu-năzi-uah   Bunăziua.

Goodbye.
lah re-ve-de-re   La revedere.

Yes./No.
dah/nu   Da./Nu.

Excuse me.
sku-zah-tsi-mă   Scuzați-mă.

May I? Do you mind?
se poah-te? per-mi-te-tsi?   Se poate? Permiteți?

Sorry. (excuse me, forgive me)
imi pah-re rău   Imi pare rău.

Please.
vă rog   Vă rog.

Thank you.
mul-tsu-mesk   Mulțumesc.

Many thanks.
mul-te mul-tsu-miri   Multe mulțumiri.

That's fine./You're welcome.
es-te în re-gu-lă/ku plă-che-re/n-ah-vetsi de che   Este în regulă./Cu plăcere./N-aveți de ce.

Greetings

Good morning.
bu-nă di-mi-neah-tsah   Bună dimineața.

Good afternoon.
bu-nă zi-uah   Bună ziua.

ROMANIAN

Good evening/night.
  bu-nă seah-rah/no
  ahp-te bu-nă.   Bună seara/Noapte bună.
How are you?
  che mai fa-che-tsi?   Ce mai faceţi?
Well, thanks.
  bi-ne mul-zu-mesk   Bine mulţumesc.

Forms of Address

Madam/Mrs	*doahm-nă*	Doamna/Dnă
Sir/Mr	*dom-nu-le*	Domnule/Dl
Miss	*dom-ni-shoah-ră*	Domnişoară/Dşoara
companion, friend	*pri-e-ten*	prieten

Small Talk
Meeting People

What is your name?
  kum vă nu-mi-tsi?   Cum vă numiţi?
My name is ...
  nu-me-le meu es-te ...   Numele meu este ...
I'd like to introduce you to ...
  ash do-ri să vă pre-zint ...   Aş dori să vă prezint ...
I'm pleased to meet you.
  sînt în-kîn-taht să vă -   Sînt încîntat să vă cunosc.
  kunosk

I (don't) like ...
  (nu) imi plah-che ...   (Nu) Imi place ...

How old are you?
   che vîr-stă ah-vetsi?   Ce vîrstă aveți?
   kî tsi ahni ah-vetsi?   Cîți ahni aveți?
I am ... years old.
   (eu) ahm ... ahni   (Eu) Am ... ani.

Note that it is not necessary to use the pronouns *eu* (I), *tu* (you), *noi* (we), etc, because the verb ending indicates the person.

Nationalities

Where are you from?
   de un-de sîn-tetsi?   De unde sînteți?

I am from ...
   sînt din ...   Sînt din ...

Australia	*ah-us-trah-li-ah*	Australia
Canada	*kah-nah-dah*	Canada
England	*ahn-gli-ah*	Anglia
Ireland	*ir-lahn-dah*	Irlanda
New Zealand	*no-uah ze-e-lahn-dă*	Noua Zeelandă
Scotland	*sko-tsi-ah*	Scoția
United States	*stah-te-le u-ni-te*	Statele Unite
Wales	*tsah-ra gah-li-lor*	Țara Galilor

Occupations

What do you do?
   ku che vă o-cu-pahtsi?   Cu ce vă ocupați?

ROMANIAN

I am a/an ...

(eu) sînt ...		(Eu) sînt ...
artist	*ahr-tist/ă*	artist/ă
businessman	*om de ah-fa-cheri*	om de afaceri
doctor	*dok-tor/me-dik*	doctor/medic
engineer	*in-gi-ner/ă*	inginer/ă
farmer	*fer-mi-er/ă*	fermier/ă
journalist	*zi-ah-rist/ă*	ziarist/ă
lawyer	*ah-vo-kaht/ă*	avocat/ă
manual worker	*mun-chi-tor* (m)	muncitor
	mun-chi-toah-re (f)	muncitoare
mechanic	*me-kah-nik*	mecanic
nurse	*ah-sis-tent/ă*	asistent/ă
	me-di-kahl/ă	medical/ă
	so-ră me-di-kah-lă (f)	soră medicală
office worker	*fun-ktsi-o-nahr/ă*	funcţionar/ă
scientist	*cher-che-tă-tor*	cercetător
	shti-in-tsi-fik	ştiinţific
student	*stu-dent/ă*	student/ă
teacher	*pro-fe-sor*	profesor
	pro-fe-soah-ră	profesoară
waiter	*kel-ner/kel-ne-ri-tsă*	chelner/chelneriţă
writer	*skri-i-tor*	scriitor
	skri-i-toah-re	scriitoare

Religion

What is your religion?

   che re-li-gi-e ah-vetsi?   Ce religie aveţi?

I am not religious.

   nu sînt re-li-gios (m)/   Nu sînt religios/
   re-li-gi-oahsă (f)   religioasă.

What does ... mean?
che în-seahm-nă ...? — Ce înseamnă ...?

Some Useful Words
Sure.
si-gur — Sigur.
Just a minute.
un mi-nut/un mo-ment — Un minut/Un moment.
It's (not) important.
(nu) es-te im-por-tahnt — (Nu) Este important.
It's (not) possible.
(nu) es-te po-si-bil — (Nu) Este posibil.
Good luck!
no-rok! — Noroc!

Signs

BAGGAGE COUNTER	GHIŞEUL PENTRU BAGAJE
CUSTOMS	VAMĂ
EMERGENCY EXIT	IEŞIRE DE URGENŢĂ
ENTRANCE	INTRARE
EXIT	IEŞIRE
FREE ADMISSION	INTRARE LIBERĂ
HOT/COLD	CALD/RECE
INFORMATION	INFORMAŢII
NO ENTRY	NU INTRAŢI/INTRAREA INTERZISĂ

I am ...
eu sînt ... — Eu sînt ...

Buddhist	*bu-dist/ă*	Budist/ă
Catholic	*kah-to-lik/ă*	Catolic/ă
Christian	*kresh-tin/ă*	Creştin/ă
Hindu	*hin-dus/să*	Hindus/ă
Jewish	*e-vreu/e-vrei-kă*	Evreu/Evreică
Muslim	*mu-sul-mahn* (m)	Musulman
	mu-sul-mah-nă (f)	Musulmană

Family
Are you married?
sîn-te-tsi kă-să-to-rit/ă — Sînteţi căsătorit/ă?
I am single. I am married.
nu sînt kă-să-to-rit/ă. — Nu sînt căsătorit/ă.
sînt kă-să-to-rit/ă — Sînt căsătorit/ă.
How many children do you have?
kî-tsi ko-pii ah-vetsi? — Cîţi copii aveţi?
I don't have any children.
nu ahm nichi un ko-pil — Nu am nici un copil.
I have a daughter/a son.
ahm o fi-i-kă/un fiu — Am o fiică/un fiu.
How many brothers/sisters do you have?
kî-tsi frahtsi/kî-te su-rori ah-vetsi? — Cîţi fraţi/cîte surori aveţi?
Is your husband/wife here?
es-te so-tsul/so-tsia ah-ichi? — Este soţul/soţia aici?

Do you have a boyfriend/
girlfriend?
  ah-vetsi un pri-e-ten/   Aveţi un prieten/o prietenă?
  o pri-e-te-nă?

brother	*frah-te*	frate
children	*ko-pii*	copii
daughter	*fii-kă*	fiică
family	*fah-mi-li-e*	familie
father	*tah-ta*	tata
grandfather	*bu-nik*	bunic
grandmother	*bu-ni-kă*	bunică
husband	*sots*	soţ
mother	*mah-mă*	mamă
sister	*so-ră*	soră
son	*fiu*	fiu
wife	*so-tsi-e*	soţie

Feelings

I am sorry. (condolence)
  imi pah-re rău   Imi pare rău.
I am grateful.
  (eu) sînt re-ku-nos-kă-tor   (Eu) Sînt recunoscător.

I am ...
  imi es-te ...   Imi este ...

cold/hot	*re-che/kahld*	rece/cald
hungry/thirsty	*foah-me/se-te*	foame/sete
right	*ahm drep-tah-te*	Am dreptate.
sleepy	*sînt som-no-ros* (m)/	Sînt somnoros/
	som-no-roah-să (f)	somnoroasă.

I am ...
  (eu) sînt ...   (Eu) sînt ...

angry	*su-pă-raht/ă*	supărat/ă
happy	*fe-ri-chit/ă*	fericit/ă
sad	*trist/ă*	trist/ă
tired	*o-bo-sit/ă*	obosit/ă
well	*bi-ne*	bine
worried	*în-gri-zho-raht/ă*	îngrijorat/ă

Language Problems

Do you speak English?
  vor-bitsi en-gle-zah?   Vorbiţi engleza?
Does anyone speak English?
  vor-besh-te chi-ne-vah   Vorbeşte cineva engleza?
  en-gle-zah?
I speak a little ...
  (eu) vor-besk pu-tsin ...   (Eu) Vorbesc puţin ...
I don't speak ...
  nu vor-besk ...   Nu vorbesc ...
I (don't) understand.
  eu (nu) în-tse-leg   Eu (nu) înţeleg.
Could you speak more slowly
please?
  ah-tsi pu-teah vor-bi mahi Aţi putea vorbi mai rar?
  rahr?
Could you repeat that?
  ah-tsi pu-teah re-pe-tah?   Aţi putea repeta?

How do you say ...?
  kum spu-netsi ...?   Cum spuneţi ...?

ROMANIAN

NO SMOKING	NU FUMAŢI/FUMATUL INTERZIS
OPEN/CLOSED	DESCHIS/INCHIS
PROHIBITED	INTERZIS
RESERVED	REZERVAT
TELEPHONE	TELEFON
TOILETS	TOALETA

Emergencies

POLICE	POLIŢIE
POLICE STATION	STAŢIE DE POLIŢIE

Help!
ah-zhu-tor!   Ajutor!
It's an emergency!
es-te o ur-gen-tsă!   Este o urgenţă!
There's been an accident!
ah fost un ahk-chi-dent!   A fost un accident!
Call a doctor!
ke-mah-tsi un dok-tor!   Chemaţi un doctor!
Call an ambulance!
ke-mah-tsi o ahm-bu-l   Chemaţi o ambulanţă!
ahn-tsa!

I've been raped!
ahm fost vi-o-lah-tă!   Am fost violată!
I've been robbed!
ahm forst zhe-fu-i-t/ă!   Am fost jefuit/ă!

Call the police!
ke-mah-tsi po-li-tsi-ah!   Chemați poliția!
Where is the police station?
un-de es-te po-li-tsi-ah?   Unde este Poliția?

Go away!
du-te!/pleah-kă!   Du-te!/Pleacă!
I'll call the police!
ahm să kem po-li-tsi-ah!   Am să chem poliția!
Thief!
hots/tîl-hahr!   Hoț/Tîlhar!

I am/My friend is ill.
eu sînt/pri-e-te-nul meu   Eu sînt/Prietenul meu
es-te bol-nahv   este bolnav.
I am lost.
sînt pier-dut   Sînt pierdut.
Where are the toilets?
un-de es-te to-ah-le-tah?   Unde este toaleta?
Could you help me please?
m-ah-tsi pu-teah   M-ați putea ajuta?
ah-zhu-tah?
May I use the telephone?
pot fo-lo-si te-le-fo-nul?   Pot folosi telefonul?
I'm sorry. I apologise.
imi pah-re rău   Imi pare rău. Imi cer scuze.
imi cher sku-ze
I didn't realise I was doing
anything wrong.
nu mi-ahm daht seah-mah   Nu mi-am dat seama
kă fahk che-vah rău   că fac ceva rău.

I didn't do it.
nu ahm fă-ku-to eu
    Nu am făcut-o eu.

I wish to contact my embassy/
consulate.
ahsh do-ri să kon-tahk-tez
ahm-bah-sah-dah/
kon-su-lah-tul
    Aş dori să contactez
ambasada/consulatul.

I speak English.
(eu) vor-besk en-gle-zah
    (Eu) Vorbesc engleza.

I have medical insurance.
(eu) ahm ah-si-gu-rah-re
me-di-kah-lă
    (Eu) Am asigurare
medicală.

My possessions are insured.
lu-kru-ri-le me-le
sînt ah-si-gu-rah-te
    Lucrurile mele
sînt asigurate.

My ... was stolen.
... meu (m)/*meah* (f) *a fost*
fu-raht/ă
    ... meu/mea a fost
furat/ă

I've lost ...
ahm pier-dut ...
    Am pierdut ...

my bags	*bah-gah-zhe-le me-le*	bagajele mele
my handbag	*po-se-tă/jeaută/*	poşetă/geaută/
	bah-gah-jul de mînă	bagajul de mînă
my money	*bah-nii mei*	banii mei
my travellers'	*che-ku-ri-le de*	cecurile de călătorie
cheques	*că-lă-to-ri-e*	
my passport	*pah-shah-por-tul meu*	paşaportul meu

ROMANIAN

Forms

name	*nu-me (le)*	nume (le)
address	*ah-dre-sah*	adresa
date of birth	*dah-tah nahsh-te-rii*	data nașterii
place of birth	*lo-kul nahsh-te-rii*	locul nașterii
age	*vîr-stah*	vîrst
sex	*se-xul*	sexul
nationality	*nah-tsi-o-nah-li-tah-teah*	naționalitatea
next of kin	*ru-dah cheah mahi ah-pro-pi-ahtă*	ruda cea mai apropiată
religion	*re-li-gi-ah*	religia
reason for travel	*mo-ti-vul kă-lă-to-ri-ei*	motivul călătoriei
profession	*pro-fe-si-ah*	profesia
marital status	*stah-tu-tul mah-tri-mo-ni-ahl/stah-reah chi-vi-lă*	statutul matri-monial/starea civilă
passport	*pah-shah-port*	pașaport
passport number	*nu-mă-rul pah-shah-por-tu-lui*	numărul pașaportului
visa	*vi-zah*	viza
identification	*ahk-te-le/ de i-den-ti-tah-te*	actele/de identitate
birth certificate	*cher-ti-fi-kaht de nahsh-te-re*	certificat de naștere
driver's licence	*per-mis de kon-du-che-re*	permis de condu-cere
car registration	*cher-ti-fi-ka-tul de in-re-gi-trah-re al*	certificatul de înregistrare al
customs	*vah-mă*	vamă

migration	*e-mi-grah-re*	emigrare
border	*fron-ti-e-ră*	frontieră

Getting Around

ARRIVALS	SOSIRI
BUS STOP	STAȚIE DE AUTOBUS
DEPARTURES	PLECĂRI
STATION	STAȚIE
SUBWAY	TUNEL/PASAJ/METROU
TICKET OFFICE	GHIȘEU/CASĂ DE BILETE
TIMETABLE	ORAR
TRAIN STATION	GARĂ

What time does the... leave/
arrive?

lah che o-ră pleah-kă/ so-sesh-te ...?	La ce oră pleacă/soseşte ...?
(aero)plane	*ah-vi-o-nul*	avionul
boat	*vah-po-rul*	vaporul
bus (city & intercity)	*ahu-to-bu-sul*	autobusul
train	*tre-nul*	trenul
tram	*trahm-vah-iul*	tramvaiul

ROMANIAN

Directions
Where is ...?

un-de es-te ...?	Unde este ...?

How do I get to ...?
kum ah-zhung lah ...?   Cum ajung la ...?

Is it far near/from here?
es-te de-pahr-te/   Este departe/
ah-proah-pe de ah-ichi?   aproape de aici?

Can I walk there?
pot să merg pe zhos   Pot să merg pe jos pînă acolo?
pînăacolo?

Can you show me (on the map)?
pu-te-tsi să-mi ah-ră-tah-   Puteţi să-mi arătaţi
tsi (pe hahr-tă)?   (pe hartă) ?

Are there other means of getting there?
sînt ahl-te mize-loah-che   Sînt alte mijloace
de trahn-sport pen-tru ah   de transport pentru
ah-zhun-ge ah-ko-lo?   ajunge acolo?

I want to go to ...
vreahu sămerg lah ...   Vreau sămerg la ...

Go straight ahead.
du-te drept î-nah-in-te   Du-te drept înainte.

It's further down.
es-te mai de-pahr-te   Este mai departe.

Turn left ...
in-toahr-che lah stîn-gah ...   Intoarce la stînga ...

Turn right ...
în-toar-che lah   Intoarce la dreapta ...
dreahp-tah ...

at the next corner.
   lah ur-mă-to-rul kolts   la următorul colț
at the traffic lights.
   lah se-mah-for   la semafor

behind	*în spah-te-le*	în spatele
in front of	*în fah-tsah*	în fața
far	*de-pahr-te*	departe
near	*ah-proah-pe*	aproape
in front of	*în fah-tsah*	în fața
opposite	*o-pus*	opus

Booking Tickets

Excuse me, where is the
ticket office?
   scu-zah-tsi-mă un-de   Scuzați-mă unde este
   es-te ghi-she-ul de   ghișeul de bilete?
   bi-le-te?
Where can I buy a ticket?
   un-de pot kum-pă-rah un   Unde pot cumpăra un bilet?
   bi-let?
I want to go to ...
   vreahu sămerg lah ...   Vreau să merg la ...
Do I need to book?
   tre-bu-ie sәre-zerv?   Trebuie să rezerv?
You need to book.
   tre-bu-ie să re-zervvahtsi   Trebuie să rezervați.
I would like to book a seat to...
   ahsh do-ri să re-serv un   Așdori să rezerv un loc la ...
   loc lah ...

I would like ...
   ahsh do-ri ...   Aş dori ...
a one-way ticket
   un bi-let dus   un bilet dus
a return ticket
   un bi-let dus în-tors   un bilet dus-întors
two tickets
   do-uă bi-le-te   două bilete
tickets for all of us
   bi-le-te pen-tru to-tsi   bilete pentru toţi
a student fare
   bi-let pen-tru stu-den-tsi bilet pentru studenţi
a child's/pensioner's fare
   bi-let pen-tru ko-pii/   bilet pentru copii/
   pen-sio-nahri   pensionari

1st class
   klah-sah în-tîi   clasa întîi
2nd class
   klah-sah ah do-uah   clasa a doua

It is full.
   es-te plin   Este plin.
Is it completely full?
   es-te kom-plet plin?   Este complet plin?
Can I get a stand-by ticket?
   pot pri-mi un bi-let în   Pot primi un bilet în
   pi-chioah-re?   picioare?

Air

CHECKING IN	CONTROL
LUGGAGE PICKUP	BAGAJE
LEFT-LUGGAGE ROOM	SALĂ PENTRU CONSE-MNAREA BAGAJELOR
REGISTRATION	INREGISTRARE

Is there a flight to ...?
es-te vre-um zbor spre ...? Este vreum zbor spre ...?
When is the next flight to ...?
kînt es-te ur-mă-to-rul Cînt este următorul
zbor spre? zbor spre ...?
How long does the flight take?
kît du-reah-ză zbo-rul? Cît durează zborul?
What is the flight number?
kah-re es-te nu-mă-rul Care este numărul zborului?
zbo-ru-lui?
You must check in at ...
tre-bu-ie sa Trebuie să vă prezentați la ...
pre-zen-ta-tsi la ...

airport tax	*tah-xa de ah-e-ro-port*	taxa de aeroport
boarding pass	*per-mi-sul de bord*	permisul de bord
customs	*vah-mă*	vamă

Bus

Bus/tram stop
stah-tsi-e de ahu-to-bus/ trahm-vahi — Stație de autobus/tramvai

Where is the bus/tram stop?
un-de es-te stah-tsi-ah de ahu-to-bus/trahm-vahi? — Unde este stația de autobus/ tramvai?

Which bus goes to ...?
kah-re ahu-to-bus merge lah ...? — Care autobus merge la ...?

Does this bus go to ...?
ah-chest ahu-to-bus merge lah ...? — Acest autobus merge la ...?

How often do buses pass by?
kît de des trec ahu-to-bu-se-le? — Cît de des trec autobusele?

Could you let me know when we get to ...?
po-tsi să-mi spui kînd ah-zhun-gem lah ...? — Poți să-mi spui cînd ajungem la ...?

I want to get off!
vreahu să ko-bor! — vreau să cobor!

What time is the ... bus?
kînt es-te ... ahu-to-bus? — Cînt este ... autobus?

next	*ur-mă-torul*	următorul
first	*pri-mul*	primul
last	*ul-ti-mul*	ultimul

Metro

METRO/UNDERGROUND	METROU
CHANGE (for coins)	SCHIMB (mărunțiș)
THIS WAY TO	SPRE/PE AICI
WAY OUT	IEȘIRE

Which line takes me to ...?
kah-re li-ni-e du-che lah ..? Care linie duce la...?
What is the next station?
kah-re es-te ur-mă-toah- Care este următoare stație?
reah stah zi-e?

Train

DINING CAR	VAGON RESTAURANT
EXPRESS	ACCELERAT
PLATFORM NO	PERON NR.
SLEEPING CAR	VAGON DE DORMIT

Is this the right platform for...?
ah-ches-tah es-te Acesta este peronul pentru ...?
pe-ro-nul pen-tru ...?

Passengers must change
trains.
pah-sah-ge-ri tre-bu-ie Pasageri trebuie
să skim-be tre-nul să schimbe trenul.

The train leaves from platform ...

tre-nul pleah-kă de la pe-ro-nul nr...

Trenulpleacă de la peronul nr. ...

Taxi

Can you take me to ...?

pu-te-tsi să mă du-che-tsi lah ...?

Puteți să mă duceți la ...?

Please take me to ...

vă rog du-che-tsi-mălah ...

Vă rog duceți -măla ...

How much does it cost to go to ...?

kît kos-ta dru-mul pînă lah ...?

Cît costadrumul pînă la ...?

Instructions

Here is fine, thank you.

ah-ichi es-te bi-ne mul-tsu-mesk

Aici este bine mulțumesc.

The next corner, please.

ur-mă-to-rul kolts vă rog

Următorul colț vă rog.

Continue!

kon-ti-nu-ă!

Continuă!

The next street to the left/right.

ur-mă-toah-reah strah-dă lah stîn-gah/dreahp-tah

Următoarea stradă la stînga/dreapta.

Stop here!

o-presh-te ah-ichi!

Oprește aici!

Please slow down.
vă rog în-che-ti-nitsi

Vă rog încetiniţi.

Please wait here.
vă rog ahsh-tep-tah-tsi ah-ichi

Vă rog aşteptaţi aici.

Some Useful Phrases

The train is delayed/
cancelled.
tre-nul es-te în-tîr-zi-aht/ah-nu-laht

Trenul este întîrziat/
anulat.

How long will it be
delayed?
kît vah în-tîr-zi-ah?

Cît va întîrzia?

There is a delay of ... hours.
ah-re o în-tîr-zi-e-re de ... o-re

Are o întîrziere de ... ore.

Can I reserve a place?
pot re-zer-va un lok?

Pot rezerva un loc?

How long does the trip
take?
kît timp du-reah-ză ex-kur-si-ah?

Cît timp durează excursia?

Is it a direct route?
es-te ru-tă di-rek-tă?

Este rută directă?

Is that seat taken?
es-te o-ku-paht skah-u-nul?

Este ocupat scaunul?

I want to get off at ...
vreahu să ko-bor lah ...

Vreau să cobor la ...

Excuse me.
sku-zah-tsi-mă   Scuzaţi-mă.
Where can I hire a bicycle?
un-de pot în-ki-riah o   Unde pot închiria o bicicletă?
bi-chi-kle-tă?

Car

DETOUR	OCOLIRE
FREEWAY	AUTO-STRADĂ
GARAGE	GARAJ
GIVE WAY	CEDEAZĂ TRECEREA
MECHANIC	MECANIC
NO ENTRY	NU INTRAŢI
NO PARKING	NU PARCAŢI
NORMAL	NORMAL
ONE WAY	SENS UNIC
REPAIRS	REPARAŢII
SELF SERVICE	AUTOSERVIRE
STOP	STOP
SUPER	SUPER
UNLEADED	FĂRĂ PLUMB

Where can I rent a car?
un-de pot în-ki-ri-ah o   Unde pot închiria o maşină?
mah-shi-nă?
How much is it ...?
kît kos-tă ...?   Cît costă ...?
daily/weekly
pe zi/pe săp-tă-mî-nă   pe zi/pe săptămînă

ROMANIAN

Does that include insurance/
mileage?

> *in-klu-de shi*
> *ah-si-gu-rahreah/kos-tul*
> *ki-loh-me-trah-gul?*

Include şi asigurarea/costul
kilometragul?

Where's the next petrol
station?

> *un-de es-te ur-mă-toah-*
> *reah stah-tsi-e de*
> *ben-zi-nă?*

Unde este următoarea
staţie de benzină?

Please fill the tank.

> *te rog um-ple-mi re-zer-*
> *vo-rul*

Te rog umple-mi rezervorul.

I want ... litres of petrol (gas).

> *vreahu ... de li-tri de*
> *ben-zi-nă*

Vreau ... de litri de benzină.

Please check the oil and
water.

> *te rog ve-ri-fi-kă u-le-iul*
> *shi ah-pah*

Te rog verifică uleiul şi apa.

How long can I park
here?

> *kît timp pot pahr-kah*
> *ah-chi?*

Cît timp pot parca aici?

Does this road lead to ...?

> *es-te ah-ches-tah*
> *dru-mul spre ...?*

Este acesta drumul spre ...?

air (for tyres)	*ah-er*	aer
battery	*bah-te-ri-e*	baterie
brakes	*frî-ne*	frîne

clutch	*bor-nă/kle-mă/* *în-ki-ză-tor/ku-plă*	bornă/clemă/ închizător/cuplă
driver's licence	*per-mis de kon-du-* *che-re*	permis de condu- cere
engine	*mo-tor*	motor
lights	*lu-mi-ni*	lumini
oil	*u-lei*	ulei
puncture	*pah-nă (pah-nă de* *kah-u-chiuk)*	pană (pană de cauciuc)
radiator	*rah-di-ah-tor*	radiator
road map	*hahr-tă ru-ti-e-ră*	hartă rutieră
tyres	*kah-u-chiu-kuri*	cauciucuri
windscreen	*pahr-briz (geahm)*	parbriz (geam)

Car Problems

I need a mechanic.
   ahm ne-vo-ie de un   Am nevoie de un mecanic.
   me-ka-nik

What's wrong with it?
   che ah-re?   Ce are?

The battery is flat.
   bah-te-ri-ah es-te   Bateria este moartă.
   moahr-tă

The radiator is leaking.
   rah-di-ah-to-rul kur-ge   Radiatorul curge.

I have a flat tyre.
   ahm un kah-u-chiuk   Am un cauciuc dezumflat.
   de-zum-flaht

It's overheating.
   es-te su-prah-în-căl-zit   Este supraîncălzit.

It's not working.
  nu mer-ge   Nu merge.

Accommodation

CAMPING GROUND	CAMPING
GUEST HOUSE	CASA DE OASPEŢI
HOTEL	HOTEL
MOTEL	MOTEL
YOUTH HOSTEL	CĂMIN PENTRU

Where is ...?
  un-de es-te ...?   Unde este ...?
a cheap hotel   *un ho-tel ief-tin*   un hotel ieftin
a good hotel   *un ho-tel bun*   un hotel bun
a nearby hotel   *un ho-tel ah-pro-*   un hotel apropiat
                 pi-aht
a clean hotel   *un ho-tel ku-raht*   un hotel curat

What is the address?
  kah-rei ah-dre-sah?   Care-i adresa?
Could you write the address,
please?
  po-tsi să-mi skrii adresa,   Poţi să-mi scrii adresa,
  te rog?   te rog?

At the Hotel

Do you have any rooms available?

ah-vetsi kah-me-reh li-be-reh?	Aveţi camere libere?

I would like ...

ahsh do-ri ...		Aş dori ...
a single room	*o kah-me-ră de o per-soah-nă*	o cameră de o persoană
a double room	*o kah-me-ră du-blă*	o cameră dublă
a room with a bathroom	*o kah-me-ră ku bah-ie*	o cameră cu baie
to share a dorm	*ah îm-păr-tsi un dor-mi-tor*	a împărţi un dormitor
a bed	*un paht*	un pat

I want a room with a

vreahu o ka-me-ră ku ...		Vreau o cameră cu ...
bathroom	*bah-ie*	baie
shower	*dush*	duş
television	*te-le-vi-zor*	televizor
window	*fe-reahs-tră*	fereastră

I'm going to stay for ...

ahm să stahu ...		Am să stau ...
one day	*o zi*	o zi
two days	*do-uă zi-le*	două zile
one week	*o săp-tă-mî-nă*	o săptămînă

Do you have identification?
ah-ve-tsi ahk-te de?
iden-ti-tah-te?

Aveţiacte de identitate?

Your membership card,
please.
le-gi-ti-mah-tsi-ah de
mem-bru, vă rog

Legitimaţia de membru,
vă rog.

Sorry, we're full.
ne pah-re rău, es-te plin

Ne pare rău, este plin.

How long will you be
staying?
kît timp ve-tsi stah?

Cît timp veţi sta?

How many nights?
kît-te nop-tsi?

Cîte nopţi?

It's ... per day/per person.
es-te ... pe zi/de
per-soah-nă

Este ... pe zi/de persoană.

How much is it per night/
per person?
kît kos-tă pe noahp-te/
de per-soah-nă?

Cît costă pe noapte/
de persoană?

Can I see it?
pot să văd?

Pot să văd?

Are there any others?
mahi sînt shi ahl-te-le?

Mai sînt şi altele?

Are there any cheaper
rooms?
sînt shi kah-me-re mah
i ief-ti-ne?

Sînt şi camere mai ieftine?

Can I see the bathroom?
pot să văd bah-iah?

Pot să văd baia?

ROMANIAN

Is there a reduction for students/children?

ex-is-tă re-du-che-re pen-tru stu-den-tsi/ko-pii?

Există reducere pentru studenți/copii?

Does it include breakfast?

in-klu-de mi-kul de-zhun?

Include micul dejun?

It's fine, I'll take it.

es-te în re-gu-lă, îl (o) iahu

Este în regulă, îl (o) iau.

I'm not sure how long I'm staying.

nu sînt si-gur kît voi stah

Nu sînt sigur/ă cît voi sta.

Is there a lift?

ex-is-tă lift?

Există lift?

Where is the bathroom?

un-de es-te bah-iah?

Unde este baia?

Is there hot water all day?

es-te ah-pă kahl-dă to ah-tă zi-uah?

Este apă caldă toată ziua?

Do you have a safe where I can leave my valuables?

ah-vetsi un se-if un-de pot lă-sah vah-lo-ri-le?

Aveți un seif unde pot lăsa valorile?

Is there somewhere to wash clothes?

pot spă-lah un-de-vah hahi-ne?

Pot spăla undeva haine?

Can I use the kitchen?

pot fo-lo-si bu-kă-tă-ri-ah?

Pot folosi bucătăria?

Can I use the telephone?

pot fo-lo-si te-le-fo-nul?

Pot folosi telefonul?

Requests & Complaints

Please wake me up at ...
vă rog, tre-zi-tsi-mă la ...   Vă rog, treziți-mă la ...

The room needs to be
cleaned.
kah-me-rah tre-bu-ie   Camera trebuie curațată.
ku-ră-tsah-tă

Please change the sheets.
vă rog skim-bah-tsi   Vă rog schimbați cear
cheahr-cheah-fu-ri-le   ceafurile.

I can't open/close the
window.
nu pot des-ki-de/în-ki-de   Nu pot deschide/închide
fe-reahs-trah   fereastra.

I've locked myself out of
my room.
m-ahm în-ku-iaht în   M-am încuiat în afara
ah-fah-rah kah-me-rei   camerei.

The toilet won't flush.
to-ah-le-tah nu   Toaleta nu funcționează.
fun-ktsi-o-neah-ză

I don't like this room.
nu-mi plah-che   Nu-mi place camera aceasta.
kah-me-rah ah-cheahs-tah

It's too small.
es-te preah mi-kă   Este prea mică.

It's noisy.
es-te zgo-mo-toah-să   Este zgomotoasă.

It's too dark.
es-te preah în-tu-ne-ko   Este prea întunecoasă.
ah-să

It's expensive.
es-te skum-pă   Este scumpă.

Some Useful Words & Phrases

I am/We are leaving ...
eu plek/noi ple-kăm ...   Eu plec/Noi plecăm ...
now/tomorrow
ah-kum/mîi-ne   acum/mîine

I would like to pay the bill.
ahsh do-ri săplă-tesk   Aş dori săplătesc nota.
no-tah

name	*nu-me*	nume
surname	*pre-nu-me*	prenume
room number	*nu-mă-rul kah-me-rei*	numărul camerei
address	*ah-dre-să*	adresă
air-conditioned	*aher kon-di-tsi-o-naht*	aer condiţionat
balcony	*bahl-kon*	balcon
bathroom	*bah-ie*	baie
bed	*paht*	pat
bill	*no-tăde plah-tă*	notăde plată
blanket	*ku-ver-tu-ră /pă-tu-ră*	cuvertură/pătură
candle	*lu-mî-nah-re*	lumînare
chair	*skah-un*	scaun
clean	*ku-raht*	curat
cupboard	*bu-fet/du-lahp*	bufet/dulap
dark	*în-tu-ne-rik*	întuneric
dirty	*mur-dahr*	murdar
double bed	*paht du-blu*	pat dublu

ROMANIAN

English	Pronunciation	Romanian
electricity	*e-lek-tri-chi-tah-te*	electricitate
excluded	*ex-klus*	exclus
fan	*ven-ti-lah-tor/* *e-vahn-tahi*	ventilator/evantai
included	*in-klus*	inclus
key	*ke-ie*	cheie
lift (elevator)	*lift*	lift
light bulb	*bek*	bec
lock (n)	*lah-kăt/ză-vor/* *în-ku-ie-toah-re*	lacăt/zăvor/ încuietoare
mattress	*sahl-teah*	saltea
mirror	*o-glin-dă*	oglindă
padlock	*lah-kăt*	lacăt
pillow	*per-nă*	pernă
quiet	*li-nish-te*	linişte
room (in hotel)	*kah-me-ră de hotel*	cameră de hotel
sheet	*cheahr-cheahf*	cearceaf
shower	*dush*	duş
soap	*să-pun*	săpun
suitcase	*vah-li-ză*	valiză
swimming pool	*bah-zin de î-not/* *pis-chi-nă*	bazin de înot/ piscină
table	*mah-să*	masă
toilet	*toah-le-tă*	toaletă
toilet paper	*hîr-ti-e i-gi-e-ni-kă*	hîrtie igienică
towel	*pro-sop/shter-gahr*	prosop/ştergar
water	*ah-pă*	apă
cold water	*ah-pă re-che*	apă rece
hot water	*ah-pă kahl-dă*	apă caldă
window	*fe-reahs-tră*	fereastră

ROMANIAN

Around Town

I'm looking for ...

kah-ut .../sînt î kă-u-tah-reah ...   Caut .../Sînt în căutarea ...

the art gallery	*gah-le-ri-ah de ahr-tă*	galeria de artă
a bank	*o bahn-kă*	o bancă
the church	*bi-se-ri-kah*	biserica
the city centre	*chen-trul o-rah-shu-lui*	centrul orașului
the ... embassy	*ahm-bah-sah-dah*	ambasada ...
my hotel	*ho-te-lul meu*	hotelul meu
the market	*piah-tsa*	piața
the museum	*mu-ze-ul*	muzeul
the police	*po-li-tsi-ah*	poliția
the post office	*posh-tah*	poșta
a public toilet	*o to-ah-le-tă pu-bli-kă*	o toaletă publică
the telephone centre	*chen-trah-lah te-le-fo-ni-kă/ te-le-foah-ne-le*	centrala telefonică/ telefoanele
the tourist inform-ation office	*bi-roul de in-for-mah-tsii pen-tru tu-rism*	biroul de informaţii pentru turism

What ... is this?

che ... es-te?   Ce ... este?

street	*strah-dă*	stradă
suburb	*su-bur-bi-e*	suburbie

For directions, see the Getting Around section, page 327.

What time does it open?
kînd se des-ki-de?   Cînd se deschide?

What time does it close?
kînd se în-ki-de?   Cînd se închide?

At the Post Office

I would like some stamps.
ahsh do-ri kî-te-vah tim-bre   Aş dori cîteva timbre.

How much is the postage?
kît es-te tah-xah posh-tah-lă?   Cît este taxa poştală?

How much does it cost to send ... to ...?
kît kos-tă să tri-mi-tsi ... lah ...?   Cît costă să trimiţi ... la ...?

I would like to send ...
ahsh do-ri să tri-mit ...   Aş dori să trimit ...

a letter	*o skri-soah-re*	o scrisoare
a postcard	*o kahr-te posh-tah-lă*	o carte poştală
a parcel	*un pah-ket*	un pachet
a telegram	*o te-le-grah-mă*	o telegramă
an aerogram	*o ah-e-ro-grah-mă*	o aerogramă
air mail	*pahr ah-vi-on*	par avion
envelope	*plik*	plic
mail box	*ku-ti-e posh-tah-lă*	cutie poştală
parcel	*pah-ket*	pachet

registered mail	*skri-soah-re*	scrisoare
	re-ko-mahn-dah-tă	recomandată
surface mail	*skri-soah cu va-po-rul*	scrisoare cu vaporul

Telephone

If you want to call abroad you must wait 30 to 45 minutes, because Romania is not connected to the international direct telephone system.

I want to ring ...
    ahsh do-ri să sun ...   Aş dori să sun ...
The number is ...
    nu-mă-rul es-te ...   Numărul este ...
I want to speak for three minutes.
    vreahu să vor-besk trei   Vreau să vorbesc trei minute.
    mi-nu-te.
How much does a three-minute call cost?
    kît kos-tă o kon-vor-bi-re   Cît costă o convorbire
    de trei mi-nu-te?   de trei minute?
How much does each extra minute cost?
    kît kos-tă fie-kah-re mi-nu   Cît costă fiecare în plus?
    în plus?
I would like to speak to Mr Perez.
    ahsh do-ri să vor-besk ku   Aş dori să vorbesc cu domnul
    dom-nul Perez   Perez.

I want to make a reverse-
charges phone call.
   ahsh do-ri o kon-vor-bi-re   Aş dori o convorbire cu
   ku tah-xă in-ver-să   taxă inversă.
It's engaged.
   es-te o-ku-paht   Este ocupat.
I've been cut off.
   ahm fost în-tre-rupt/ă   Am fost întrerupt/ă.

At the Bank

It's difficult to transfer money from your bank to a Romanian
bank, so you should take sufficient money with you.

I want to exchange some
money/travellers' cheques.
   vreahu să skimb che-vah   Vreau să schimb ceva bani/
   bahni/che-ku-ri   cecuri.
What is the exchange
rate?
   kah-re es-te rah-tah   Care este rata de schimb?
   de schimb?
How many lei per
dollar?
   kî-tsi lei pen-tru un   Cîţi lei pentru un dolar?
   do-lahr?
Can I have money transferred
here from my bank?
   se pot trahn-sfe-rah   Se pot transfera bani aici din
   bah-ni ah-ichi din   banca mea?
   bahn-kah meah?

How long will it take to
arrive?

kît du-reah-ză pî-nă   Cît durează pînă ajung?
ah-zhung?

Has my money arrived yet?

ahu ah-zhuns bah-nii mei? Au ajuns banii mei?

bankdraft	*bi-let de bahn-kă po-li-tsă*	bilet de bancă poliţa
bank notes	*bahn-kno-te*	bancnote
cashier	*kah-si-er*	casier
coins	*mo-ne-de*	monede
credit card	*kahr-te de kre-dit*	carte de cerdit
exchange	*skimb*	schimb
loose change	*mă-runt/mă-run-zish*	mărunt/mărunţis
signature	*sem-nă-tu-ră*	semnătură

Sightseeing

Do you have a guidebook/
local map?

ah-vetsi un ghid/   Aveţi un ghid/o hartă locală?
o hahr-tă lokah-lă?

What are the main attractions?

kah-re sînt prin-chi- Care sînt principalele atracţii?
pah-le-le ah-trahk-tsii

What is that?

che es-te ah-cheahs-tah? Ce este aceasta?

How old is it?

kît de veki (m)/*ve-ke* (f) Cît de vechi/veche este?
es-te?

sleeping bag	*sahk de dor-mit*	sac de dormit
stove	*so-bă/kup-tor*	sobă/cuptor
water bottle	*plos-kă*	ploscă

Food

Work for Romanians begins at 7 am and ends at 3 to 3.30 pm. People generally have a break (pauză de masă) when they eat a sandwich snack, or drink coffee, but they don't leave their offices. At 4 pm they have lunch.

Most eating places in Romania have recognisable names, such as 'snack bar'. Here are some useful words:

restaurant cu autoservire − self-service restaurant
bufet lacto − milk bar
restaurant de categoria întîi − 1st-class restaurant
restaurant de lux − deluxe restaurant
restaurant lactovegetarian − vegetarian restaurant

Table for ..., please.
   mah-să pen-tru ..., vărog   Masă pentru ..., vărog.
Can I see the menu please?
   pot ve-deah me-ni-ul,   Pot vedea meniul, vă rog?
   vă rog?
I would like the set lunch, please.
   ahsh do-ri prîn-zul, vărog   Aș dori prînzul, vărog.
What does it include?
   che in-klu-de?   Ce include?

Can I take photographs?
   pot fo-to-grah-fi-ah?   Pot fotografia?
What time does it open/close?
   kînd se des-ki-de/în-ki-de?   Cînd se deschide/înde?

ancient	*veki/ahn-tik*	vechi/antic
archaeological	*ahr-he-o-lo-gik*	arheologic
beach	*plah-zhă*	plajă
building	*klă-di-re*	clădire
castle	*kahs-tel*	castel
cathedral	*kah-te-drah-lă*	catedrală
church	*bi-se-ri-kă*	biserică
concert hall	*sah-lă de kon-chert*	sală de concert
library	*bi-bli-o-te-kă*	bibliotecă
main square	*piah-tsa prin-chi-pah-lă*	piața principală
market	*piah-tsa*	piața
monastery	*mă-năs-ti-re*	mănăstire
monument	*mo-nu-ment*	monument
mosque	*mos-kee*	moschee
old city	*ve-kiul o-rahsh*	vechiul oraș
palace	*pah-laht*	palat
opera house	*o-pe-rah/ klă-di-reah o-pe-rei*	opera/ clădirea operei
ruins	*ru-i-ne*	ruine
stadium	*stah-di-on*	stadion
statues	*stah-tui*	statui
synagogue	*si-nah-go-gă*	sinagogă
temple	*tem-plu*	templu
university	*u-ni-ver-si-tah-te*	universitate

ROMANIAN

Entertainment

What's there to do in the evenings?

che se poah-te fah-che seah-rah?	Ce se poate face seara?

Are there any discos?

sînt dis-ko-techi?	Sînt discoteci?

Are there places where you can hear local folk music?

sînt lo-kuri un-de se poah-te ahs-kul-tah mu-zi-kă po-pu-lah-ră?	Sînt locuri unde se poate asculta muzică populară?

cinema	*chi-ne-mah*	cinema
concert	*kon-chert*	concert
discotheque	*dis-ko-te-kă*	discotecă
theatre	*teah-tru*	teatru

In the Country

Weather

What's the weather like?

kum es-te tim-pul?	Cum este timpul?

The weather is ... today.

tim-pul es-te ... ahzi	Timpul este ... azi.

Will it be ... tomorrow?

vah fi ... mîi-ne?	Va fi ... mîine?

cloudy	*no-ros*	noros
cold	*re-che*	rece
foggy	*che-tsos*	cetos
frosty	*ge-ros*	geros
hot	*kahld*	cald
raining	*plo-ios*	ploios
snowing	*nin-ge*	ninge
sunny	*în-so-rit*	însorit
windy	*ku vînt/suf-lă vîn-tul*	cu vînt/suflă vîntul

Camping

Am I allowed to camp here?

pt să kahm-pez ah-ichi?	Pot să campez aici?

Is there a campsite nearby?

ah-vetsi vre-un kahm-ping în ah-pro-pi-e-re?	Aveți vreun camping în apropiere?

backpack	*ruk-sahk*	rucsac
can opener	*des-fă-kă-tor de kon-ser-ve*	desfăcător de conserve
compass	*în-tin-de-re, ku-prins*	întindere, cuprir
crampons	*krahm-poah-ne*	crampoane
firewood	*lem-ne de fok*	lemne de foc
gas cartridge	*lahm-pă ku gaz*	lampă cu gaz
hammock	*hah-mak*	hamac
ice axe	*pi-o-let*	piolet
mattress	*sahl-teah*	saltea
penknife	*bri-cheag*	briceag
rope	*frîn-ghi-e/sfoah-ră*	frînghie/sfo
tent	*kort*	cort
tent pegs	*tsă-rush*	țăruș
torch (flashlight)	*fă-kli-e/tor-tsă*	făclie/tort

Is service included in the bill?
es-te in-klus ser-vi-chiul   Este inclus serviciul în notă?
în no-tă?
Not too spicy.
nu preah kon-di-men-taht   Nu prea condimentat.

breakfast	*mik de-zhun*	mic dejun
lunch	*de-zhun, prînz*	dejun, prînz
dinner	*cină*	chi-nă
ashtray	*skru-mi-e-ră*	scrumieră
the bill	*no-ta*	nota
cup	*cheahsh-kă*	ceaşcă
dessert	*de-sert*	desert
drink	*bă-u-tu-ră*	băutură
fork	*fur-ku-li-tsă*	furculiţă
fresh	*proahs-păt*	proaspăt
glass	*pah-hahr*	pahar
knife	*ku-zit·*	cuţit
plate	*fahr-fu-ri-e*	farfurie
spicy	*kon-di-men-taht*	condimentat
spoon	*lin-gu-ră*	lingură
stale	*veki, în-ve-kit*	vechi, învechit
sweet	*dul-che*	dulce
teaspoon	*lin-gu-ri-tsă*	linguriţă
toothpick	*sko-bi-toah-re*	scobitoare

Vegetarian Meals
Vegetarian restaurants are not common and often have a very small menu.

ROMANIAN

I am a vegetarian.
eu sînt ve-ge-tah-ri-ahn Eu sînt vegetarian.

I don't eat meat.
eu nu mă-nînk kahr-ne Eu nu mănînc.

I don't eat chicken, fish or ham.
eu nu mă-nînk pui, sahu pesh-te, sahu shun-kă Eu nu mănînc pui, sau peşte, sau şuncă.

Soups
Ciorbă/Supă

bean soup	*ciorbă de fasole*
clear soup	*supă*
fish soup	*ciorbă de peste*
noodle soup	*supă cu tăiţei*
potato soup	*supă de cartofi*
vegetable soup	*supă de legume*

Meat, Fish & Poultry
Carne & Peşte

beefsteak	*bifteč*
duck	*raţă*
fish	*peşte*
goulash	*gulaş*
roast beef	*friptură de vacă*
roast chicken	*friptură de pui*
roast meat	*friptură*

Vegetable
Legume

beans	*fasole*
cabbage	*varză*
cauliflower	*conopida*

cucumber	*castravete*
garlic	*usturoi*
green beans	*fasole verde*
green peas	*mazăre verde*
green pepper	*ardei gras*
lettuce	*salată verda*
mushroom	*ciupercă*
onion	*ceapă*
potato	*cartof*
spinach	*spanac*

Rice & Pasta

macaroni	*macaroane*
rice	*orez*
spaghetti	*spaghete*

Salads & Garnish — Salată şi Garnitură

cold meat salad	*salată de boeuf*
cucumber salad	*salată de castraveţi*
eggplant salad	*salată de vinete*
lettuce and tomato salad	*salată verde cu roşii*
oriental salad	*salată orientală*
pickled cucumbers	*castraveţi muraţi*
pickles	*murături*
salad	*salată*

Methods of Cooking

boiled	*fiert*
chopped	*tocat*
fried	*prăjiţi*

ROMANIAN

| grilled | *grătar* |
| mashed | *piure* |

Fruit	**Fructe**
apples	*mere*
bananas	*banane*
grapes	*struguri*
oranges	*portocale*
peaches	*piersici*
plums	*prune*

Desserts	**Desert**
biscuits	*biscuiti*
cake	*prăjitură*
dessert	*desert*
doughnuts	*gogoşi*
nuts	*nuci*
ice cream	*îngheţată*
pancakes	*clătite*
pastry	*produse de patiserie*
pie	*plăcintă*
pudding	*budincă*
stewed fruit	*compot*
sweet biscuit	*pişcot/biscuit*

Breakfast & Dinner

A Romanian breakfast consists of a selection of the following foods, with tea, milk, white and black coffee. Dinner very much resembles breakfast, although without the black coffee.

bread	*pîne*
butter	*unt*
cheese	*brînză*
fried eggs	*ouă prăjite*
jam	*gem*
marmelade	*marmeladă*
poached eggs	*ouă ochiuri*
salami	*salam*
soft/hard boiled eggs	*ouă fierte moi/tari*

Lunch – 1st Course   Dejun/Prînz – Primul Fel

ciorbă de burtă
  White soup made of a small quantity of vegetables and large quantities of beef tripe. *Ciorbă* means sour soup and is typical of many Romanian dishes.

ciorbă de perisoare
  Soup made with vegetables and balls of minced meat.

ciorbă de văcuță
  Soup of vegetables and beef.

ciorbă
  Soup made out of vegetables (carrots, onion, green pepper), meat (pork, beef or poultry) with minced parsley. Some people like to eat it with sour cream.

supă cu tăieţei
  Clear soup (with vermicelli) or noodle soup native to Transylvania.

Lunch – 2nd Course　　　　Dejun/Prînz – Felul Doi

sarmale

Stuffed cabbage with minced pork meat, rice, spices. Each leaf of the cabbage (fresh or sour) is stuffed with this mixture and then rolled up. It is usually served with sour cream and hominy, 'mămăligă' (coarsely ground maize flour). The hominy is served also with cottage cheese/fresh cheese, 'brînză', and sour cream or milk.

friptură de porc cu salată

Roast pork with vegetable salad.

The third course consists of pancakes, fruit or pastry. A specifically Romanian dish served at picnics or on weekends is *mititei*: minced pork and mutton meat with spices. It is roasted on a grill and served with mustard.

Nonalcoholic Drinks	Băuturi Nealcoolice
black coffee	*cafea*
cold	*rece*
ice	*gheaţ*
fruit juice	*suc de fructe*
juice	*suc*
milk	*lapte*
mineral water	*apă minerală*
soda	*sifon*
soft drinks	*băuturi răcoritoare*
tea	*ceai*
water	*apă*
white coffee	*cafea cu lapte*

ROMANIAN

Alcoholic Drinks

	Băuturi Alcoolice
beer	*bere*
black beer	*bere neagră*
white beer	*bere blondă*
brandy	*ţuica*
cognac	*coniac*
liqueur	*lichior*
plum brandy – very strong	*ţuieă*
wine	*vin*
red wine	*vin roşu*
white wine	*vin alb*
whisky	*whisky*

Shopping

How much (is it)?
  kît kos-tă?   Cît costă?

bookshop	*li-bră-ri-e*	librărie
camera shop	*mah-gah-zin*	magazin
clothing store	*mah-gah-zin de*	magazin de
	îm-bră-kă-min-te	îmbrăcăminte
delicatessen	*de-li-kah-te-se*	delicatese
general store,	*mah-gah-zin ge-ne-*	magazin general/
shop	*rahl/u-ni-ver-sahl*	universal
laundry	*spă-lă-to-ri-e*	spălatorie
market	*piah-tsă*	piaţă
newsagency/	*ah-gen-zi-e de shti-ri/*	agenţie de ştiri/
stationers	*pah-pe-tă-ri-e*	papetărie
pharmacy	*fahr-mah-chi-e*	farmacie

ROMANIAN

shoeshop	mah-gah-zin de în-kăl-tsă-min-te	magazin de încălţăminte
souvenir shop	mah-gah-zin de kah-do-uri	magazin de cadouri
supermarket	su-per-mah-gah-zin/ su-per-mahr-ket	supermagazin/ supermarket
vegetable shop	ah-pro-zahr	aprozar

I would like to buy ...
ahsh do-ri să kum-păr ...   Aş dori să cumpăr ...

Do you have others?
ah-vetsi ahlt-che-vah?   Aveţi altceav?

I don't like it.
nu îmi plah-che   Nu îmi place.

Can I look at it?
pot să mă uit?   Pot să mă uit?

I'm just looking.
doahr mă uit   Doar mă uit.

Can you write down the price?
pu-te-tsi să-mi skri-etsi pre-tsul?   Puteţi să-mi scrieţi preţul?

Do you accept credit cards?
ahk-chep-tahtsi kăr-ti de kre-dit?   Acceptaţi cărţi de credit?

Could you lower the price?
pu-te-tsi skă-deah din prets?   Puteţi scădea din preţ?

I don't have much money.
nu ahm des-tui bahni   Nu am destui bani.

Can I help you?
vă pot ah-zhu-tah?   Vă pot ajuta?
Will that be all?
ah-cheahs-tah es-te tot?   Aceasta este tot?
Would you like it wrapped?
do-ritsi să-l îm-pah-ke-tez?   Doriţi să-l împachetez?
Sorry, this is the only one.
imi pah-re rău, es-te   Imi pare rău, este singurul
sin-gu-rul (sin-gu-rah)   (singura).
How much/many do you
want?
kî-tsi/kî-te do-ri-tsi?   Cîţi/cîte doriţi?

Souvenirs

earrings	*cher-chei*	cercei
handicraft	*ahr-ti-zah-naht*	artizanat
necklace	*ko-li-er*	colier
pottery	*o-bi-ek-te de o-lă-rit*	obiecte de olărit
ring	*i-nel*	inel
rug	*kahr-pe-tă, ko-vor*	carpetă, covor

Clothing

clothing	*îm-bră-kă-min-te, hahi-ne*	îmbrăcăminte, haine
coat	*pahl-ton*	palton
dress	*ro-ki-e*	rochie
jacket	*zhah-ke-tă*	jachetă
jumper (sweater)	*pu-lo-ver, sve-ter*	pulovăr, sveter
shirt	*tri-kou, kă-mah-shă*	tricou, cămaşă
shoes	*pahn-to-fi*	pantofi

skirt	*fus-tă*	fustă
trousers	*pahn-tah-loni*	pantaloni

It doesn't fit.
   nu es-te bun/nu mer-ge   Nu este bun/Nu merge.

It is too ...
   es-te preah ...   Este prea ...

big/small	*mah-re/mik*	mare/mic
short/long	*skurt/lung*	scurt/lung
tight/loose	*strîmt/ lahrg*	strîmt/ larg

Materials

cotton	*bum-bahk*	bumbac
handmade	*lu-kraht de mî-nă/ mah-nu-ahl*	lucrat de mînă/ manual
leather	*pi-e-le*	piele
of brass	*din bronz/ah-lah-mă*	din bronz/alamă
of gold	*din ah-ur*	din aur
of silver	*din ahr-gint*	din argint
pure alpaca	*ahl-pah-ka pu-ră*	alpaca pură
silk	*mă-tah-se*	mătase
wool	*lî-nă*	lînă

Colours

black	*ne-gru*	negru
blue	*ahl-bahs-tru*	albastru
brown	*mah-ro*	maro
green	*ver-de*	verde

ROMANIAN

pink	roz	roz
purple	pur-pu-riu	purpuriu
red	ro-shu	roşu
white	ahlb	alb
yellow	gahl-ben	galben

Toiletries

comb	piep-ten (piep-te-ne)	piepten (pieptene)
condoms	pre-zer-vah-ti-ve	prezervative
deodorant	de-o-do-rahnt	deodorant
hairbrush	pe-ri-e de păr	perie de păr
moisturising cream	kre-mă grah-să	cremă grasă
razor	lah-mă	lamă
sanitary napkins	sher-ve-tse-le i-gi-e-ni-che	şerveţele igienice
shampoo	shahm-pon	şampon
shaving cream	kre-mă de rahs	cremă de ras
soap	să-pun	săpun
sunblock cream	kre-mă de soah-re	cremă de soare
tampons	tahm-poah-ne	tampoane
tissues	fe-she	feşe
toilet paper	hîr-ti-e i-gi-e-ni-kă	hîrtie igienică
toothbrush	pe-ri-e de din-tsi	perie de dinţi
toothpaste	pahs-tă de din-tsi	pastă de dinţi

Stationery & Publications

| map | hahr-tă | hartă |
| newspaper | zi-ahr | ziar |

ROMANIAN

newspaper in English	zi-ah-re în en-gle-ză	ziare în engleză
novels in English	ro-mah-ne în en-gle-ză	romane în engleză
paper	hîr-ti-e	hîrtie
pen (ballpoint)	sti-lou (pix)	stilou (pix)
scissors	foahr-fe-kă	foarfecă

Photography

How much is it to process this film?

   kît du-reah-ză pro-che-sah-reah fil-mu-lui? — Cît durează procesarea filmului?

When will it be ready?

   kînd vah fi gah-tah? — Cînd va fi gata?

I'd like a film for this camera.

   ahsh do-ri un film pen-tru ah-chest ah-pah-raht — Aş dori un film pentru acest aparat.

B&W (film)	ahlb-ne-gru	alb-negru
camera	ah-pah-raht fo-to-grah-fik	aparat fotografic
colour (film)	ko-lor (film)	color (film)
film	film	film
flash	blitz	blitz
lens	len-ti-le	lentile
light meter	di-ah-frahg-mă	diafragmă

Smoking

A packet of cigarettes.
  un pah-ket de tsi-gări Un pachet de ţigarări.
Are these cigarettes strong/
mild?
  sînt ah-ches-te tsi-gări Sînt aceste ţigări tari/slabe?
  tahri/slah-be?
Do you have a light?
  ah-ve-tsi un fok? Aveţi un foc?

cigarette papers	*fo-i-ză de tsi-gah-ră*	foiţă de ţigară
cigarettes	*tsi-gări*	ţigări
filtered	*ku fil-tru*	cu filtru
lighter	*slah-be/u-shoah-re*	slabe/uşoare
matches	*ki-bri-turi*	chibrituri
menthol	*men-to-lah-te*	mentolate
pipe	*pi-pă*	pipă
tobacco (pipe)	*tu-tun*	tutun

Sizes & Comparisons

small	*mik*	mic
big	*mah-re*	mare
heavy	*greu*	greu
light	*u-shor*	uşor
more	*mahi mult*	mai mult
less	*mahi pu-tsin*	mai puţin
too much/many	*preah mult/mul-te*	prea mult/multe
many	*mul-te*	multe
enough	*des-tul*	destul
a little bit	*un pik/pu-tsin*	un pic/puţin

Health

Every Romanian village and town has a health facility. In the cities there are hospitals and clinics. The prices for medicines are quite low.

Where is the ...?
   un-de es-te ...?   Unde este ...?

doctor	*dok-to-rul*	doctorul
hospital	*spi-tah-lul*	spitalul
chemist	*fahr-mah-chis-tul*	farmacistul
dentist	*den-tis-tul*	dentistul

I am sick
   sînt bol-nav   Sînt bolnav.

My friend is sick.
   pri-e-te-nul meu es-te   Prietenul meu este bolnav.
   bol-nahv

Could I see a female doctor?
   ahsh pu-teah ve-deah o   Aş putea vedea o doctoriţă?
   dok-to-ri-tsă?

What's the matter?
   kah-re es-te pro-ble-mah?   Care este problema?
   che s-ah în-tîm-plaht?   Ce s-a întîmplat?

Where does it hurt?
   che vă doah-re?   Ce vă doare?

It hurts here.
   mădoah-re ah-ichi   Mă doare aici.

My ... hurts.
   mă doah-re ...   Mă doare ...

ROMANIAN

Parts of the Body

ankle	*glez-nah*	glezna
arm	*brah-tsul*	brațul
back	*spah-te-le*	spatele
chest	*piep-tul*	pieptul
ear	*u-re-keah*	urechea
eye	*o-kiul*	ochiul
finger	*de-ge-tul*	degetul
foot	*lah-bah pi-chio-nu-lui*	laba piciorului
hand	*mî-nah*	mîna
head	*kah-pul*	capul
heart	*i-ni-mah*	inima
leg	*pi-chio-rul*	piciorul
mouth	*gu-rah*	gura
nose	*nah-sul*	nasul
ribs	*koahs-te-le*	coastele
skin	*pie-leah*	pielea
spine	*ko-loah-nah ver-te-brah-lă*	coloana vertebrală
teeth	*din-tsii*	dinții
throat	*gî-tul*	gîtul

Ailments

I have ...

eu ahm ...		Eu am ...
an allergy	*o ah-ler-gi-e*	o alergie
anaemia	*ah-ne-mi-e*	anemie
a burn	*o ahr-su-ră*	o arsură
a cold	*o ră-cheah-lă*	o răceală
constipation	*kon-sti-pah-tsi-e*	constipație

a cough	*o tu-se/ră-cheach-lă*	o tuse/răceală
diarrhoea	*di-ah-ree*	diaree
fever	*fe-bră*	febră
a headache	*o du-re-re de kahp*	o durere de cap
hepatitis	*he-pah-ti-tă*	hepatită
indigestion	*in-di-ges-ti-e*	indigestie
an infection	*o in-fek-tsi-e*	o infecție
influenza	*gri-pă*	gripă
lice	*pă-duki*	păduchi
low/high blood pressure	*hi-po/ hi-per-ten-si-u-ne*	hipo/hipertensiune
a pain	*o du-re-re*	o durere
sore throat	*du-re-re de gît*	durere de gît
sprain	*o ră-su-chi-re/ lu-xah-tsi-e*	o răsucire/luxație
a stomachache	*o du-re-re de sto-mahk*	o durere de stomac
sunburn	*ahr-su-ră de soah-re*	arsură de soare
a venereal disease	*o boah-lăve-ne-ri-kă*	o boalăvenerică
worms	*vier-mi in-tes-ti-nahli*	viermi intestinali

Some Useful Words & Phrases

I'm ...

(eu) sînt ...		(Eu) Sînt ...
diabetic	*di-ah-be-tik*	diabetic
epileptic	*e-pi-lep-tik*	epileptic
asthmatic	*ahst-mah-tik*	astmatic

I'm allergic to antibiotics/
penicillin.

*(eu) sînt ah-ler-gik
ă lah ahn-ti-bi-o-ti-che/
pe-ni-chi-li-nă*

(Eu) Sînt alergic
ă la antibiotice/
penicilină.

I'm pregnant.

(eu) sînt grah-vi-dă

(Eu) Sînt gravidă.

I'm on the pill.

*iahu pi-lu-le
an-ti-kon-chep-tsio-nah-le*

Iau pilule anticoncepționale.

I haven't had my period for
... months.

*nu ahm ah-vut
men-stru-ah-tsi-e de... luni*

Nu am avut
menstruație de ... luni.

I have been vaccinated.

*(eu) ahm fost vahk-chi-
naht/ă*

(Eu) Am fost vaccinat/ă

I have my own syringe.

*(eu) ahm si-rin-gă
pro-prie*

(Eu) Am siringă proprie.

I feel better/worse.

*(eu) măsimt mahi bi-ne/
rău.*

(Eu) Măsimt mai bine/rău.

accident	*ahk-chi-dent*	accident
addiction	*vi-chiu/pah-si-u-ne*	viciu/pasiune
antibiotics	*ahn-ti-bi-o-ti-che*	antibiotice
antiseptic	*ahn-ti-sep-tik*	antiseptic
aspirin	*ahs-pi-ri-nă*	aspirină
bandage	*bahn-dahzh*	bandaj
bite	*mush-kă-tu-ră/*	mușcătura

blood pressure	*ten-si-u-ne*	tensiune
blood test	*tes-tul sîn-ge-lui*	testul sîngelui
contraceptive	*kon-trah-chep-ti-ve*	contraceptive
injection	*in-zhek-tsi-e*	injecţie
injury	*rah-nă/le-zi-u-ne*	rană/leziune
medicine	*me-di-kah-ment*	medicament
menstruation	*men-stru-ah-tsi-e*	menstruaţie
nausea	*greah-tsă/*	greaţă/ameţeală
	ah-me-tseah-lă	
oxygen	*o-xi-gen*	oxigen
vitamins	*vi-tah-mi-ne*	vitamine
wound	*plah-gă/rah-nă*	plagă/rană

At the Chemist

I need medication for ...
ahm ne-vo-ie de me-di-   Am nevoie de
kah-men-te pen-tru ...   medicamente pentru ...
I have a prescription.
ahm o re-tse-tă   Am o reţetă.

At the Dentist

I have a toothache.
ahm o du-re-re de din-tsi   Am o durere de dinţi.
I've lost a filling.
mi-ah că-zut o plom-bă   Mi-a căzut o plombă.
I've broken a tooth.
mi-ahm spahrt un din-te   Mi-am spart un dinte.
My gums hurt.
mădor gin-gi-i-le   Mădor gingiile.

I don't want it extracted.

nu vreahu să o ex-trahg   Nu vreau să o extrag.

Please give me an anaesthetic.

vă rog dah-tsi-mi un   Vă rog daţi-mi un anestezic.
ah-nes-te-zik

Time & Dates

Romanians use both the 12-hour and 24-hour clocks. The 24-hour clock is the more formal system used in print and conversation. The 12-hour system is more casual.

Telling the time is very simple! You only need to say the hour and after that the minutes, and between the hour and minutes you can introduce *şi,* 'and'. For example, 4.05 is *patru şi cinci.*

What time is it?

che o-ră es-te?   Ce oră este?

What date is it today?

che dah-tă es-te ahs-tăzi?   Ce dată este astăzi?

It is ... am/pm

es-te ... ah-em/pe-em   Este ... am/pm

in the morning	*di-mi-neah-tsah*	dimineaţa
in the afternoon	*du-pă-ah-miah-zah*	după-amiaza
in the evening	*seah-rah*	seara

Days of the Week

Monday	*lu-ni*	Luni
Tuesday	*mahr-tsi*	Marţi

Wednesday	*mier-kuri*	Miercuri
Thursday	*zhoi*	Joi
Friday	*vi-neri*	Vineri
Saturday	*sîm-bă-tă*	Sîmbătă
Sunday	*du-mi-ni-kă*	Duminică

Months

January	*iah-nu-ah-ri-e*	Ianuarie
February	*fe-bru-ah-ri-e*	Februarie
March	*mahr-ti-e*	Martie
April	*ah-pri-li-e*	Aprilie
May	*mahi*	Mai
June	*iu-ni-e*	Iunie
July	*iu-li-e*	Iulie
August	*ahu-gust*	August
September	*sep-tem-bri-e*	Septembrie
October	*ok-tom-bri-e*	Octombrie
November	*no-iem-bri-e*	Noiembrie
December	*de-chem-bri-e*	Decembrie

Seasons

summer	*vah-ră*	vară
autumn	*toahm-nă*	toamnă
winter	*iahr-nă*	iarnă
spring	*pri-mă-vah-ră*	primăvară

Present

| today | *ahs-tăzi* | astăzi |
| this morning | *ahzi di-mi-neah-tsa* | azi dimineață |

tonight	*în noahp-teah ah-cheahs-tah*	în noaptea aceasta
this week	*săp-tă-mî-nah ah-cheahs-ta*	săptămîna aceasta
this year	*ah-nul ah-ches-ta*	anul acesta
now	*ah-kum*	acum

Past

yesterday	*ieri*	ieri
day before yesterday	*ah-lahl-tă-ieri*	alaltăieri
yesterday morning	*ieri di-mi-neah-tsa*	ieri dimineaţa
last night	*noahp-teah tre-ku-tă*	noaptea trecută
last week/year	*săp-tă-mî-nah tre-ku-tă*	săptămîna trecută

Future

tomorrow	*mîi-ne*	mîine
day after tomorrow	*poi-mîi-ne*	poimiine
tomorrow morning	*mîi-ne di-mi-neah-tsa*	mîine dimineaţă
tomorrow afternoon/ evening	*mîi-ne du-pă-ah-miah-ză/ seah-ră*	mîine după-amiază/ seară
next week	*săp-tă-mî-nah vi-i-toah-re*	săptămîna viitoare
next year	*ah-nul vi-i-tor*	anul viitor

During the Day

afternoon	*du-pă-ah-miah-ză*	după-amiază
dawn	*în zori*	în zori
day	*zi*	zi
early	*de-vre-me*	devreme
midnight	*mie-zul nop-tsii*	miezul nopţii
morning	*di-mi-naeh-tsah*	dimineaţa
night	*noahp-teah*	noaptea
noon	*ah-miah-zah*	amiază
sundown	*ahs-fin-tsit*	asfinţit
sunrise	*ră-să-rit*	răsărit

Numbers & Amounts

0	*ze-ro*	zero
1	*u-nu*	unu
2	*doi*	doi
3	*trei*	trei
4	*pah-tru*	patru
5	*chinchi*	cinci
6	*shah-se*	şase
7	*shahp-te*	şapte
8	*opt*	opt
9	*no-uă*	nouă
10	*ze-che*	zece
20	*do-uă-zechi*	douăzeci
30	*trei-zechi*	treizeci
40	*pah-tru-zechi*	patruzeci
50	*chinchi-zechi*	cincizeci
60	*shahi-zechi*	şaizeci
70	*shahp-te-zechi*	şaptexeci

80	*opt-zechi*	optzeci
90	*no-uă-zechi*	nouăzeci
100	*o su-tă*	o sută
1000	*o mi-e*	o mie
one million	*un mi-li-on*	un milion
1st	*pri-mul*	primul (1-ul)
2nd	*ahl doi-leah*	al doilea (al 2-lea)
3rd	*ahl trei-leah*	al treilea (al 3-lea)
1/4	*un sfert/o pă-tri-me*	un sfert/o pătrime
1/3	*o tre-i-me*	o treime
1/2	*zhu-mă-tah-te/*	jumătate/o doime
	o do-i-me	
3/4	*trei sfer-turi/*	trei sferturi/
	trei pă-trimi	trei pătrimi

Some Useful Words

a little (amount)	*pu-tsin*	puţin
double	*du-blu*	dublu
a dozen	*o du-zi-nă*	o duzină
Enough!	*des-tul!*	Destul!
few	*chî-te-vah*	cîteva
less	*pu-tsin*	puţin
many	*mul-tsi/mul-te*	mulţi/multe
more	*mahi mult/mul-tă*	mai mult/multă
once	*o dah-tă*	o dată
percent	*pro-chent*	procent
some	*kî-te-vah*	cîteva
too much	*preah mult*	prea mult
twice	*de do-uăori*	de douăori

Abbreviations

C.E.	Comunitatea Europeană	EU
Dl	Domnul	Mr
D-na	Doamna	Mrs
D-şoara	Domnişoara	Miss
e.n./î.e.n.	era noastră/înaintea erei noastre	AD/BC
N/S	Nord/Sud	Nth/Sth
O.N.U.	Organizaţia Naţiunilor Unite	UN
SIDA		AIDS
Str	strada	St
S.U.A.	Statele Unite ale Americii	USA

ROMANIAN

Slovak

Introduction

The Slovak language belongs to the Western branch of the Slavonic languages, and is the standard language of the six million people living in Slovakia, as well as nearly two million people living beyond the country's borders.

Slovak evolved into a separate Slavonic language between the 9th and the 15th centuries, and was associated with the development of a national Slovak culture at a time when Slovakia's territory and the surrounding regions were dominated by Latin at religious, administrative and literary level. In the 17th century Slovakia found itself at the eastern border of Christian Europe, and the rules of Slovak were written down for the first time. However, Slovak emerged only in the mid-19th century in the course of a national revival as a uniform literary language.

Of all Slavonic languages the one which bears the closest resemblance to Slovak is Czech. This should come as no surprise, since Slovakia and the Czech lands have strong ties dating back to the 9th century and the Great Moravian Empire, where one common language (Old Church Slavonic) was in use. Modern Slovak and Czech are, in general, mutually understandable, but you are well advised not to substitute one for the other. The linguistic territory of each language includes many regional dialects, and these form a continuum across present and past political boundaries, so that, for example, the East Slovak dialect is closer to the West Ukrainian dialect than to the standard Czech language.

Standard Slovak recognizes two forms of address corresponding to English 'you': formal *Vy* and more familiar *ty*. This phrasebook uses the polite form *Vy*, since in Slovak it is considered the appropriate form when initiating conversation or addressing strangers.

Pronunciation

Slovak is basically a phonetic language (ie written as it sounds) and not as difficult as it may look at first sight. It may help to remember that Slovak makes use of only four diacritical marks; the two found most frequently are the length mark (for example **é**) and the softening mark (for example **ď**), and the other two are limited to the letters **ä** and **ô**.

Vowels

The Slovak language has six short vowels **a, ä, e, i, o, u, y** and five long vowels **á, é, í, ó, ú, ý**. It is important to observe their different pronunciation, as detailed below, since vowel length may determine the meaning of a word.

a	as the 'u' in 'cup'	**á**	as the 'a' in 'father'
ä	as the 'a' in 'fat'	**é**	as the 'ea' in 'bear'
e	as in 'bed'	**í**	as the 'ee' in 'feet'
i	as the 'y' in 'sorry'	**ó**	as the 'a' in 'mall'
o	as in 'pot'	**ú**	as the 'oo' in 'choose'
u	as the 'oo' in 'book'	**ý**	as the 'ee' in 'feet'
y	as the 'i' in 'bit'		

Diphthongs

There are four diphthongs in Slovak: three diphthongs **ia, ie, iu** which are pronounced phonetically, and the diphthong **ô** which is pronounced 'uo' like the sound in 'swan'.

Consonants

The consonants **b**, **d**, **f**, **g**, **l**, **m**, **n**, **s**, **v**, **z** are pronounced approximately as in English.

c	as the 'ts' in 'lots'
č	as the 'ch' in 'China'
ch	is similar to the Scottish 'ch' in 'loch' or German 'ch' in 'Nacht'
ď, ť, ň, ľ	correspond to the English sounds 'dy, ty, ny, ly' in 'during', 'tutor', 'new', 'lure'
dz	is similar to the 'ds' in 'roads' or Italian 'z' in 'zero'
dž	as the 'j' in 'jeans'
h	as the 'h' in 'hand' but pronounced more forcefully
j	as the 'y' in 'yes'
k, p, t	are never aspirated
ĺ, ŕ	long ĺ and ŕ are given as a test piece for students of the Slovak language; they are semi-vowels, found in words such as *stĺp*, *vŕba*, *tŕň*
q, w, x	only exist in words of foreign origin and are pronounced approximately as in their original language.
r	is rolled as in Scottish
š	as the 'sh' in 'shoe'

Slovak speakers refer to their language lovingly as *l'úbozvučná slovenčina* ('sweet sounding Slovak') in recognition of its melodious quality which, for example, does not allow two consecutive long syllables, and avoids heavy emphasis on any word. Stress always falls on the first syllable, but is far less strong than in other languages, including English.

Greetings & Civilities
Top 10 Useful Phrases
Hello.
doh-bree dyeny	Dobrý deň

Goodbye.
doh vidyeny-nyiah	Do videnia.

Yes./No.
aa-noh/nyieh	Áno./Nie.

Excuse me.
prepaach-tyeh	Prepáčte.

May I? Do you mind?
smyiem? dovoh-leetyeh?	Smiem? Dovolíte?

Sorry. (Forgive me.)
prepaach-tyeh, proh-seem	Prepáčte, prosím.

Please.
proh-seem	Prosím.

Thank you.
dyakuh-yem	Ďakujem.

Many thanks.
dyakuh-yem (vely-mih) pek-neh	Ďakujem (veľmi) pekne.

That's fine. You're welcome.
nyieh yeh zah cho	Nie je za čo.
proh-seem	Prosím.

Greetings

Good morning.
doh-brair raano Dobré ráno.

Good afternoon.
doh-bree dyeny Dobrý deň.

Good evening.
doh-bree veh-cher Dobrý večer.

Good night.
doh-broo nots Dobrú noc.

How are you?
akoh sah maa-tyeh ? Ako sa máte?

Well, thanks.
dyakuh-yem dobreh Ďakujem, dobre.

Forms of Address

Madam/Mrs	*pah-nyih*	Pani
Sir/Mr	*paan*	Pán
Miss	*slech-nah*	Slečna
friend	*pryiah-tyely* (m)	Priateľ
	pryiah-tyely-kah (f)	Priateľka

Small Talk
Meeting People

What is your name?
akoh sah voh-laa-tyeh? Ako sa voláte?

My name is ...
voh-laam sah ... Volám sa ...

I'd like to introduce you to ...
dovoly-tyeh abih som Dovoľte, aby som
vaas predstah-vil Vás predstavil. Toto je ...
totoh yeh ...

I'm pleased to meet you.
tyeshee mah　　　　　　Teší ma.

Age
How old are you?
koly-koh maa-teh rokohw?　Koľko máte rokov?
I am ... years old.
maam ... rokohw　　　　　Mám ... rokov.

Nationalities
Where are you from?
odkyialy styeh ?　　　　Odkiaľ ste?
I am from ...
som z ...　　　　　　　Som z ...

Australia	*ahwstraa-lyieh*	Austrálie
Canada	*kanah-dih*	Kanady
England	*anglitz-kah*	Anglicka
Ireland	*eer-skah*	Írska
New Zealand	*novair-hoh zair-landuh*	Nového Zélandu
Scotland	*shkawht-skah*	Škótska
USA	*oo-es-ah (spoyeh-neekh shtaa-tohw ameritz-keekh)*	USA (Spojených štátov amerických)
Wales	*wheyl-suh*	Walesu

Occupations
What do you do?
choh robee-tyeh ?　　　Čo robíte?

I am a/an ...

(yah) som ...	(Ja) som ...
artist	*oomeh-lets* (m)	umelec
	oomel-kinya (f)	umelkyňa
business person	*podnyih-kah-tyely* (m)	podnikateľ
	podnyih-kah-tyely-kah (f)	podnikateľka
doctor	*dok-tor* (m)	doktor
	dok-tor-kah (f)	doktorka
engineer	*inzhih-nyier* (m)	inžinier
	inzhih-nyier-kah (f)	inžinierka
farmer	*roly-nyeek* (m)	roľník
	roly-nyeech-kah (f)	roľníčka
journalist	*novih-naar* (m)	novinár
	novih-naar-kah (f)	novinárka
lawyer	*praav-nyik* (m)	právnik
	praav-nyich-kah (f)	právnička
manual worker	*robot-nyeek* (m)	robotník
	robot-nyeech-kah (f)	robotníčka
mechanic	*mekhah-nik* (m)	mechanik
	mekhah-nich-kah (f)	mechanička
nurse	*osheh-trovah-tyely* (m)	ošetrovateľ
	osheh-trovah-tyely-kah (f)	ošetrovateľka
office worker	*oorad-nyeek* (m)	úradník
	oorad-nyeech-kah (f)	úradníčka
scientist	*vedyets-kee pratsov-nyeek* (m)	vedecký pracovník
	vedyets-kaa pratsov-nyeech-kah (f)	vedecká pracovníčka

student	*shtuh-dent* (m)	študent
	shtuh-dent-kah (f)	študentka
teacher	*oochih-tyely* (m)	učiteľ
	oochih-tyely-kah (f)	učiteľka
waiter	*chash-nyeek* (m)	čašník
	chash-nyeech-kah (f)	čašníčka
writer	*spisoh-vah-tyely* (m)	spisovateľ
	spisoh-vah-tyely-kah (f)	spisovateľka

Religion

What is your religion?
> *akair-hoh styeh (vyieroh) viznah-nyiah ?*   Akého ste (viero-)vyznania?

I am not religious.
> *som bez viznah-nyiah*   Som bez vyznania.

I am ...
> *(yah) som ...*   (Ja) som ...

Buddhist	*boodhih-stah* (m)	budhista
	bood-hist-kah (f)	budhistka
Catholic	*kahtoh-leek* (m)	katolík
	kahtoh-leech-kah (f)	katolíčka
Protestant	*evanyieh-lik* (m)	evanjelik
	evanyieh-lich-kah (f)	evanjelička
Christian	*kres-tyan* (m)	kresťan
	kres-tyan-kah (f)	kresťanka
Hindu	*hindoo-istah* (m)	hinduista
	hindoo-ist-kah (f)	hinduistka
Jewish	*zhid* (m)	žid
	zhidohv-kah (f)	židovka

| Muslim | *mos-lim* (m) | moslim |
| | *mos-lim-kah* (f) | moslimka |

Family

Are you married?
   steh zhenah-tee? (m)   Ste ženatý?
   steh vidah-taa? (f)   Ste vydatá ?
I am single.
   som slobod-nee (m)   Som slobodný.
   som slobod-naa (f)   Som slobodná.
I am married.
   som zhenah-tee (m)   Som ženatý.
   som vidah-taa (f)   Som vydatá.
How many children do you have?
   koly-koh maa-tyeh dyeh-tyee?   Koľko máte detí?
I don't have any children.
   nye-maam (zhiad-neh) dyeh-tih   Nemám (žiadne) deti.
I have a daughter/a son.
   maam tsair-ruh/sinah   Mám dcéru/syna.
How many brothers/sisters do you have?
   koly-koh maa-teh brah-tohw/seh-styier?   Koľko máte bratov/sestier?
Is your husband/wife here?
   vaash man-zhel/vaa-shah man-zhel-kah yeh tuh?   Váš manžel/Vaša manželka je tu?

Do you have a boyfriend/
girlfriend?
   maa-teh priah-tyeh-lyah/   Máte priateľa/priateľku?
   priah-tyely-kuh?

brother	*braht*	brat
daughter	*tsair-rah*	dcéra
family	*rodyih-nah*	rodina
father	*oh-tyets*	otec
grandfather	*stah-ree oh-tyets*	starý otec
grandmother	*stah-raa mat-kah*	stará matka
husband	*man-zhel*	manžel
mother	*mat-kah*	matka
sister	*seh-strah*	sestra
son	*sin*	syn
wife	*manzhel-kah*	manželka

Feelings

I like .../I don't like ...
   maam raad ... (m)   Mám rád ...
   maam radah ... (f)/   Mám rada .../
   nyeh-maam raad ... (m)   Nemám rád ...
   nyeh-maam radah ... (f)   Nemám rada ...

I am ...

cold/hot	*yeh mih zimah/ tyep-loh*	Je mi zima/teplo.
hungry/thirsty	*maam hlahd/smed*	Mám hlad/smäd.
in a hurry	*ponaa-hlyam sah*	Ponáhľam sa.
right	*maam prahv-duh*	Mám pravdu.

sleepy	*som ospah-lee* (m)/	Som ospalý/
	ospah-laa (f)	ospalá.

I am ...

angry	*hnye-vaam sah*	Hnevám sa.
happy	*som shtyast-nee* (m)	Som šťastný/
	shtyast-naa (f)	šťastná.
sad	*som smut-nee* (m)	Som smutný/
	smut-naa (f)	smutná.
tired	*som oonah-vehnee*	Som unavený/
	(m)/*oonah-vehnaa* (f)	unavená.
well	*tsee-tyim sah dob-reh*	Cítim sa dobre.
worried	*ohbaa-vam sah*	Obávam sa.

I am sorry. (condolence)
    lyutuh-yem   Ľutujem.
I am grateful.
    som vdyach-nee (m)/   Som vďačný/
    vdyach-naa (f)   vďačná.

Language Problems
Do you speak English?
    hovoh-ree-tyeh   Hovoríte po anglicky?
    poh ahnglits-kih ?
Does anyone (here) speak
English?
    hovoh-ree (tuh) nyiek-toh   Hovorí (tu) niekto
    poh ahnglits-kih ?   po anglicky?
I speak a little ...
    yah hovoh-reehm   Ja hovorím trocha (po) ...
    tro-kha (poh ...)

SLOVAK

I don't speak ...
nyeh-hovoh-reehm
(poh ...)

Nehovorím (po) ...

I (don't) understand.
rozuh-miehm/
nyeh-rozuh-miehm

Rozumiem./Nerozumiem.

Could you speak more
slowly please?
muoh-zhetyeh proh-
seem hoh-vohrity
pohmal-shyieh ?

Môžete prosím hovoriť
pomalšie?

Could you repeat that?
muoh-zhetyeh toh zo
pa-kovaty ?

Môžete to zopakovať?

How do you say ...?
akoh sah povyieh ?

Ako sa povie ...?

What does ... mean?
choh znameh-naa ?

Čo znamená ...?

I speak ...
hovoh-reehm poh ...

Hovorím po ...

Arabic	*arab-skih*	arabsky
Danish	*daan-skih*	dánsky
Dutch	*holand-skih*	holandsky
English	*anglits-kih*	anglicky
Finnish	*feen-skih*	fínsky
French	*fran-tsooz-kih*	francúzsky
German	*nyemetz-kih*	nemecky
Italian	*talyian-skih*	taliansky
Japanese	*yapon-skih*	japonsky

Some Useful Phrases

Sure.
oorchih-tyeh   Určite!

Just a minute.
ohkam-zhik   Okamžik.

It's (not) important.   To (nie) je dôležité.
toh (nyieh) yeh
duole-zhitair

It's (not) possible.   To (nie) je možné.
toh (nyieh) yeh
mozh-nair

Wait!
pochkay (sing)/   Počkaj!/
pochkay-tyeh (pl)   Počkajte!

Good luck!
fshet-koh naylep-shyieh   Všetko najlepšie!

Signs

BAGGAGE COUNTER	PODAJ BATOŽÍN
CHECK-IN COUNTER	ODBAVOVANIE
	CESTUJÚCICH
CUSTOMS	COLNICA
	(COLNÁ KONTROLA)
EMERGENCY EXIT	NÚDZOVÝ VÝCHOD
ENTRANCE	VCHOD
EXIT	VÝCHOD
FREE ADMISSION	VOĽNÝ (BEZPLATNÝ)
	VSTUP

HOT/COLD (WATER)	HORÚCA/STUDENÁ (VODA)
INFORMATION	INFORMÁCIE
NO ENTRY	ZÁKAZ VSTUPU/VSTUP ZAKÁZANÝ
NO SMOKING	ZÁKAZ FAJČENIA
OPEN/CLOSED	OTVORENÉ/ ZATVORENÉ
OPENING HOURS	OTVÁRACIE HODINY
PROHIBITED	ZAKÁZANÉ
RESERVED	REZERVOVANÉ
TELEPHONE	TELEFÓN
TOILETS	ZÁCHODY/WC/ TOALETY

Emergencies

POLICE	POLÍCIA
POLICE STATION	STANICA POLÍCIE

Help!
   pomots   Pomoc!
It's an emergency!
   potreh-buyem pomots!   Potrebuje pomoc!
There's been an accident!
   stalah sah nyeh-hodah!   Stala sa nehoda!

SLOVAK

Call a doctor!
zahvolai-tyeh doktoh-rah/ Zavolajte doktora/lekára!
lekaa-rah!

Call an ambulance!
zahvolai-tyeh Zavolajte záchranku!
zaakhran-koo!

I've been raped.
bolah som Bola som znásilnená.
znaasil-nyenaah

I've been robbed.
ohkrad-lih mah Okradli ma.

Call the police!
zahvolai-tyeh polee-tsyiuh! Zavolajte políciu!

Where is the police station?
gdyeh yeh poli-tsaynaa Kde je policajná stanica?
stanyih-tsa?

Go away!
khody prech (sg)/ Choď preč!/Choďte preč!
khody-tyeh prech (pl)

I'll call the police!
zahvoh-laam polee-tsyiuh ! Zavolám políciu!

Thief!
zlodyey Zlodej!

I am ill.
(yah) som khoree (m) (Ja) som chorý.
(yah) som khoraa (f) (Ja) som chorá.

My friend is ill.
muoy pryia-tyely yeh Môj priateľ je chorý.
khoree (m)
moya pryia-tyely-kah yeh Moja priateľka je chorá.
khoraa (f)

I am lost.
    nye-viznaahm sah tuh   Nevyznám sa tu.
Where are the toilets?
    gdyeh soo tuh zaa-khodih ?   Kde sú tu záchody?
Could you help me please?
    muo-zhetye mih (proh-   Môžete mi (prosím) pomôcť?
    seem) poh-muotsty ?
Could I please use the tele-
phone?
    muo-zhem (proh-seem)   Môžem (prosím) použiť
    pohw-zhity teleh-fawn ?   telefón?
I'm sorry. I apologise.
    prepaach-tyeh proh-seem   Prepáčte, prosím.
I didn't realise I was doing
anything wrong.
    nyeh-oovedoh-mil (m)/   Neuvedomil/Neuvedomila
    nyeh-oovedoh-milah (f)   som si, že robím niečo
    som sih zheh roh-beam   nesprávne.
    nyieh-cho nye-spraavneh
I didn't do it.
    yah som toh nyeh-oorobil Ja som to neurobil/
    (m)/*nyeh-oorobilah* (f)   neurobila.
I wish to contact my embassy/
consulate.
    zhelaam sih hoh-vohrity Želám si hovoriť so zastu-
    zoh zastuh-pityely-stvom piteľstvom mojej krajiny.
    moyey krayih-nih
I have medical insurance.
    maam nyemotsen-skair   Mám nemocenské poistenie.
    poh-istyenyieh

My possessions are insured.
  moyah batoh-zhinah yeh   Moja batožina je poistená.
  poh-istyenaa

My ... was stolen.
  ookrad-lih mih   Ukradli mi ...
I've lost my ...
  strahtyil som ... (m)   Stratil som ...
  strahtyil-lah som ... (f)   Stratila som ...

bags	*batoh-zhinuh*	batožinu
handbag	*tash-kuh/kabel-kuh*	tašku/kabelku
money	*penyiah-zeh*	peniaze
travellers'	*tses-tohv-nair*	cestovné šeky
cheques	*sheh-kih*	
passport	*tses-tohv-nee pahs*	cestovný pas
next of kin	*(nai-blizh-shee)*	(najbližší)
	pree-buznee	príbuzní

My blood group is (A, B, O positive/negative).
  mohyah krvnaa skupih-nah Moja krvná skupina
  yeh (aa, bair, awh poh zi- je (A, B, O pozitívna/
  teev-nah/neh -ga-teev-nah) negatívna).

Forms

name/surname	*menoh/pryieh-zviskoh*	meno/priezvisko
address	*adreh-sah*	adresa
date of birth	*daatum*	dátum narodenia
	naroh-dyenyiah	

place of birth	*myiestoh naroh-dyenyiah*	miesto narodenia
age	*vek*	vek
sex	*poh-hlavyieh*	pohlavie
nationality/ citizenship	*naarod-nosty/ shtaat-nah pree-slush-nosty*	národnosť/ štátna príslušnosť
religion	*vyieroh-vizna-nyieh*	vierovyznanie
reason for travel	*oochel tses-tih*	účel cesty
profession	*povoh-lanyieh*	povolanie
marital status	*stav (rohdyin-nee)*	stav (rodinný)
passport	*tses-tohv-nee pahs*	cestovný pas
passport number	*cheesloh tses-tohv-nairhoh pahsuh*	číslo cestovného pasu
visa	*veezum*	vízum
tourist card	*toorist- itskee preh-oo-kahz*	turistický preukaz
identification	*preh-oo-kahz totozh-nostih*	preukaz totožnosti
birth certificate	*rodnee list*	rodný list
driver's licence	*vodyich-skee preh-oo-kahz*	vodičský preukaz
car owner's title	*doklah-dih oh vlast-nyeetst-veh motoroh-vair-hoh vozid-lah*	doklady o vlastníctve motoro-vého vozidla
car registration	*reghistrach-nair doklah-dih motor oh-vairhoh vozid-lah*	registračné doklady motorového vozidla
customs	*tsol-naa pre hlyiad-kah*	colná prehliadka

immigration	*pri-styahoh-valets-*	prisťahovalecké
	kair zaalezhi-tostyih	záležitosti
border	*shtaat-nah hranyi-tsa*	štátna hranica

Getting Around

ARRIVALS	PRÍCHODY
BUS STOP	AUTOBUSOVÁ
	ZASTÁVKA
DEPARTURES	ODCHODY
STATION	STANICA
SUBWAY	PODZEMNÁ DRÁHA/
	METRO
TICKET OFFICE	PREDAJ CESTOVNÝCH
	LÍSTKOV
TIMETABLE	CESTOVNÝ PORIADOK
TRAIN STATION	ŽELEZNIČNÁ STANICA

What time does the ... leave/
arrive?

kedih ot-khaa-dzah/	Kedy odchádza/prichádza ...?
pri-khaa-dzah ...?	
aeroplane	*lyieh-tadloh*	lietadlo
boat	*lody*	loď
(city) bus	*(mest-skee)*	(mestský) autobus
	owtoh-buhs	
(intercity) bus	*(medzih-mest-skee)*	(medzimestský)
	owtoh-buhs	autobus

train	*vlakh*	vlak
tram	*elek-trich-kah*	električka

Directions

Where is ...?
gdyeh yeh ...? — Kde je ...

How do I get to ...?
akoh sah dostah-nyem doh ...? — Ako sa dostanem do ...?

Is it far from/near here?
yeh toh od-tyialy-toh dya-lekoh/bleez-koh ? — Je to odtiaľto ďaleko/blízko?

Can I walk there?
daa sah tam easty peshih ? — Dá sa tam ísť peši?

Can you show me (on the map)?
muo-zhetyeh mih uh-kaazaty (nah mapeh) — Môžete mi ukázať (na mape)?

Are there other means of getting there?
akoh sah tam daa eshtyeh dos-taty ? — Ako sa tam dá ešte dostať?

I want to go to ...
khtsehm easty doh — Chcem ísť do ...

Go straight ahead.
khody-tyeh rovnoh dya-lay — Choďte rovno ďalej.

It's two blocks down.
soo toh od-tyialy-toh dveh uhlih-tse — Sú to odtiaľto dve ulice.

Turn left ...
zaboch-tyeh vlya-voh — Zabočte vľavo ...

Turn right ...
    zaboch-tyeh fpra-voh   Zabočte vpravo ...
at the next corner.
    nah nasleh-duh-yootsom   na nasledujúcom rohu.
    rohuh
at the traffic lights.
    na krizho-vatkeh zoh   na križovatke so svetlami.
    svetlah-mih

behind/in front of	*zah/ pred*	za/pred
far/near	*dya-lehkoh/bleez-koh*	ďaleko/blízko
in front of	*pred*	pred
opposite	*oh-protyih*	oproti

Booking Tickets

Excuse me, where is the ticket office?
    gdyeh yeh pre-dai   Kde je predaj cestovných
    tses-tohv-neekh least-   lístkov, prosím?
    kohw proh-seem ?
Where can I buy a ticket?
    gdyeh sih muo-zhem   Kde si môžem kúpiť cestovný
    koo-pity tses-tohv-nee   lístok?
    leas-tok ?
I want to go to ...
    khtsem easty do   Chcem ísť do ...
Do I need to book?
    potreh-buyem   Potrebujem miestenku?
    myies-tyenkuh ?
You need to book.
    potreh-buyetye   Potrebujete miestenku.
    myies-tyenkuh

I would like to book a seat to ...
    myies-tyenkuh do ...   Miestenku do ... prosím.
    proh-seem

I would like ...
    proh-seem sih   Prosím si ...

a one-way ticket	*yednoh-smernee leas-tok*	jednosmerny lístok
a return ticket	*spyiatoch-nee leas-tok*	spiatočný lístok
two tickets	*dvah least-kih*	dva lístky
tickets for all of us	*least-kih preh naas fshet-keekh*	lístky pre nás všetkých
a student's fare	*shtudent-skee leas-tok*	študentský lístok
a child's fare	*dyet-skee leas-tok*	detský lístok
pensioner's fare	*leas-tok preh duo-khod-tsohw*	lístok pre dôchodcov

1st class
    prvaa tryieh-dah   prvá trieda
2nd class
    dru-haa tryieh-dah   druhá trieda
It is full.
    fshet-koh yeh obsah-dyenair   Všetko je obsadené.
Is it completely full?
    nyieh yeh tuh nich voly-nee ?   Nie je tu nič voľné?
Can I get a stand-by ticket?
    muo-zhem tuh dos-taty stend-baay leas-tok ?   Môžem tu dostať 'stand-by' lístok?

Air

CHECKING IN	PREZENTÁCIA/ ODBAVOVANIE CESTUJÚCICH
LUGGAGE PICKUP REGISTRATION	VÝDAJ BATOŽÍN REGISTRÁCIA

Is there a flight to ...?
  yeh let doh ...? Je let do ...?
When is the next flight to ...?
  kedih yeh nai-blizh-shee
  let doh ...? Kedy je najbližší let do ...?
How long does the flight take?
  akoh dlhoh tr-vaa
  tentoh let ? Ako dlho trvá tento let?
What is the flight number?
  akair chees-loh maa
  tentoh let ? Aké číslo má tento let?
You must check in at ...
  pred od-letom sah Pred odletom sa musíte
  muh-seetye dos-tavity dostaviť k prezentácii ku ...
  k prezen-taatsiyi kuh ...

airport tax	*letisht-nee poh-platok*	letištný poplatok
boarding pass	*palub-nee leas-tok*	palubný lístok
customs	*tsol-naa kon-trolah*	colná kontrola

Bus

BUS/TRAM STOP	ZASTÁVKA AUTOBUSOV / ELEKTRIČIEK

Where is the bus/tram stop?
gdyeh yeh tuh zas-taavkah owtoh-buhsuh/ elek-trichkih ?
Kde je tu zastávka autobusu/ električky?

Which bus goes to ...?
ktoh-reem owtoh-buhsom sah dos-tanyem doh ?
Ktorým autobusom sa dostanem do ...?

Does this bus go to ...?
idyeh tentoh owtoh-buhs doh ...?
Ide tento autobus do ...?

How often do buses pass by?
akoh chas-toh tuh yaz-dyiah owtoh-buhsih ?
Ako často tu jazdia autobusy?

What time is the ... bus?
kedih pree-dyeh ... owtoh-buhs ?
Kedy príde ... autobus ?

next	*nasleh-duhyoo-tsih*	nasledujúci
first	*pr-vee*	prvý
last	*poh-slednee*	posledný

Could you let me know when
we get to ...?

   muo-zhetyeh mah
   proh-seem upoh-zornyity
   kedih buh-dyemeh v ...?

Môžete ma prosím upozorniť,
keď budeme v ...?

I want to get off!

   khtsem vih-stoopyity

Chcem vystúpiť!

Metro

METRO/UNDERGROUND	METRO/PODZEMNÁ DRÁHA
CHANGE (for coins)	DROBNÉ (MINCE)
THIS WAY TO	TÝMTO SMEROM
WAY OUT	K VÝCHODU

Which line takes me to ...?

   ktoh-rohw lin-kohw sah
   dos-tahnyem doh ...?

Ktorou linkou sa
dostanem do ...?

What is the next station?

   akoh sah volaa nah-
   sleduhyoo-tsah
   stanyi-tsah?

Ako sa volá nasledujúca
stanica?

Train

DINING CAR	JEDÁLENSKÝ VOZEŇ
EXPRESS	EXPRES/ RÝCHLIK
PLATFORM NO	NÁSTUPIŠTE ČÍSLO
SLEEPING CAR	SPACÍ VOZEŇ

Is this the right platform
for ...?
    yeh toh spraav-neh   Je to správne nástupište do ...?
    naah-stupish-tyeh doh ...?
Passengers must ...
    tsestuh-yootsih muhsyiah ... Cestujúci musia ...

change trains	*pres-toopity nah*	prestúpiť na ...
change	*preysty nah inair*	prejsť na iné
platforms	*naah-stupish-tyeh*	nástupište

The train leaves from
platform ...
    vlak od-khaatzah z   Vlak odchádza z nástupišťa ...
    naah-stupish-tyah ...

dining car	*yedaa-lenskee vozeny*	jedálenský vozeň
express	*eks-pres/ reekh-lick*	expres/rýchlik
local	*lokaal-nih vlakh*	lokálny vlak
sleeping car	*spah-tsee vozeny*	spací vozeň

Taxi

Can you take me to ...?
*muo-zhetyeh mah
zavyiesty doh ...?*

Môžete ma zaviesť do ...?

Please take me to ...
*zavestyeh mah proh-seem
doh ...*

Zavezte ma prosím do ...

How much does it cost to go to ...?
*koly-koh toh budyeh
staaty doh ...?*

Koľko to bude stáť do ...?

Instructions

Here is fine, thank you.
potyialy-toh stachee

Potiaľ to stačí.

The next corner, please.
*azh poh nai-blizh-shee
rokh proh-seem*

Až po najbližší roh, prosím.

Continue!
*poh-krachuy-tyeh
v yaz-dyeh*

Pokračujte v jazde!

The next street to the left/right.
*nah-sleduyoo-tsa ulitsa
vlyah-voh/ fprah-voh*

Nasledujúca ulica vľavo/
vpravo.

Stop here!
*zah-stavtyeh tuh
proh-seem*

Zastavte tu, prosím.

Please slow down.
spomal-tyeh proh-seem

Spomaľte, prosím.

Please wait here.
*pochkay-tyeh tuh
proh-seem*

Počkajte tu, prosím.

Some Useful Phrases

The train is delayed.
vlak maa meshkah-nyieh

Vlak má meškanie.

The train is cancelled.
vlak bol zruh-sheh-nee

Vlak bol zrušený.

How long will it be delayed?
*akoh dlhoh budyeh
meshkaty ?*

Ako dlho bude meškať?

There is a delay of ... hours.
meshkah-nyieh budyeh ...

Meškanie bude ...

Can I reserve a place?
*muo-zhem sih rezer-
vohvaty myiestyen-kuh?*

Môžem si rezervovať
miestenku?

How long does the trip take?
akoh dlhoh tr-vaa tsestah?

Ako dlho trvá cesta?

Is it a direct route?
*yeh toh pryiah-meh
spoyeh-nyieh?*

Je to priame spojenie?

Is that seat taken?
ob-sadyenair?

Obsadené?

I want to get off at ...
khtsem vih-stoopity v ...

Chcem vystúpiť v ...

Excuse me.
preh-paachtyeh

Prepáčte.

Where can I hire a bicycle?
*gdyeh sah tuh daa
poh-zhichaty
bih-tsih-kehl ?*

Kde sa tu dá požičať bicykel?

Car

DETOUR	OBCHÁDZKA
FREEWAY	DIAĽNICA
GARAGE/WORKSHOP	AUTOOPRAVOVŇA
GIVE WAY	DAJ PREDNOSŤ V JAZDE
MECHANIC	(AUTO)MECHANIK
NO ENTRY	ZÁKAZ VJAZDU
NO PARKING	ZÁKAZ PARKOVANIA
NORMAL	NORMÁL
ONE WAY	JEDNOSMERNÁ DOPRAVA
REPAIRS	AUTOOPRAVY
SELF SERVICE	SAMOOBSLUHA
STOP	STOP/ ZASTAVIŤ/ STÁŤ
SUPER	SUPER
UNLEADED	NATURAL

Where can I rent a car?
  gdyeh sih muo-zhem
  preh-nayaty owtoh?   Kde si môžem prenajať auto?
How much is it daily/weekly?
  koly-koh toh stoh-yee
  nah dyeny/teezh-dyeny?   Koľko to stojí na deň/ týždeň?
Does that include insurance/mileage?
  yeh v tse-nyeh za-hrnuh-tai   Je v cene zahrnuté
  poh-istyeh-nyieh/   poistenie/kilometráž ?
  kiloh-metraazh ?

SLOVAK

Where's the next petrol station?
gdyeh yeh nai-blizh-shyieh Kde je najbližšie benzínové
benzee-novair cher-pahd- čerpadlo?
loh ?

Please fill the tank.
pl-noo naa-drzh Plnú nádrž, prosím.
proh-seem

I want ... litres of petrol (gas).
potreh-buyem ... lit-rohw Potrebujem ... litrov benzínu.
ben-zeenuh

Please check the oil and water.
skon-troluy-tyeh proh-seem Skontrolujte prosím
hlah-dyinuh aw-leyah ah hladinu oleja a vody.
vodih

How long can I park here?
akoh dlhoh tuh muo-zhem Ako dlho tu môžem
par-kovaty? parkovať ?

Does this road lead to?
veh-dyieh taa-toh Vedie táto cesta do ...?
tses-tah doh?

air (for tyres)	*stlah-cheh-nee vz-dukh/ kom-preh-sor*	stlačený vzduch/ kompresor
battery	*bah-tair-ryiah*	batéria
brakes	*brz-dih*	brzdy
clutch	*spoy-kah*	spojka
driver's licence	*voh-dyich-skee preh-oo-kaz*	vodičský preukaz
engine	*moh-tor*	motor

lights	*sveht-laa*	svetlá
oil	*aw-ley*	olej
puncture	*preh-pikh-nootaa*	prepichnutá
	pneu-mah-tikah/	pneumatika/
	deh-fekt (fam)	defekt
radiator	*khlah-dyich*	chladič
road map	*owtoh-mapah*	automapa
tyres	*pneu-mah-tikih*	pneumatiky
windscreen	*pred-nair skloh*	predné sklo

Car Problems

I need a mechanic.
   potreh-buyem pomots
   owtoh-mekhah-nikah
Potrebujem pomoc auto-
mechanika.

What make is it?
   akaa yeh toh znach-kah
   (owtah)?
Aká je to značka (auta)?

The battery is flat.
   bah-tair-ryiah yeh
   vih-bihtaa
Batéria je vybitá.

The radiator is leaking.
   khlah-dyich tyeh-chyieh
Chladič tečie.

I have a flat tyre.
   maam preh-pikh-nutoo
   pneu-mah-tikuh
   maam deh-fekt (fam)
Mám prepichnutú
pneumatiku.
Mám defekt.

It's overheating.
   moh-tor sah
   preh-hryieh-vah
Motor sa prehrieva.

It's not working.
   neh-fuhn-guhyeh toh
Nefunguje to.

Accommodation

CAMPING GROUND	KEMPING/TÁBORISKO
GUEST HOUSE	PENZIONÁT
HOTEL	HOTEL
MOTEL	MOTEL
YOUTH HOSTEL	TURISTICKÁ
	UBYTOVŇA MLÁDEŽE

I am looking for ...
hlyah-daam Hľadám ...
Where is a ...?
gdyeh yeh ...? Kde je ... ?
cheap hotel *lahts-nee hoh-tel* lacný hotel
good hotel *kvahlit-nee hoh-tel* kvalitný hotel
nearby hotel *hoh-tel nah-blees-kuh* hotel nablízku
clean hotel *dobreh uhdr-zhyia-* dobre udržiavaný
  vah-nee hoh-tel hotel

What is the address of ... ?
ah-kaa yeh adreh-sah Aká je adresa toho ... ?
tohoh ...?
Could you write the address, please?
muo-zhetyeh mih Môžete mi prosím napísať tú
proh-seem nah-peesaty adresu?
too adreh-suh ?

At the Hotel

Do you have any rooms
available?

maa-tyeh voly-nair izbih?   Máte voľné izby?

I would like ...

poh-trebuhyem ...   Potrebujem ...

a single room	*yednoh-luozhkoh-voo izbuh*	jednolôžkovú izbu
a double room	*izbuh preh dveh ohsoh-bih*	izbu pre dve osoby
a room with a bathroom	*izbuh s koo-pely-nyohw*	izbu s kúpeľňou
to share a dorm	*(spoloch-noo) izbuh nah uhbitov-nyih*	(spoločnú) izbu na ubytovni
a bed	*pos-tyely*	posteľ

I want a room with a ...

muo-zhetyeh mih daty izbuh ...   Môžete mi dať izbu ...

bathroom	*s koo-pelynyohw*	s kúpeľňou
shower	*zoh spr-khohw*	so sprchou
television	*s teleh-veeznim prih-yeemachom*	s televíznym prijimačom
window	*s oknom*	s oknom

I'm going to stay for ...

zoh-stanyem tuh ...   Zostanem tu ...

one day	*yeden dyeny*	jeden deň
two days	*dvah dnyih*	dva dni
one week	*yeden teezh-dyeny*	jeden týždeň

I'm not sure how long I'm staying.

    nyeh-vyiem eshtyeh akoh   Neviem ešte ako dlho tu
    dlhoh tuh zoh-stanyem   zostanem.

Do you have identification?

    maa-tyeh preh-oo-kaz   Máte preukaz totožnosti?
    totozh-nostyih?

Your membership card, please.

    vaash chlen-skee   Váš členský preukaz, prosím.
    preh-oo-kaz proh-seem

Sorry, we're full.

    zhyialy smeh pl-nee   Žiaľ, sme plní.

How long will you be staying?

    akoh dlhoh tuh zoh-   Ako dlho tu zostanete?
    stanyeh-tyeh?

How many nights?

    koly-koh nohtsee ?   Koľko nocí?

It's ... per day/per person.

    stoh-yee toh ... nah dyeny/ Stojí to ... na deň/osobu.
    oh-sobuh

How much is it per night/per person?

    koly-koh toh stoh-yee   Koľko to stojí na deň/
    nah dyeny/oh-sobuh?   osobu?

Can I see it?

    muo-zhem toh (proh-seem) Môžem to (prosím) vidieť?
    vi-dyiety?

Are there any others?

    maa-tyeh eshtyeh ih-nair   Máte ešte iné na výber?
    nah vee-ber?

Do you have any cheaper
rooms?
   maa-tyeh ih lats-   Máte aj lacnejšie izby?
   nyey-shyieh izbih?

Can I see the bathroom?
   muo-zhem vih-dyiety   Môžem vidieť kúpeľňu?
   koo-pelynyu?

Is there a reduction for
students/children?
   mah-yoo shtuden-tyih/   Majú študenti/deti zľavu?
   dyetyih zlyah-vuh?

Does it include breakfast?
   soo rah-nyaikih   Sú raňajky zahrnuté v cene?
   zahrh-nuhtair f tse-nyeh?

It's fine, I'll take it.
   doh-breh, beh-ryiem toh Dobre, beriem to.

Is there a lift?
   yeh tam vee-tyakh?   Je tam výťah?

Where is the bathroom?
   gdyeh yeh koo-pelynyah? Kde je kúpeľňa?

Is there hot water all day?
   yeh horoo-tsah vodah   Je horúca voda po celý deň?
   poh tselee dyeny?

Do you have a safe where
I can leave my valuables?
   maa-tyeh treh-zor (saife) Máte trezor (safe) na uloženie
   nah uh-lozheh-nyieh   cenností?
   tsen-nos-tyee?

Is there somewhere to wash
clothes?
   muo-zhem sih nyiegdyeh Môžem si niekde oprať
   opraty obleh-chenyieh? oblečenie?

Can I use the kitchen?
 muo-zhem poh-uzheevaty Môžem používať kuchyňu?
 kukhih-nyuh?
Can I use the telephone?
 muo-zhem poh-uzheevaty Môžem používať telefón?
 teleh-fawn?

Requests & Complaints

Please wake me up at ...
 zoh-boody-tyeh mah Zobuďte ma (prosím) o ...
 (proh-seem) oh ...
The room needs to be cleaned.
 izbuh trebah vih-chistyity Izbu treba vyčistiť.
Please change the sheets.
 vih-menytyeh (proh-seem) Vymeňte (prosím) posteľnú
 postyely-noo byehlih-zeny bielizeň.
I can't open/close the window.
 nyeh-muo-zhem oh-tvohrity Nemôžem otvoriť /zatvoriť
 /zah-tvohrity oknoh okno.
I've locked myself out of my
room.
 vim-kohl (m)/ *vim-klah* (f) Vymkol/Vymkla
 som sah z izbih som sa z izby.
The toilet won't flush.
 zaa-khod nyeh-splah- Záchod nesplachuje.
 khooyeh
I don't like this room.
 taa-toh izbah sah mih Táto izba sa mi nepáči.
 nyeh-paachih
It's too small.
 yeh pree-lish malaa Je príliš malá.

It's noisy.
yeh hlooch-naa   Je hlučná.
It's too dark.
yeh pree-lish tmah-vaa   Je príliš tmavá.
It's expensive.
yeh drahaa   Je drahá.

Some Useful Words & Phrases

I am leaving ...
ot-khaa-dzam ...   Odchádzam ...
We are leaving ...
ot-khaa-dzameh ...   Odchádzame ...
now/tomorrow
teraz/zai-trah   teraz/zajtra

I would like to pay the bill.
khtsel (m)/ *khtselah* (f) *bih*   Chcel/Chcela by
som vih-rovnaty ooh-chet   som vyrovnať účet.

name	*menoh (krst-nee)*	meno (krstné)
surname	*pryieh-zviskoh*	priezvisko
room number	*chees-loh izbih*	číslo izby
address	*adreh-sah*	adresa
air-conditioned	*klimah-tih-zaatsyiah*	klimatizácia
balcony	*bal-koohn*	balkón
bathroom	*koo-pelynyah*	kúpeľňa
bed	*pos-tyely*	posteľ
bill	*ooh-chet*	účet
blanket	*prih-kreev-kah*	prikrývka

candle	*svyiech-kah*	sviečka
chair	*stolich-kah/kres-loh*	stolička/kreslo
clean	*chis-tee* (m)	čistý
	chis-taa (f)	čistá
	chis-taihr (neut)	čisté
cupboard	*ot-kladah-tsee pryieh-stor*	odkladací priestor
dark	*tmah-vee* (m)	tmavý
	tmah-vaa (f)	tmavá
	tmah-vair (neut)	tmavé
dirty	*shpinah-vee* (m)	špinavý
	shpinah-vaa (f)	špinavá
	shpinah-vair (neut)	špinavé
double bed	*dvoh-yih-taa postyely*	dvojitá posteľ
electricity	*elek-trinah*	elektrina
excluded	*bez ...*	bez ...
fan	*ventih-laator*	ventilátor
included	*vraa-tah-nyeh/ fchee-tah-nyeh*	vrátane/včitane
key	*klyooch*	kľúč
lift (elevator)	*vee-tyakh*	výťah
light bulb	*zhyiah-rohw-kah*	žiarovka
lock (n)	*zaam-kah*	zámka
mattress	*matrats*	matrac
mirror	*zrkad-loh*	zrkadlo
padlock	*vih-satsyiah zaam-kah*	visacia zámka
pillow	*van-koosh*	vankúš
quiet	*tyikhoh*	ticho
room (in hotel)	*(hohtel-ohvaa) iz-bah*	(hotelová) izba
sheet	*plakh-tah*	plachta

shower	*spr-khah*	sprcha
soap	*midloh*	mydlo
suitcase	*kufohr*	kufor
swimming pool	*bazairn*	bazén
table	*stuol*	stôl
toilet	*zaa-khod/*	záchod/
	toah-letah/vair-tsair	toaleta/WC
toilet paper	*zaa-khod-ohvee*	záchodový
	(toah-letnee)	(toaletný) papier
	pah-pyier	
towel	*utyeh-raak*	uterák
water	*vodah*	voda
cold water	*studyeh-naa vodah*	studená voda
hot water	*horoo-tsah vodah*	horúca voda
window	*oknoh*	okno

Around Town

I'm looking for ...
hlyah-daam ...   Hľadám ...

the art gallery	*galair-ryiuh*	galériu
a bank	*bankuh*	banku
the church	*kostol*	kostol
the city centre	*stred (tsen-truhm)*	stred (centrum)
	mestah	mesta
the ... embassy	*shtaat-neh zastuh-*	štátne zastu-
	pityehly-stvoh ...	piteľstvo ...
my hotel	*muoy hohtel*	môj hotel
the market	*trkh*	trh
the museum	*moo-zeum*	múzeum

SLOVAK

the police	*polee-tsyiuh*	políciu
the post office	*posh-tuh*	poštu
a public toilet	*vereih-nair*	verejné záchody
	zaa-khodih	
the telephone	*teleh-fawn-nuh*	telefónnu centrálu
centre	*tsentraa-luh*	
the tourist	*infor-mahchnair*	informačné
information	*stredyis-koh preh*	stredisko
office	*turis-tohw*	pre turistov

What time does it open?
  od koly-kei yeh otvoh-renair? — Od koľkej je otvorené ?

What time does it close?
  doh koly-kei yeh otvoh-renair? — Do koľkej je otvorené ?

What ... is this?
  akoh sah voh-laa? — Ako sa volá ...?

| street | *taa-toh uhli-tsa* | táto ulica |
| suburb | *taa-toh shtvr-ty* | táto štvrť |

Note: For directions, see the Getting Around section, page 398.

At the Post Office

I would like to send ...
  khtsel (m)/*khtseh-lah* (f) — Chcel/Chcela by som
  bih som pos-laty ... — poslať ...

| a letter | *list* | list |
| a postcard | *pohlyad-nitsu* | pohľadnicu |

| a parcel | *bah-leak* | balík |
| a telegram | *teleh-grahm* | telegram |

I would like some stamps.
khtsel (m)/*khtseh-lah* (f)   Chcel/Chcela by som
bih som koo-pity znaam-kih   kúpiť známky.
How much is the postage?
koly-koh yeh posh-   Koľko je poštovné ?
tohv-nair?

How much does it cost to
send ... to ...?
koly-koh stoh-yee ... doh ...? Koľko stojí ... do ... ?

an aerogram	*airoh-grahm*	aerogram
air mail	*letyets-kaa posh-tah*	letecká pošta
envelope	*obaal-kah*	obálka
mailbox	*poshtoh-vaa*	poštová schránka
	skhraan-kah	
parcel	*bah-leak*	balík
registered mail	*dopoh-ruche-nyeh*	doporučene
surface mail	*obichai-nohw*	obyčajnou poštou
	posh-tohw	

Telephone

I want to ring ...
khtsem teleh-fohnoh-vaty ... Chcem telefonovať ...
The number is ...
chees-loh yeh   Číslo je ...
I want to speak for three
minutes.
buh-dyem hoh-vohrity trih Budem hovoriť tri minúty.
minoo-tih

How much does a three-minute
call cost?
> *koly-koh stoh-yee troi-
> minoo-tohvee hoh-vor?*

Koľko stojí trojminútový
hovor ?

How much does each extra
minute cost?
> *koly-koh stoh-yee kazh-daa
> minoo-tah nah-vishe?*

Koľko stojí každá minúta
navyše ?

I would like to speak to
Mr Perez.
> *muo-zhem hoh-vohrity
> s paa-nom pe-re-zom?*

Môžem hovoriť s pánom
Perezom ?

I want to make a reverse-
charges phone call.
> *khtsem teleh-fohnoh-vaty
> nah ooh-chet volah-nair-
> hoh chees-lah*

Chcem telefonovať na účet
volaného čísla.

It's engaged.
> *yeh op-sadyeh-nair*

Je obsadené.

I've been cut off.
> *muoy hoh-vor bol
> preh-rushe-nee*

Môj hovor bol prerušený.

At the Bank

I want to exchange some
money/traveller's cheques.
> *khtsem vih-meh-nyihty
> peh-nyiah-zeh/
> tses-tohv-nair shekih*

Chcem vymeniť peniaze/
cestovné šeky

What is the exchange rate?
> *akee yeh vee-men-nee kurz*

Aký je výmenný kurz?

How many crowns per dollar?
koly-koh koh-roohn   Koľko korún dostanem za
dostah-nyem zah yeden   jeden dolár?
doh-laar ?

Can I have money transferred
here from my bank?
muo-zhem sem trahns-   Môžem sem transferovať
feroh-vaty peh-nyiah-zeh   peniaze z mojej banky?
z mohyay bankih?

How long will it take to arrive?
kedih toh muo-zhem   Kedy to môžem očakávať?
ocha-kaavaty?

Has my money arrived yet?
ob-drzha-lih styeh uzh   Obdržali ste už moje
moyeh peh-nyiah-zeh?   peniaze?

bank draft	*bankoh-vaa zmen-kah*	banková zmenka
bank notes	*bankov-kih*	bankovky
cashier	*poklad-nyeek* (m)	pokladník
	poklad-nyeech-kah (f)	pokladníčka
coins	*min-tseh*	mince
credit card	*ooveh-rohvaa*	úverová (kreditná)
	(kredit-naa) kartah	karta
exchange	*zmeh-naa-reny*	zmenáreň
loose change	*drob-nair/min-tse*	drobné/mince
signature	*(vlastnoh-ruchnee)*	(vlastnoručný)
	pod-pis	podpis

Sightseeing

Do you have a guidebook/
local map?

maa-tyeh tses-tohv-noo   Máte cestovnú príručku/
pree-ruchkuh/myiest-nuh   miestnu mapu?
mapuh ?

What are the main attractions?

akair soo tuh turist-itskair   Aké sú tu turistické
za-ooyee-mah-vostih ?   zaujímavosti?

What is that?

cho yeh toh ?   Čo je to?

How old is it?

akoh yeh toh stah-rair ?   Ako je to staré?

Can I take photographs?

muo-zhem fotoh-gra-   Môžem fotografovať?
foh-vaty ?

What time does it open/close?

oh koly-kay otvaa-rahyoo/   O koľkej otvárajú /zatvárajú?
zah-tvaa-rahyoo ?

ancient	*staroh-bilee* (m)	starobylý
	staroh-bilaa (f)	starobylá
	staroh-bilair (neut)	starobylé
archaeological	*arkheoloh-ghi-tskee* (m)	archeologický
	arkheoloh-ghi-tskaa (f)	archeologická
	arkheoloh-ghi-tskair (neut)	archeologické
beach	*plaazh*	pláž

building	*budoh-vah*	budova
castle	*hrad/zaa-mok*	hrad/zámok
cathedral	*kateh-draalah*	katedrála
church	*kostol*	kostol
concert hall	*kon-tsert-naa syieny*	koncertná sieň
library	*knyizh-nyitsa*	knižnica
main square	*hlav-nair-naa-mestyieh*	hlavné námestie
market	*trkh*	trh
monastery	*klaash-tor*	kláštor
monument	*pah-mat-nyeek*	pamätník
mosque	*meshi-tah*	mešita
old city	*stah-raa chasty mestah*	stará časť mesta
palace	*palaats*	palác
opera house	*operah*	opera
ruins	*zroo-tsa-nyihnih*	zrúcaniny
stadium	*shtah-diyawn*	štadión
statues	*sokhih*	sochy
synagogue	*sinah-gawhgah*	synagóga
temple	*khraam*	chrám
university	*uhnih-ver-zitah*	univerzita

Entertainment

What's there to do in the evenings?

kam sah daa easty poh vecheh-rokh? Kam sa dá ísť po večeroch?

Are there any discos?

soo tuh diskoh-taihkih? Sú tu diskotéky?

Are there places where you
can hear local folk music?

daa sah tuh nyieh-gdyeh   Dá sa tu niekde ísť počúvať
easty pochoo-vaty   ľudovú hudbu?
lyudoh-voo hoodbuh?

How much does it cost to
get in to the ...?

koly-koh yeh vstup-nair ...? Koľko je vstupné ... ?

cinema	*(doh) kinah*	(do) kina
concert	*(na) kon-tsert*	(na) koncert
discotheque	*(na) diskoh-taihkuh*	(na) diskotéku
theatre	*(do) dyivah-dlah*	(do) divadla

In the Country

Weather

What's the weather like?

akair yeh pocha-syieh?   Aké je počasie?

The weather is ... today.

dnyes yeh ...   Dnes je ...

Will it be ... tomorrow?

budyeh zai-trah ...?   Bude zajtra ...?

cloudy	*zamrah-chenair*	zamračené
cold	*zimah*	zima
foggy	*hmlis-toh*	hmlisto
frosty	*mraaz*	mráz
hot	*horoo-tsoh*	horúco
raining	*pr-shaty*	pršať
snowing	*snyeh-zhity*	snežiť
sunny	*sl-nyech-noh*	slnečno
windy	*vetyer-noh*	veterno

Camping

Am I allowed to camp here?
    muo-zhem tuh stanoh-vaty? Môžem tu stanovať?
Is there a campsite nearby?
    yeh tuh nableez-kuh   Je tu nablízku táborisko?
    taaboh-riskoh?

backpack	*plets-nyiak*	plecniak
can opener	*otvaa-rach nah konzer-vih*	otvárač na konzervy
compass	*kom-pahs*	kompas
crampons	*skobih*	skoby
firewood	*palivoh-vair dreh-voh*	palivové drevo
gas cartridge	*naa-plny doh plinoh-vairhoh vahrih-cha*	náplň do plynového variča
hammock	*(visuh-tair) luozh-koh*	(visuté) lôžko
ice axe	*horoh-lezets-kee cha-kan*	horolezecký čakan
mattress	*mah-trahts*	matrac
penknife	*vretskoh-vee nuozh*	vreckový nôž
rope	*poh-vraz/ lanoh*	povraz/lano
tent	*stahn*	stan
tent pegs	*stahno-vair kolee-kih*	stanové kolíky
torch (flashlight)	*bater-kah*	baterka
sleeping bag	*spah-tsee vahk*	spací vak
stove	*varich*	varič
water bottle	*flah-sha nah voduh*	fľaša na vodu

Food

breakfast	*ranyai-kih*	raňajky
lunch	*obed*	obed
dinner	*vecheh-rah*	večera

Table for ..., please.
stuol preh ... proh-seem Stôl pre ... prosím.
Can I see the menu please?
muo-zhem dos-taty Môžem dostať jedálny lístok?
yedaal-nih leas-tok ?
I would like the set lunch,
please.
ponuh-kuh dnyah Ponuku dňa, prosím.
proh-seem
What does it include?
cho yeh ftom zahr-nuhtair? Čo je v tom zahrnuté?
Is service included in the bill?
yeh obslu-hah zahr-nuhtaa Je obsluha zahrnutá v cene?
ftse-nyeh?
Not too spicy please.
meh-nyay koreh-nyiah Menej korenia, prosím.
proh-seem

Vegetarian

I am a vegetarian.
(yah) som veghe-tahryiaan (Ja) som vegetarián.
I don't eat meat.
nyeh-yem masoh Nejem mäso.

I don't eat chicken or fish
  or ham.
  nyeh-yem kurah-tsyieh   Nejem kuracie mäso, ryby ani
  masoh ribih ahnyih   šunku.
  shun-kuh

Some Useful Words

ashtray	*popol-nyeek*	popolník
the bill	*ooh-chet*	účet
a cup	*shaal-kah*	šálka
dessert	*mooch-nyik/*	múčnik/zákusok
	zaa-kuh-sok	
a drink	*naa-poy*	nápoj
a fork	*vidlich-kah*	vidlička
fresh (food)	*cherst-vair (yedloh)*	čerstvé (jedlo)
a glass	*poh-haar*	pohár
a knife	*nuozh*	nôž
a plate	*tah-nyier*	tanier
spicy (food)	*shtyip-lyah-vaih/*	štipľavé/
	koreh-nyistair	korenisté (jedlo)
	(yedloh)	
a spoon	*lizhi-tsah*	lyžica
stale (food)	*nyieh tselkom*	nie celkom čerstvé
	cherst-vair (yedloh)	(jedlo)
sweet (food)	*slad-kair (yedloh)*	sladké (jedlo)
teaspoon	*lih-zhich-kah*	lyžička
toothpick	*shpahraa-tkoh*	špárátko

Slovak Cuisine

Food in Slovakia reflects the myriad of influences which has
shaped this part of Europe. During your stay you will find dishes

which you may have learned to appreciate elsewhere, such as Austrian strudel, Czech dumplings, German sauerkraut, French crépes and Hungarian goulash, but you'll always find them prepared with a special Slovak touch. You may even have tasted a Slovak speciality without knowing: *Liptovská bryndza* (Liptauer cheese, named after the Liptov region in Central Slovakia), and *medovníky*, honey cakes with ginger, are eaten throughout the world. Less well-known but equally delicious are dishes such as *kapustnica* (sauerkraut soup), *lokše* (potato pancakes), *haruľa* (spicy potato puffs) *živánska* (marinated pork roasted with layers of onion, garlic, bacon and vegetables), and many varieties of local freshwater fish with names such as *sumec*, *zubáč*, *šťuka* and *hlavátka*.

Modern Slovak cooks have not forgotten traditional recipes - they are well worth discovering!

Dobrú chuť!	*(doh-broo khuty)*	Bon appétit!
Na zdravie!	*(nah zdrah-vyieh)*	Cheers!

Soups — Polievky

beef soup	*hovädzí vývar*
chicken soup	*kuracia polievka*
fish soup	*rybacia polievka*
vegetable soups:	*zeleninové polievky:*
asparagus	*špargľová*
bean	*fazuľová*
cauliflower	*karfiolová*
celeriac	*zelerová*
leek	*pórová*
pea	*hrášková*

potato	*zemiaková*
spinach	*špenátová*
tomato	*rajčiaková*
with ...	*s ...*
dumplings	*knedlíčkami*
gnocchi	*haluškami*
noodles (vermicelli)	*rezancami*
rice	*ryžou*

Starters & Snacks — Predjedlá

cheese platter (including local mountain cheese varieties)	*syrový tanier (oštiepok aparenica)*
chicken salad with mayonnaise	*kurací šalát s majonézou*
goose liver with apples	*husacia pečeň s jablkam*
green salad with goat cheese	*hlávkový šalát s oštiepkom*
open sandwich	*dánsky chlebíček*
with ...	
ham	*so šunkou*
herring	*so sleďom*
smoked salmon	*s údeným lososom*
salami platter with fresh/ pickled vegetables	*salámový tanier s oblohou*
salad Niçoise	*šalátová misa Nicé*
scrambled eggs with onion	*miešane vajíčka na cibuľke*

Fish — Ryby

braised carp in red sauce	*kapor v paprikovej omáčke*
carp braised in wine	*kapor na víne*
fillet of fish fried in breadcrumbs	*vyprážané rybacie filé*
trout fried in butter	*pstruh pečený na masle*

SLOVAK

bookshop	*predai*	predaj kníh
camera shop	*fotoh-(potreh-bih)*	foto(potreby)
clothing store	*odyeh-vih*	odevy
delicatessen	*lahuod-kih*	lahôdky
general store	*ob-khod zoh z*	obchod so
	myiesha-neem	zmiešaným
	tovah-rom	tovarom
laundry	*praa-chov-nya*	práčovňa
market	*trkh*	trh
newsagency/	*novih-nih*	noviny
stationer's	*ah chahso-pisih/*	a časopisy/
	pahpyier-nitstvoh	papiernictvo
pharmacy	*lekaa-reny*	lekáreň
shoeshop	*obuv*	obuv
souvenir shop	*darche-kih/ suveh-*	darčeky/suveníry
	neerih	
supermarket	*samoh-obslu-hah*	samoobsluha
vegetable shop	*zele-nyinah ah*	zelenina a
	ovoh-tsyieh	ovocie

I would like to buy ...
   khtsel (m)/*khtseh-lah* (f) *bih*   Chcel/Chcela by
   som koo-pity ...   som kúpiť ...
Do you have others?
   maa-tyeh ih-nair nah vee-ber?   Máte iné na výber?
I don't like it.
   toh sah mih nyeh-pozdaa-vah   To sa mi nepozdáva.
Can I look at it?
   muo-zhem toh vih-dyiety?   Môžem to vidieť?
I'm just looking.
   len sah tahk pozeh-raam   Len sa tak pozerám.

Meat

Gypsy style grilled beef
roast beef with ham and eggs

steak
veal escalopes with cream and
  mushrooms
Wiener schnitzel

Mäso

cigánska roštenka
roštenka so šunkou a
vajcom
biftek
teľacie medailónky na
smotane a hríboch
vyprážaný rezeň

Poultry

chicken braised in red sauce
fried chicken
turkey breast stuffed with
  mushrooms and almonds

Hydina

kurací paprikáš
vyprážané kurča
morčacie prsia na hríboch
as mandľovou plnkou

Game

pheasant soup
rabbit/hare in a cream sauce
roast partridge
venison in red wine

Divina

polievka z bažanta
zajac na smotane
pečená jarabica
srnčie mäso s červeným
vínom

Pasta, Rice & Vegetarian Dishes

cauliflower soufflé
fried cheese with tartare sauce

risotto with vegetables
spaghetti/macaroni with tomato
  sauce and cheese

Cestoviny, Ryža a Bezmäsite Jedlá

karfiolový nákyp
vyprážaný syr s tatarskou
omáčkou
zeleninové rizoto
špagety/makaróny na
taliansky spôsob

tagliatelle with cottage
cheese and fried bacon

*široké rezance s tvarohom
a slaninou*

Salads
beetroot
cabbage
celeriac and carrot
cucumber
lettuce
mixed
potato
sauerkraut
tomato
Wallachian/Russian (mixed
vegetables, salami, eggs and
mayonnaise)

Šaláty
cviklový
kapustový
zelerový s mrkvou
uhorkový
hlávkový
z miešanej zeleniny
zemiakový
zo sudovej (kyslej) kapusty-
rajčiakový /paradajkový
vlašský /ruský

Side Dishes
bread and pastry
potato chips
rice
roast potatoes

Prílohy
chlieb a pečivo
zemiakové hranolky
ryža
opekané zemiaky

Desserts
apple strudel
bread pudding
cherry soufflé
chestnut cream
chocolate gâteau
doughnuts

Múčniky
jablkovýá závin
žemľovka
čerešňová bublanina
gaštanové pyréchocolate
čokoládová torta
šišky

fruit cake

pancakes with chocolate
and cream
rice soufflé
roulade
shortbread

ovocný (biskupský)
chlebíček
palacinky s čokoládou
ašlahačkou
ryžový nákyp
čokoládová roláda
maslové (drobné čajové)
pečivo

Drinks
beer (bottled/draught)
carbonated water
coffee
espresso/short black
fruit juice
hot chocolate
liqueurs
mineral water
spirits
tea
Turkish coffee
Vienna coffee (with cream)

water
wine (white/red)
young (green) wine

Nápoje
pivo (fľaškové/čapované)
sóda
káva
espresso
ovocná šťava
kakao/varená čokoláda
likéry
minerálna voda
destiláty
čaj
turecká káva
viedenská káva
(so šľahačkou)
voda
víno (biele/červene)
burčák/burčiak

Shopping
How much is it?
 koly-koh toh stoh-yee ?   Koľko to stojí ?

Can you write down the price?
muo-zhetyeh mih napee- saty tsenuh? Môžete mi napísať cenu?

Do you accept credit cards?
muo-zhem plah-tyity ooveh-rovohw kar-tohw? Môžem platiť úverovou kartou?

Could you lower the price?
muo-zhetyeh znyee-zhity tsenuh? Môžete znížiť cenu?

I don't have much money.
nyeh-maam veh-lyah penyah-zee Nemám veľa peňazí.

Can I help you?
cho sih zhelaa-tyeh? Čo si želáte?

Will that be all?
toh yeh fshet-koh? To je všetko?

Would you like it wrapped?
zhelaa-tyeh sih toh zabah-lity? Želáte si to zabaliť?

Sorry, this is the only one.
zhyialy ih-nair nyeh-maameh Žiaľ, iné nemáme.

How much/many do you want?
koly-koh (kuh-sohw) sih zhelaa-tyeh? Koľko (kusov) si želáte?

Souvenirs

earrings	*naa-ush-nyitse*	náušnice
handicraft	*umelets-koh-pryieh-mihsel-nair veerob-kih*	umelecko priemyselné výrobky
necklace	*naahr-dyelnyeek*	náhrdelník
pottery	*kerah-mikah*	keramika

| ring | *prs-tyeny* | prsteň |
| rug | *pokroh-vets* | pokrovec |

Clothing

clothing	*odyeh-vih*	odevy
coat	*kah-baat*	kabát
dress	*shah-tih*	šaty
jacket	*sakoh*	sako
jumper	*sveh-ter*	sveter
shirt	*kosheh-lyah*	košeľa
shoes	*topaan-kih*	topánky
skirt	*suk-nyah*	sukňa
trousers	*nohah-vitseh*	nohavice

It's too ...

yeh toh pree-lish ...		Je to príliš ...
big	*vely-kair*	veľké
small	*mah-lair*	malé
short	*kraat-keh*	krátke
long	*dl-hair*	dlhé
tight	*ooz-keh*	úzke
loose	*voly-nair*	voľné

| It doesn't fit. | *nyeh-sedyee toh* | Nesedí to. |

Materials

cotton	*bavl-nah*	bavlna
handmade	*ruch-naa veeroh-bah*	ručná výroba
leather	*kozha*	koža
of brass	*moh-sadz*	mosadz

SLOVAK

of gold	*zlatoh*	zlato
of silver	*stryieh-broh*	striebro
silk	*hod-vaab*	hodváb
wool	*vl-nah*	vlna

Colours

black	*chyier-nah*	čierna
blue	*behlah-saa/ mod-raa*	belasá/modrá
brown	*hnyeh-daa*	hnedá
green	*zeleh-naa*	zelená
orange	*orahn-zhohvaa*	oranžová
pink	*ruzhoh-vaa*	ružová
purple	*nakhoh-vaa/ fiya-lovaa*	nachová/fialová
red	*cherveh-naa*	červená
white	*byieh-lah*	biela
yellow	*zhl-taa*	žltá

Toiletries

comb	*hreh-beny*	hrebeň
condoms	*prezer-vahtee-vih/ kon-doh-mih*	prezervatívy/ kondómy
deodorant	*dezoh-dorant*	dezodorant
hairbrush	*kefah nah vlasih*	kefa na vlasy
moisturising cream	*hidrah-touch-nee krairm*	hydratačný krém
razor (blade)	*zhilet-kah*	žiletka
sanitary napkins	*vlozh-kih*	vložky
shampoo	*sham-pohn*	šampón

shaving cream	*krairm nah holeh-nyieh*	krém na holenie
soap	*midloh*	mydlo
sunblock cream	*opa-lyovah-tsee krairm s fil-trom*	opaľovací krém s filtrom
tampons	*tahm-pohnih*	tampóny
tissues	*vrets-kohw-kih*	vreckovky
toilet paper	*toalet-nee/zaakhoh-dovee pah-pyier*	toaletný/záchodový papier
toothbrush	*zub-naa kef-kah*	zubná kefka
toothpaste	*zub-naa pahs-tah*	zubná pasta

Stationery & Publications

map	*mahpah*	mapa
newspaper	*novih-nih*	noviny
newspaper in English	*novih-nih v anglich-tyinyeh*	noviny v angličtine
novels in English	*beleh-tryiah v anglich-tinyeh*	beletria v angličtine
paper	*pah-pyier*	papier
pen (ballpoint)	*vech-nair peh-roh*	večné pero
scissors	*nozhnih-tse*	nožnice

Photography

How much is it to process this film?

koly-koh stoh-yee vivoh-lanyieh tokh-toh fill-muh? Koľko stojí vyvolanie tohto filmu?

When will it be ready?
kedih toh buh-dyeh hotoh-vair? — Kedy to bude hotové?

I'd like a film for this camera.
maa-tyeh film doh tokh-toh fotoh-ahpah-raa-tuh? — Máte film do tohto fotoaparátu?

B&W (film)	*chyier-noh-byielih film*	čiernobiely film
camera	*fotoh-ahpah-raat*	fotoaparát
colour (film)	*fareb-nee film*	farebný film
film	*film*	film
flash	*blesk*	blesk
lens	*obyek-teev*	objektív
light meter	*ekspoh-zih-mehter*	expozimeter

Smoking

A packet of cigarettes, please.
bahlee-chek tsiga-ryiet proh-seem — Balíček cigariet, prosím.

Are these cigarettes strong/mild?
soo toh sil-nair/ yem-nair tsiga-retih? — Sú to silné/jemné cigarety?

Do you have a light?
muo-zhetyeh mih pripaa-lity? — Môžete mi pripáliť?

cigarette papers	*tsiga-retoh-vair pah-pyieh-reh*	cigaretové papiere

cigarettes	*tsiga-retih*	cigarety
filtered	*tsiga-retih s fil-trom*	cigarety s filtrom
lighter	*zapah-lyoh-vach*	zapaľovač
matches	*zaa-palkih*	zápalky
menthol	*mentoloh-vair*	mentolové cigarety
	tsiga-retih	
pipe	*fy-kah*	fajka
tobacco (pipe)	*fy-koh-vee tabak*	fajkový tabak

Sizes & Comparisons

small	*mah-lee* (m)	malý
	mah-laa (f)	malá
	mah-lair (neut)	malé
big	*vely-kee* (m)	veľký
	vely-kaa (f)	veľká
	vely-kair (neut)	veľké
heavy	*tyazh-kee* (m)	ťažký
	tyazh-kaa (f)	ťažká
	tyazh-kair (neut)	ťažké
light	*lyakh-kee* (m)	ľahký
	lyakh-kaa (f)	ľahká
	lyakh-kair (neut)	ľahké
more	*vyiats*	viac
less	*meh-nyeay*	menej
too much/many	*pree-lish velyah*	príliš veľa
many	*mnohoh/ velyah*	mnoho/veľa
enough	*dosty*	dosť
also	*tyiezh*	tiež
a little bit	*troh-khah*	trocha

SLOVAK

Health

Where is ...?

	gdyeh yeh ...?	Kde je ... ?
the doctor	*dok-tor/lekaar*	doktor /lekár
the hospital	*nyemots-nyitsah*	nemocnica
the chemist	*lekaar-nyik*	lekárnik
the dentist	*zoob-nee lekaar*	zubný lekár

I am sick.

som kho-ree (m)	Som chorý.
som kho-raa (f)	Som chorá.

My friend is sick.

muoy pryiah-tyely yeh kho-ree (m)	Môj priateľ je chorý.
moh-yah pryiah-tyely-kah yeh kho-raa (f)	Moja priateľka je chorá.

Could I see a female doctor?

muo-zhem hoh-vohrity zoh zhe-nohw-lekaar-kohw ?	Môžem hovoriť so ženou-lekárkou?

What's the matter?

cho vaas traa-pih ?	Čo Vás trápi ?

Where does it hurt?

gdyeh toh boh-lee ?	Kde Vás to bolí ?

It hurts here.

tuh mah boh-lee	Tu ma bolí.

My ... hurts.

boh-lee mah ...	Bolí ma ...

Parts of the Body

ankle	*chleh-nok*	členok
arm	*rukah*	ruka (rameno a dlaň)
back	*khr-baat*	chrbát
chest	*hrudyi*	hruď
ear	*ukhoh*	ucho
eye	*okoh*	oko
finger	*prst*	prst
foot	*nohah/*	noha/chodidlo
	kho-dyid-loh	
hand	*rukah*	ruka (len časť sdlaňou)
head	*hlah-vah*	hlava
heart	*srd-tse*	srdce
leg	*noh-hah*	noha (celá)
mouth	*oos-tah*	ústa
nose	*nos*	nos
ribs	*reh-braa*	rebrá
skin	*koh-zha/*	koža/pokožka
	pokozh-kah	
spine	*khrb-tyih-tsa*	chrbtica
stomach	*zhaloo-dok*	žalúdok
teeth	*zoobih*	zuby
throat	*hrd-loh*	hrdlo

Ailments

I have ...

an allergy	*maam aler-ghiuh*	Mám alergiu.

a blister	*maam otlahk*	Mám otlak.
a burn	*maam popaa-leh-nyinuh*	Mám popáleninu.
a cold	*maam naad-khuh*	Mám nádchu.
constipation	*maam zaap-khuh*	Mám zápchu.
a cough	*maam kah-shely*	Mám kašeľ.
diarrhoea	*maam hnach-kuh*	Mám hnačku.
fever	*maam horooch-kuh*	Mám horúčku.
a headache	*bohlee mah hla-vah*	Bolí ma hlava.
hepatitis	*maam zhl-touch-kuh*	Mám žltačku.
indigestion	*maam pokah-zenee zhaloo-dok*	Mám pokazený žalúdok.
an infection	*maam naa-kaz-livoo khoroh-buh*	Mám nákazlivú chorobu.
influenza	*maam khreep-kuh*	Mám chrípku.
lice	*maam fshih*	Mám vši.
low/high blood pressure	*maam nyeez-kih/ visoh-kee krv-nee tlak*	Mám nízky/vysoký krvný tlak.
a pain	*maam boles-tyih*	Mám bolesti.
sore throat	*bohlee mah hrd-loh*	Bolí ma hrdlo.
sprained my ...	*vitkohl* (m)/*vitklah* (f) *som sih ...*	Vytkol/Vytkla som si ...
a stomachache	*bohlee mah zhaloo-dok*	Bolí ma žalúdok.
sunburn	*maam ooh-pahl*	Mám úpal.
a veneral disease	*maam pohlav-noo khoro-buh*	Mám pohlavnú chorobu.
worms	*maam chrev-neekh parah-zitohw*	Mám črevných parazitov.

Some Useful Words & Phrases

I'm ...

maam ...   Mám ...

diabetic	*tsuk-rof-kuh*	cukrovku
epileptic	*epi-lepsyiuh*	epilepsiu
asthmatic	*asth-muh*	astmu

I'm allergic to
   som aler-ghits-kee nah ... (m) Som alergický na ...
   som aler-ghits-kaa nah ... (f) Som alergická na ...

antibiotics	*antih-biyoh-tihkaa*	antibiotiká
penicillin	*penih-tsileen*	penicilín

I'm pregnant.
   som tyehot-naa   Som tehotná.
I'm on the pill.
   pohw-zheevam hormoh-   Používam hormonálnu
   naal-nuh anti-   antikoncepciu.
   kon-tseptsyiuh
I haven't had my period for
(two) months.
   uzh (dvah) mehsiyah-tse   Už (dva) mesiace som nemala
   som nyeh-malah   menštruáciu.
   men-shtru-aatsyiuh
I have my own syringe.
   maam vlast-noo   Mám vlastnú injekčnú
   in-yekch-noo   striekačku.
   stryieh-kach-kuh

I feel better/worse.
> *tsee-tyim sah lep-shyieh/*   Cítim sa lepšie/horšie.
> *hor-shyieh*

accident	*nyeh-hodah*	nehoda
addiction	*nar-koh-maanyiah/*	narkománia/
	toksi-koh-maanyiah	toxikománia
antibiotics	*anti-biyoh-tihkaa*	antibiotiká
antiseptic	*anti-septih-khum*	antiseptikum
aspirin	*aspih-reen*	aspirín
bandage	*ob-vaz*	obväz
bite (animal)	*poh-hriz-nutyieh*	pohryznutie
bite (insect)	*ushtyip-nutyieh*	uštipnutie
blood pressure	*krv-nee tlak*	krvný tlak
blood test	*krv-naa skoosh-kah*	krvná skúška
contraceptives	*proh-stryied-kih*	prostriedky proti
	protih pocha-tyiuh	počatiu
injection	*in-yek-tsyiah*	injekcia
injury	*porah-nyeh-nyieh*	poranenie
itch	*svr-beh-nyieh*	svrbenie
medicine	*lyiek*	liek
menstruation	*men-shtru-aatsyiah*	menštruácia
nausea	*zhaloo-dochnaa nyeh-*	žalúdočná
	voly-nosty	nevoľnosť
oxygen	*kis-leak*	kyslík
vitamins	*vitah-meanih*	vitamíny

At the Chemist

I need medication for ...
> *potreh-buyem lyiek nah ...*   Potrebujem liek na ...

I have a prescription.
   maam lekaar-skih pred-pis   Mám lekársky predpis
   (reh-tsept)   (recept).

At the Dentist
I have a toothache.
   boh-lyiah mah zoobih   Bolia ma zuby.
I've lost a filling.
   vih-padlah mih plom-bah   Vypadla mi plomba.
I've broken a tooth.
   zloh-mil sa mih zoob   Zlomil sa mi zub.
My gums hurt.
   boh-lyiah mah dyas-naa   Bolia ma ďasná.
I don't want it extracted.
   nyeh-khtsem sih toh   Nechcem si to nechať
   nyeh-khaty vih-trh-nooty   vytrhnúť.
Please give me an anaesthetic.
   uh-mrrt-vityeh mih toh   Umŕtvite mi to, prosím.
   proh-seem

Time & Dates
What time is it?
   koly-koh yeh hoh-dyeen ?   Koľko je hodín ?
It is ... o'clock
   yeh (jeh-dnah) hodih-nah   Je (jedna) hodina.
   soo (dveh, trih, shtih-rih)   Sú (dve, tri, štyri) hodiny.
   hodyih-nih
   yeh (pety ...) hoh-dyeen   Je (päť ...) hodín.

in the morning
   dopoh-luh-dnyah/   dopoludnia/predpoludním
   pred-poluh-dnyeem
in the afternoon
   popoh-ludnyee   popoludní
in the evening
   veh-cher   večer
What date is it today ?
   koly-kairhoh yeh dnyes ?   Koľkého je dnes ?

Days of the Week

Monday	*pon-dyelok*	pondelok
Tuesday	*uh-torok*	utorok
Wednesday	*stre-dah*	streda
Thursday	*shtvr-tok*	štvrtok
Friday	*piah-tok*	piatok
Saturday	*soboh-tah*	sobota
Sunday	*nye-dye-lya*	nedeľa

Months

January	*yanooh-aar*	január
February	*februh-aar*	február
March	*maretz*	marec
April	*apreel*	apríl
May	*maai*	máj
June	*yoon*	jún
July	*yool*	júl
August	*ow-goost*	august
September	*septem-behr*	september

October	*oktoh-behr*	október
November	*nohvem-behr*	november
December	*detzem-behr*	december

Seasons

summer	*letoh*	leto
autumn	*yeseny*	jeseň
winter	*zimah*	zima
spring	*yahr*	jar

Present

today	*dnyes*	dnes
this morning	*dnyes raa-noh*	dnes ráno
tonight	*dnyes veh-cher*	dnes večer
this week/year	*tentoh teezh-dyeny/ rok*	tento týždeň/rok
now	*teras*	teraz

Past

yesterday	*fcheh-rah*	včera
day before yesterday	*pred-fcheh-rom*	predvčerom
last night	*minuh-loo notz*	minulú noc
last week/year	*minuh-lee teezh-dyeny/ rok*	minulý týžden/rok

SLOVAK

Future

tomorrow	*zai-trah*	zajtra
day after tomorrow	*poh-zai-trah*	pozajtra
tomorrow morning	*zai-trah raa-noh*	zajtra ráno
next week	*buhdoo-tzi teezh-dyeny*	budúci týždeň
next year	*buhdoo-tzi rok*	budúci rok

During the Day

afternoon	*popoh-ludnyie*	popoludnie
dawn,	*ooh-svit*	úsvit
day	*dyeny*	deň
early	*skoh-roh*	skoro
early morning	*skoh-roh raa-noh*	skoro ráno
midnight	*pol-notz*	polnoc
morning	*raa-noh*	ráno
night	*notz*	noc
noon	*poluh-dnyie*	poludnie
sunrise	*vee-khod sln-kah*	východ slnka
sunset	*zaa-pad sln-kah*	západ slnka

Numbers

0	*noolah*	nula
1	*yeh-den*	jeden
2	*dvah*	dva
3	*trih*	tri
4	*shtih-rih*	štyri

5	*pety*	päť
6	*shesty*	šesť
7	*seh-dyem*	sedem
8	*oh-sem*	osem
9	*dye-vety*	deväť
10	*dye-sahty*	desať
20	*dvah-tsahty*	dvadsať
30	*trih-tsahty*	tridsať
40	*shtih-rih-tsahty*	štyridsať
50	*pety-dyeh-syiat*	päťdesiat
60	*shez-dyeh-syiat*	šesťdesiat
70	*seh-dyem-dyeh-syiat*	sedemdesiat
80	*oh-sem-dyeh-syiat*	osemdesiat
90	*dyeh-vaty-dyeh-syiat*	deväťdesiat
100	*stoh*	sto
1000	*tyih-seetz*	tisíc
one million	*milih-yawhn*	milión
1st	*pr-vee* (m)	prvý
	pr-vaa (f)	prvá
	pr-vair (neut)	prvé
2nd	*druh-hee* (m)	druhý
	druh-haa (f)	druhá
	druh-hair (neut)	druhé
3rd	*treh-tyee* (m)	tretí
	treh-tyiah (f)	tretia
	treh-tyieh (neut)	tretie
1/4	*shtvr-tyih-nah*	štvrtina
1/3	*treh-tyih-nah*	tretina
1/2	*poloh-vitzah*	polovica
3/4	*trih shtvr-tyeh*	tri štvrte

Some Useful Words

double	*dvoy-moh*	dvojmo
a dozen	*tuhtzet*	tucet
Enough!	*dosty!/stah-cheeh !*	dosť!/stači!
few	*maa-loh*	málo
less	*meh-nyay*	menej
many	*mnohoh/veh-lyah*	mnoho/veľa
more	*vyiah-tzyey*	viacej
once	*yeden-kraat/yeden raz*	jedenkrát/jeden raz
a pair	*paar*	pár
percent	*per-tzen-toh*	percento
some	*nyieh-koly-koh*	niekoľko
too much	*pree-lish veh-lyah*	príliš veľa
twice	*dvah-kraat/dvah razih*	dvakrát/dva razy

Abbreviations

AIDS	AIDS
atď.	etc.
Austr.	Australia
ca (cca)	approx.
CK	travel agency
cm/m/km	cm/m /km(s)
g/kg	gm/kg
h. (hod.)/min./sek.	hr(s)/ min /sec
Juž. Afrika	RSA
n.l./pr. n.l.	AD/BC
NZ	NZ
OSN/ EU	UN/EC
Sev. /Juž./ Záp. /Vých.	Nth/Sth /West/ East
Sk (slovenská koruna)	crown (unit of currency)
ŠPZ	Car Reg. No.
SR	Slovak Republic
t.č.	at present (now)
tel. č.	Ph. No.
t.j.	i.e.
t.r.	this year
Ul. /Nám./Nábr.	St. /Sq./Quay
USA/Kan.	USA/Canada
V. Brit. (GB)	UK

Index

Bulgarian

Czech

Hungarian

Polish

Romanian

Slovak

Language Survival Kits

Australian phrasebook

Arabic (Egyptian) phrasebook

Arabic (Moroccan) phrasebook

Brazilian phrasebook

Burmese phrasebook

Cantonese phrasebook

Eastern Europe phrasebook
Covers Bulgarian, Czech, Hungarian, Polish, Romanian and Slovak.

Fijian phrasebook

Hindi/Urdu phrasebook

Indonesian phrasebook

Japanese phrasebook

Korean phrasebook

Mandarin Chinese phrasebook

Mediterranean Europe phrasebook
Covers Albanian, Greek, Italian, Macedonian, Maltese, Serbian & Croatian and Slovene.

Nepali phrasebook

Pidgin phrasebook

Pilipino phrasebook

Quechua phrasebook